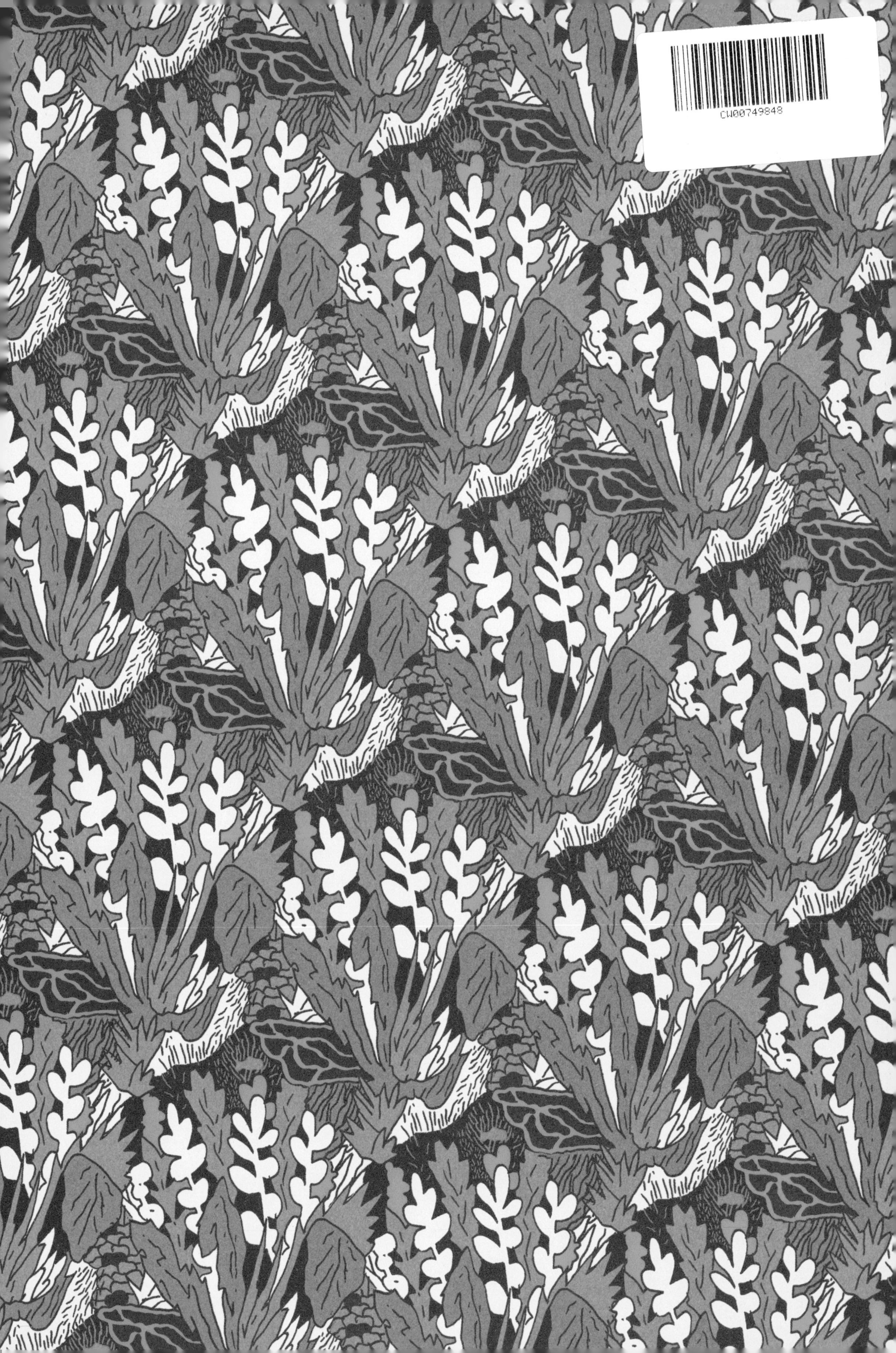

BIOGRAFIKTION

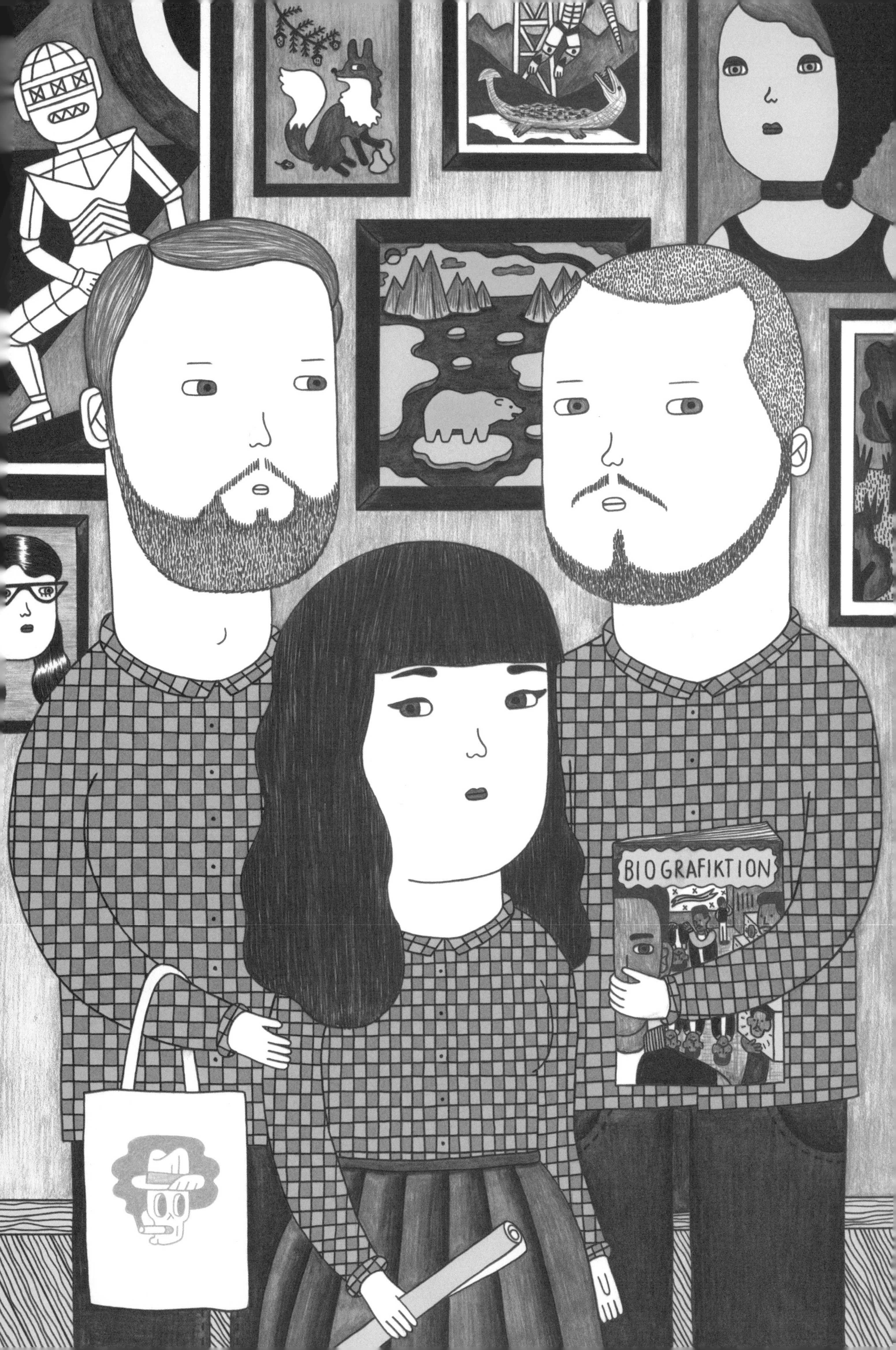
BIOGRAFIKTION

PUDGY PAUL BY ANA ALBERO

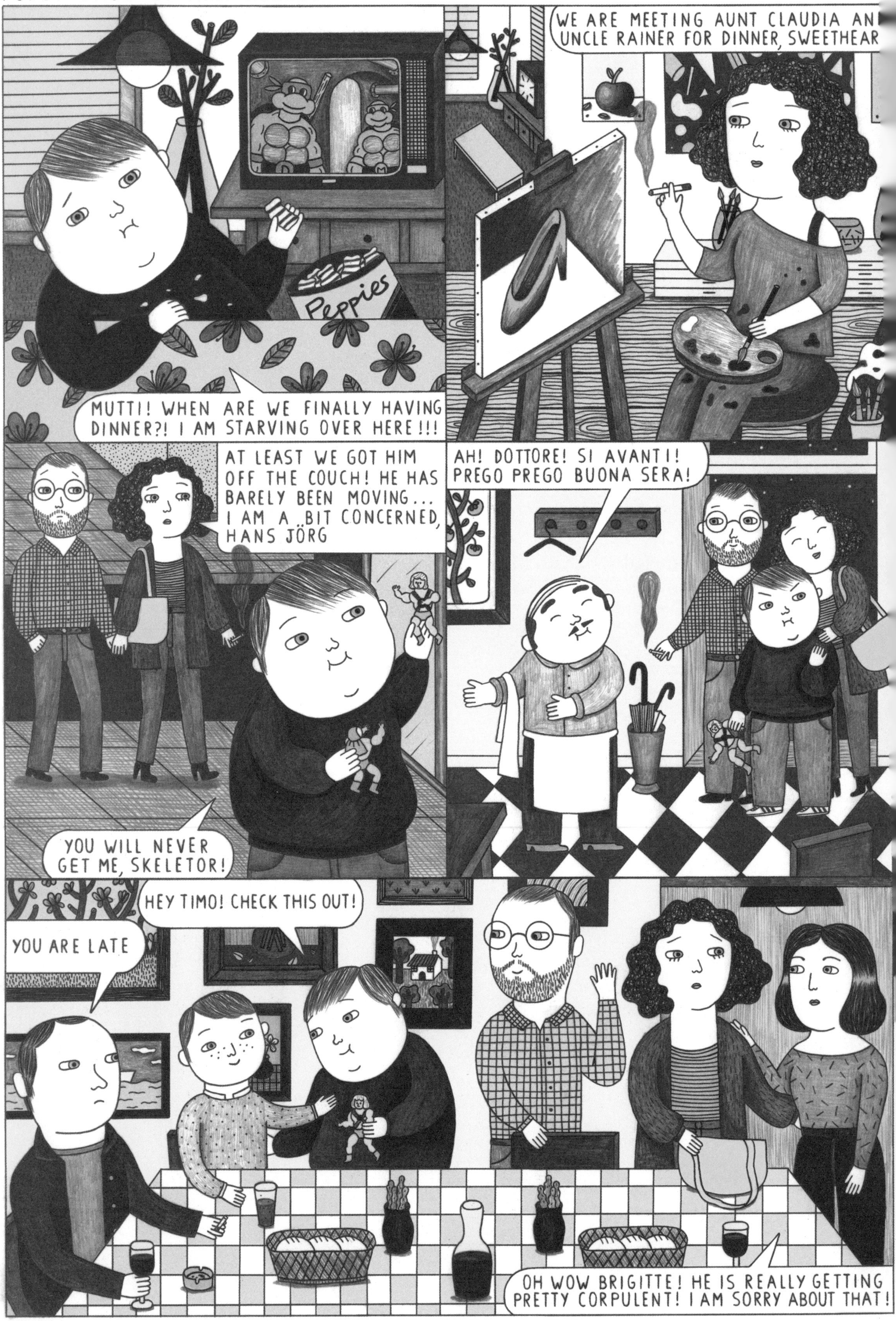
MUTTI! WHEN ARE WE FINALLY HAVING DINNER?! I AM STARVING OVER HERE!!!
Peppies
WE ARE MEETING AUNT CLAUDIA AN
UNCLE RAINER FOR DINNER, SWEETHEAR
AT LEAST WE GOT HIM OFF THE COUCH! HE HAS BARELY BEEN MOVING... I AM A BIT CONCERNED, HANS JÖRG
YOU WILL NEVER GET ME, SKELETOR!
AH! DOTTORE! SI AVANTI! PREGO PREGO BUONA SERA!
YOU ARE LATE
HEY TIMO! CHECK THIS OUT!
OH WOW BRIGITTE! HE IS REALLY GETTING PRETTY CORPULENT! I AM SORRY ABOUT THAT!

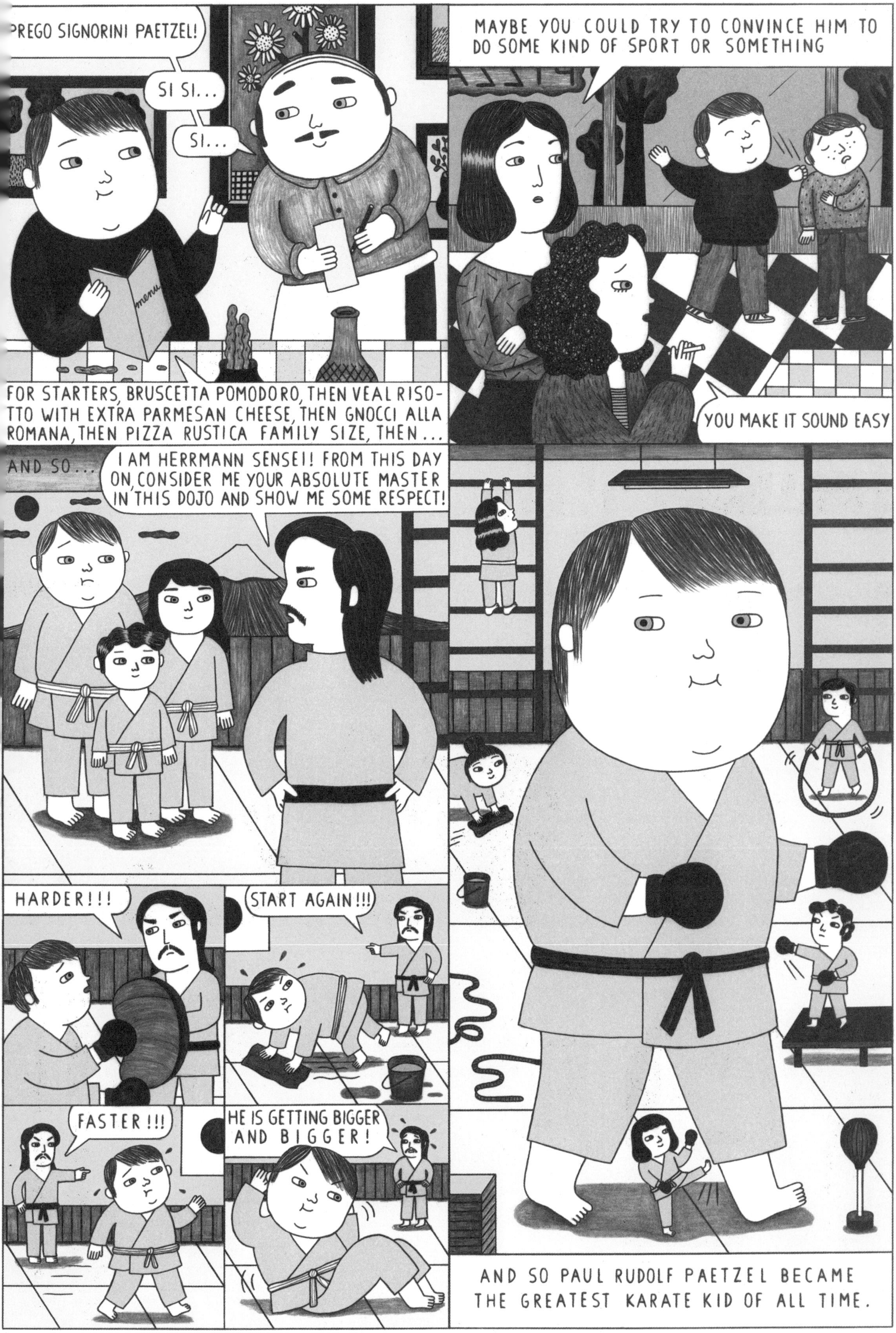
PREGO SIGNORINI PAETZEL!
SI SI...
SI...
FOR STARTERS, BRUSCETTA POMODORO, THEN VEAL RISOTTO WITH EXTRA PARMESAN CHEESE, THEN GNOCCI ALLA ROMANA, THEN PIZZA RUSTICA FAMILY SIZE, THEN...
MAYBE YOU COULD TRY TO CONVINCE HIM TO DO SOME KIND OF SPORT OR SOMETHING
YOU MAKE IT SOUND EASY
AND SO...
I AM HERRMANN SENSEI! FROM THIS DAY ON, CONSIDER ME YOUR ABSOLUTE MASTER IN THIS DOJO AND SHOW ME SOME RESPECT!
HARDER!!!
START AGAIN!!!
FASTER!!!
HE IS GETTING BIGGER AND BIGGER!
AND SO PAUL RUDOLF PAETZEL BECAME THE GREATEST KARATE KID OF ALL TIME.

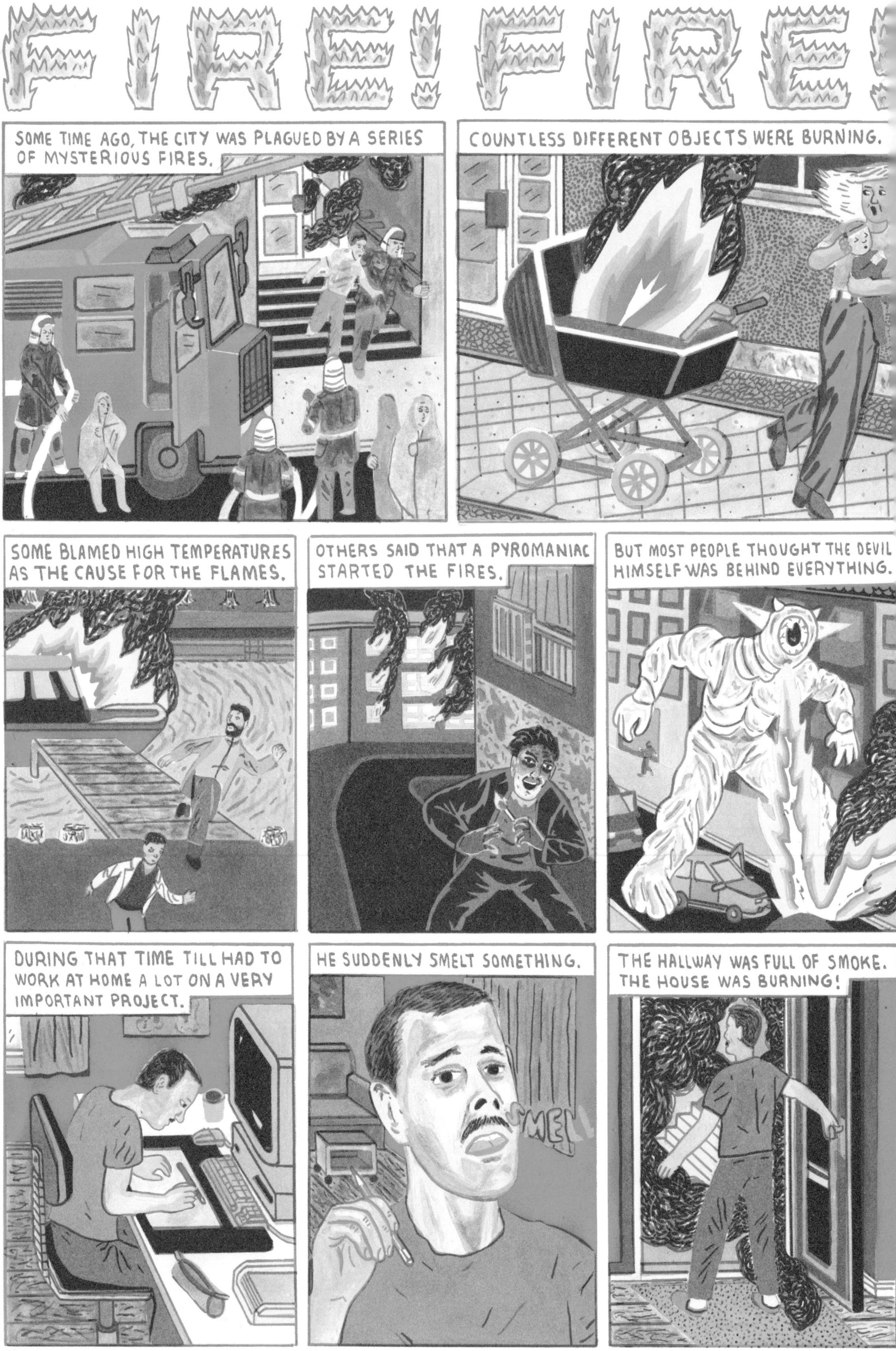
FIRE! FIRE!
SOME TIME AGO, THE CITY WAS PLAGUED BY A SERIES OF MYSTERIOUS FIRES.
COUNTLESS DIFFERENT OBJECTS WERE BURNING.
SOME BLAMED HIGH TEMPERATURES AS THE CAUSE FOR THE FLAMES.
OTHERS SAID THAT A PYROMANIAC STARTED THE FIRES.
BUT MOST PEOPLE THOUGHT THE DEVIL HIMSELF WAS BEHIND EVERYTHING.
DURING THAT TIME TILL HAD TO WORK AT HOME A LOT ON A VERY IMPORTANT PROJECT.
HE SUDDENLY SMELT SOMETHING.
THE HALLWAY WAS FULL OF SMOKE. THE HOUSE WAS BURNING!

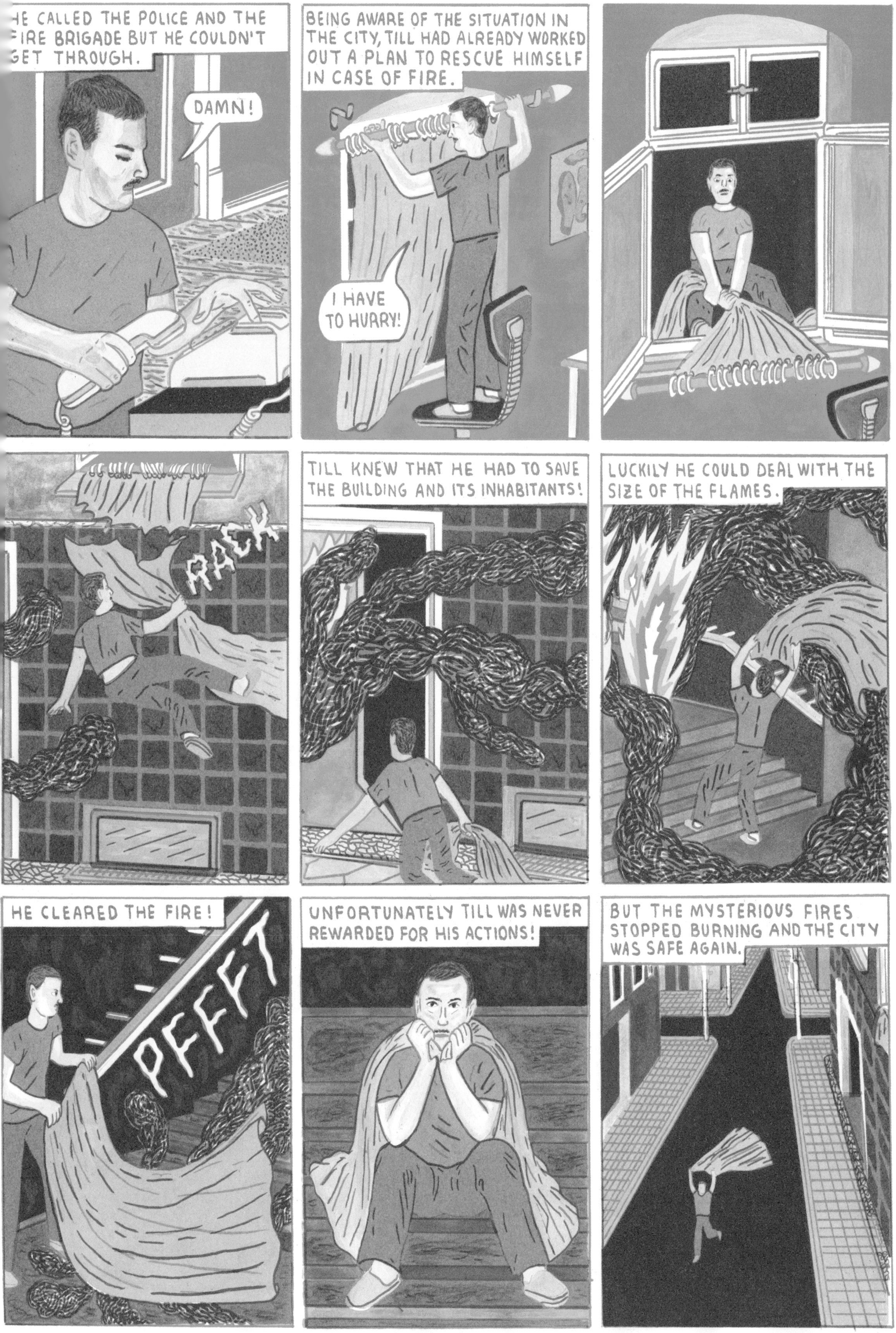
HE CALLED THE POLICE AND THE FIRE BRIGADE BUT HE COULDN'T GET THROUGH.
DAMN!
BEING AWARE OF THE SITUATION IN THE CITY, TILL HAD ALREADY WORKED OUT A PLAN TO RESCUE HIMSELF IN CASE OF FIRE.
I HAVE TO HURRY!
RACK
TILL KNEW THAT HE HAD TO SAVE THE BUILDING AND ITS INHABITANTS!
LUCKILY HE COULD DEAL WITH THE SIZE OF THE FLAMES.
HE CLEARED THE FIRE!
PFFFT
UNFORTUNATELY TILL WAS NEVER REWARDED FOR HIS ACTIONS!
BUT THE MYSTERIOUS FIRES STOPPED BURNING AND THE CITY WAS SAFE AGAIN.

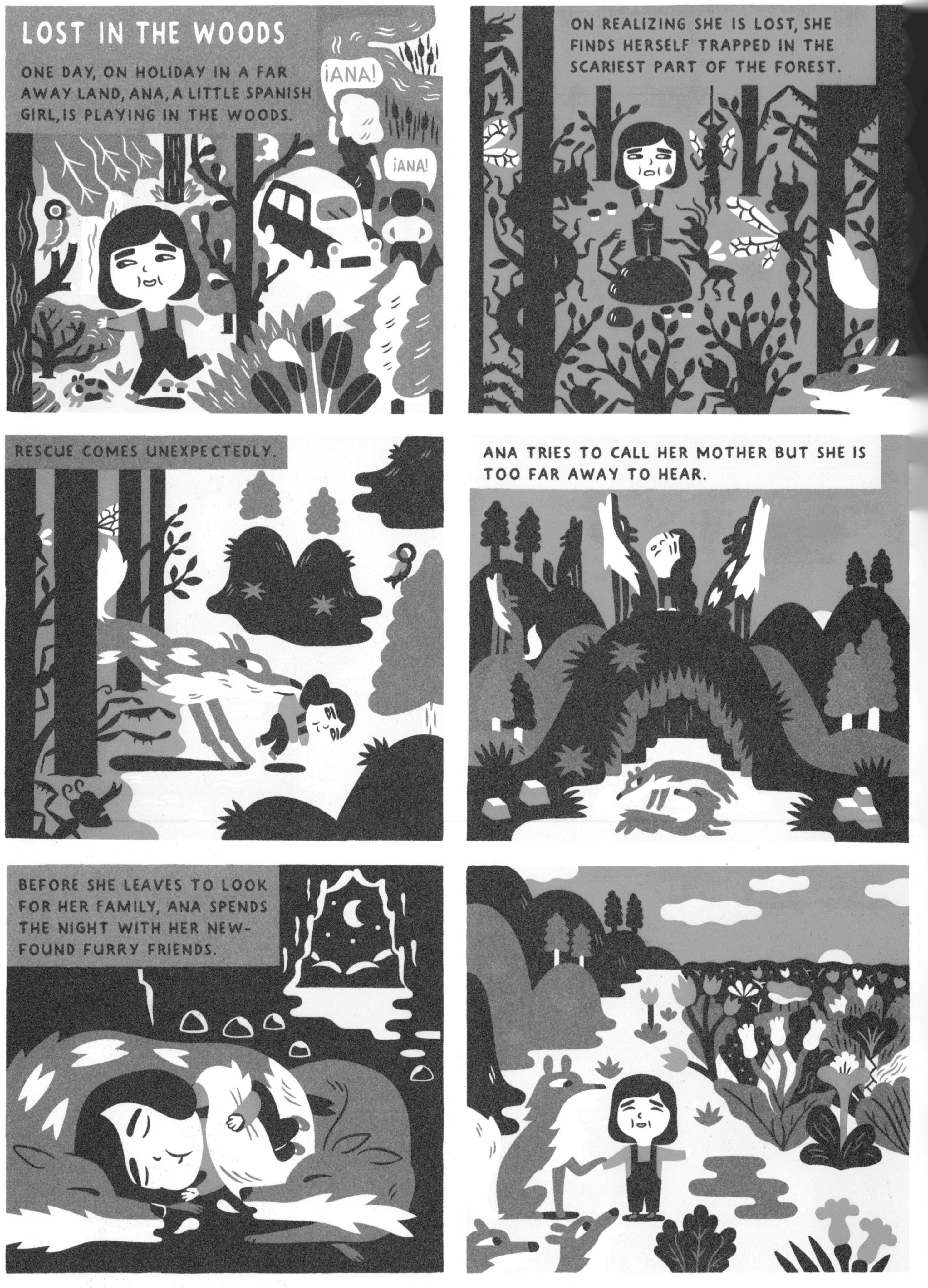
LOST IN THE WOODS
ONE DAY, ON HOLIDAY IN A FAR AWAY LAND, ANA, A LITTLE SPANISH GIRL, IS PLAYING IN THE WOODS.
¡ANA!
¡ANA!
ON REALIZING SHE IS LOST, SHE FINDS HERSELF TRAPPED IN THE SCARIEST PART OF THE FOREST.
RESCUE COMES UNEXPECTEDLY.
ANA TRIES TO CALL HER MOTHER BUT SHE IS TOO FAR AWAY TO HEAR.
BEFORE SHE LEAVES TO LOOK FOR HER FAMILY, ANA SPENDS THE NIGHT WITH HER NEW-FOUND FURRY FRIENDS.

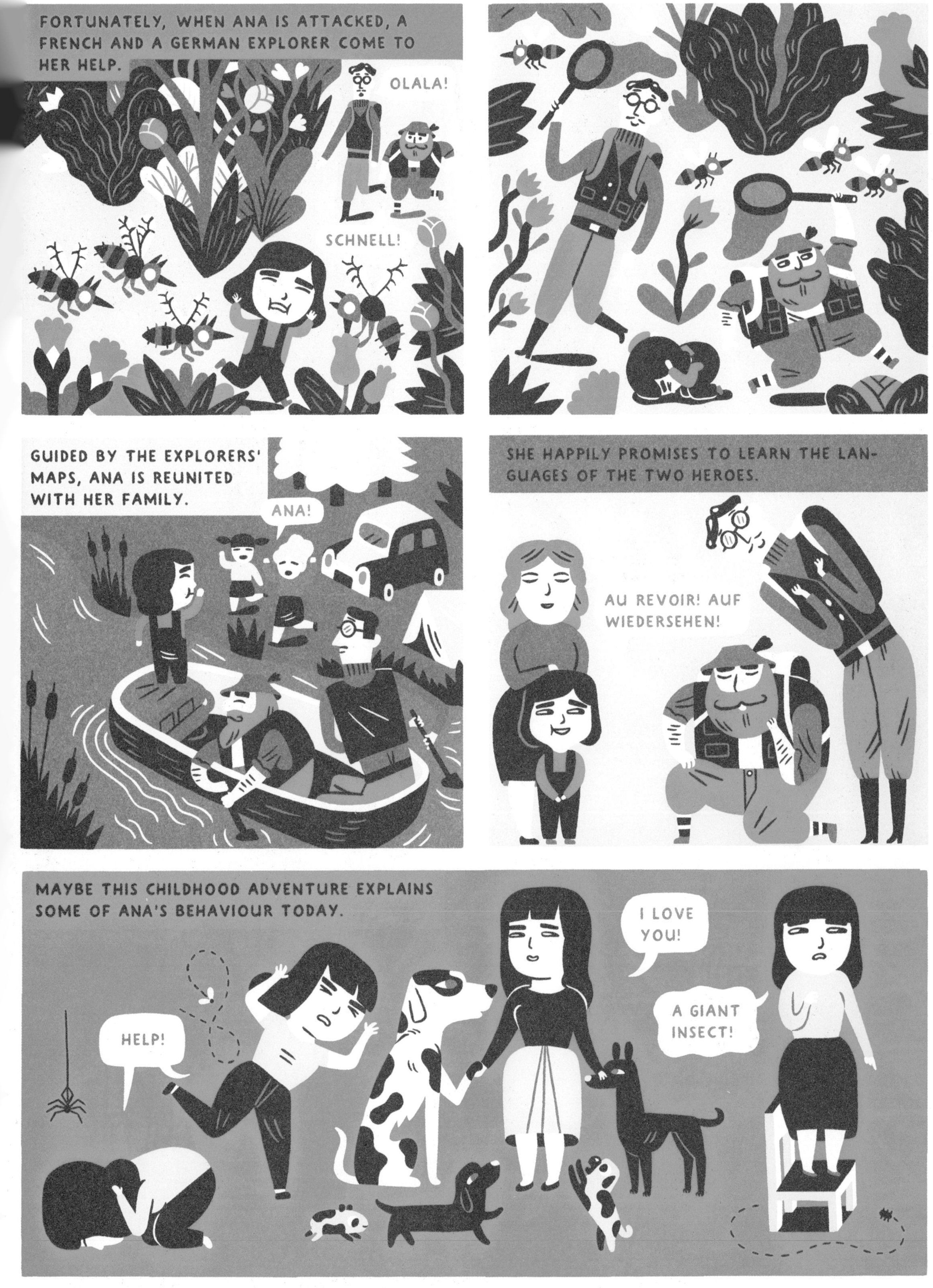
FORTUNATELY, WHEN ANA IS ATTACKED, A FRENCH AND A GERMAN EXPLORER COME TO HER HELP.
OLALA!
SCHNELL!
GUIDED BY THE EXPLORERS' MAPS, ANA IS REUNITED WITH HER FAMILY.
ANA!
SHE HAPPILY PROMISES TO LEARN THE LANGUAGES OF THE TWO HEROES.
AU REVOIR! AUF WIEDERSEHEN!
MAYBE THIS CHILDHOOD ADVENTURE EXPLAINS SOME OF ANA'S BEHAVIOUR TODAY.
HELP!
I LOVE YOU!
A GIANT INSECT!

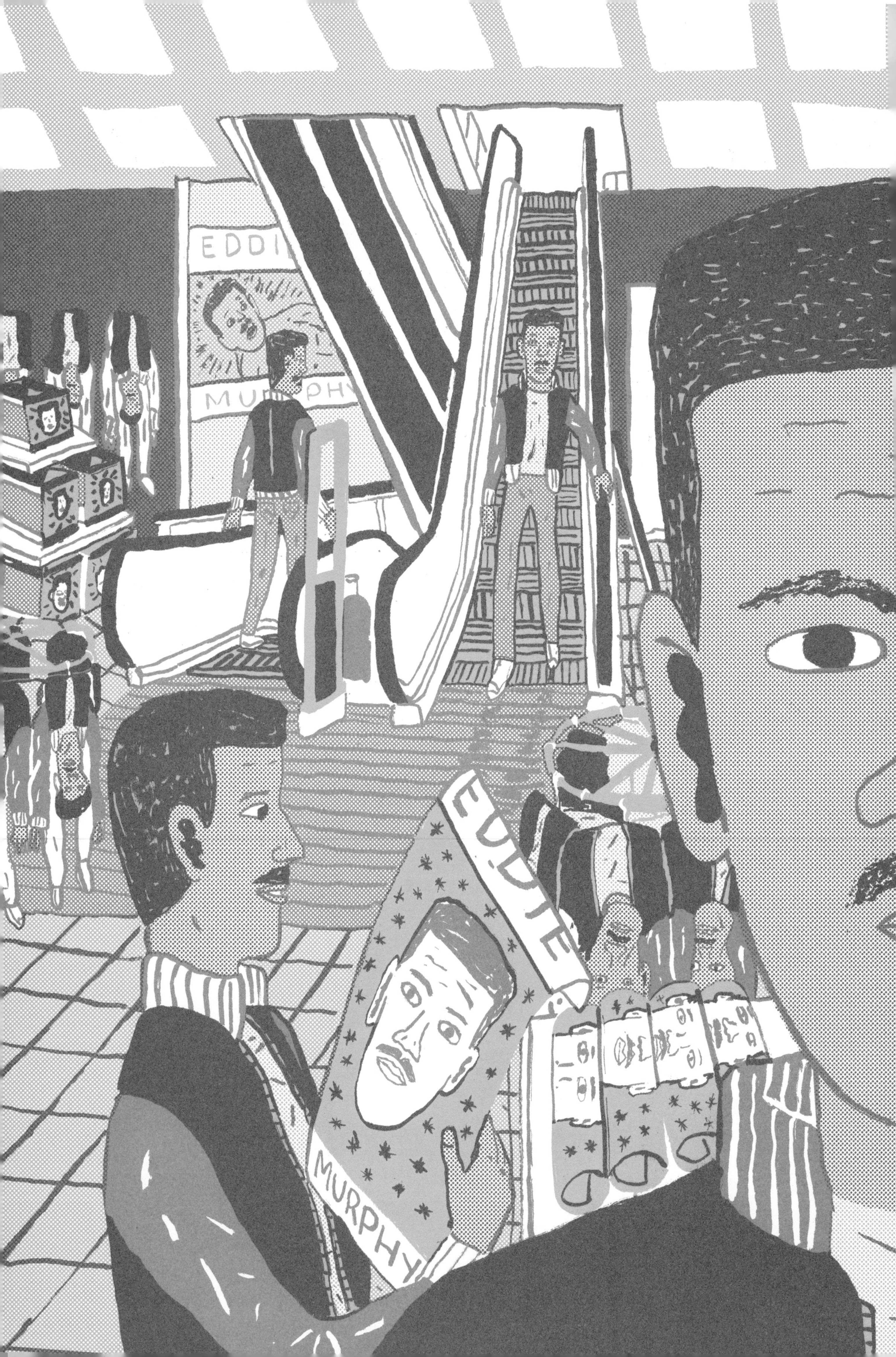
EDDI
MURPHY
EDDIE
MURPHY

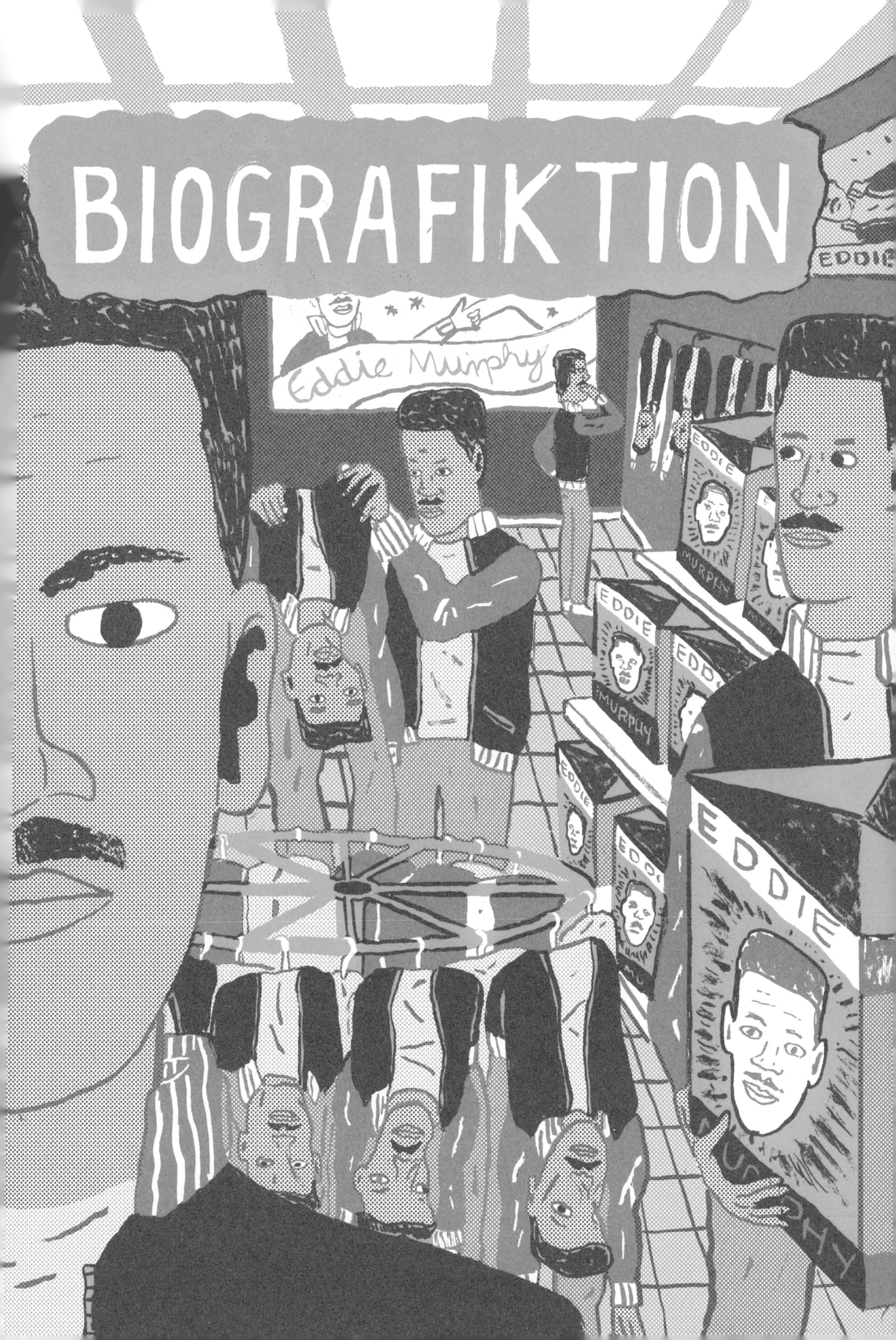
BIOGRAFIKTION
Eddie Murphy
EDDIE
EDDIE
MURPHY
EDDIE
MURPHY
EDDIE
EDDIE

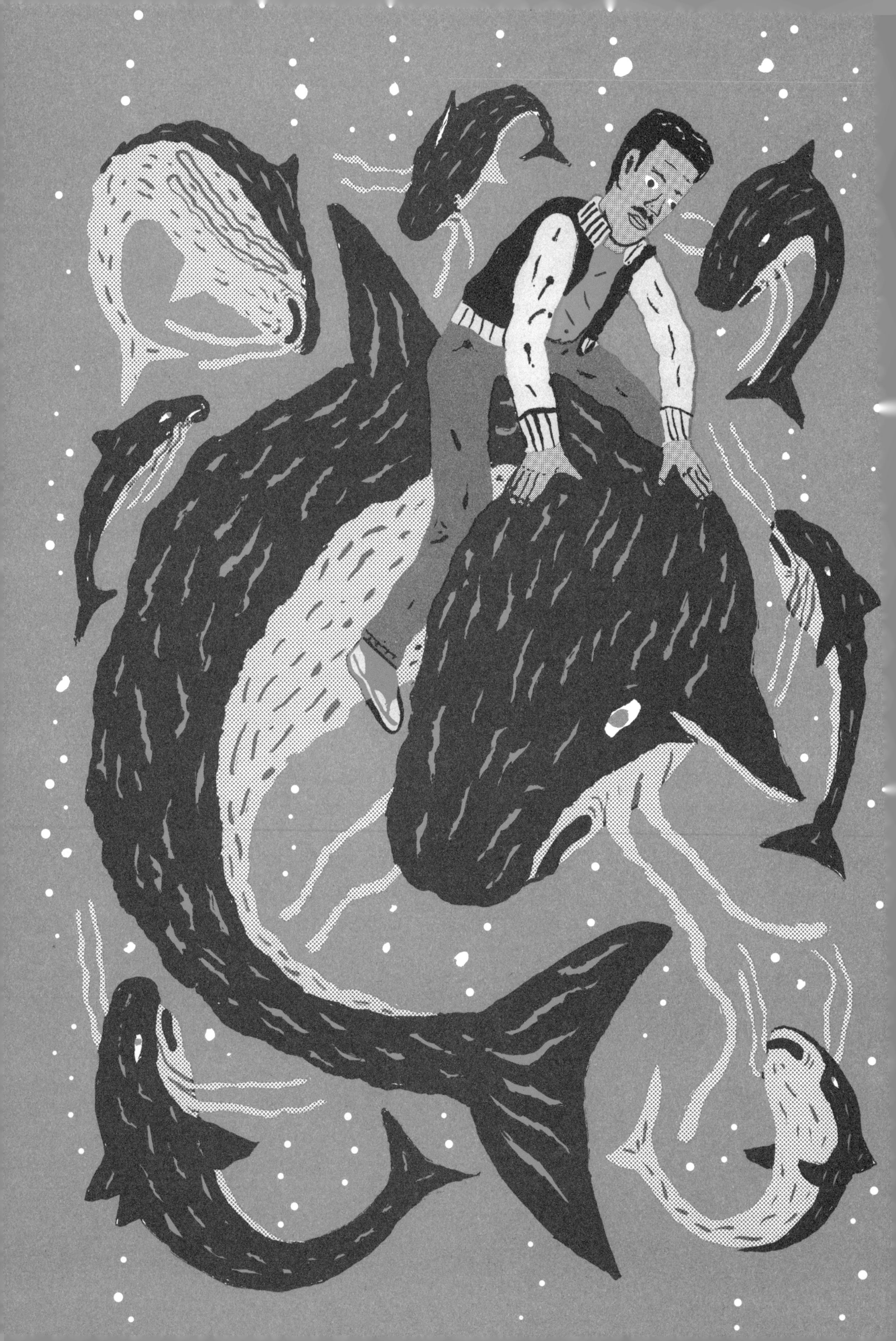

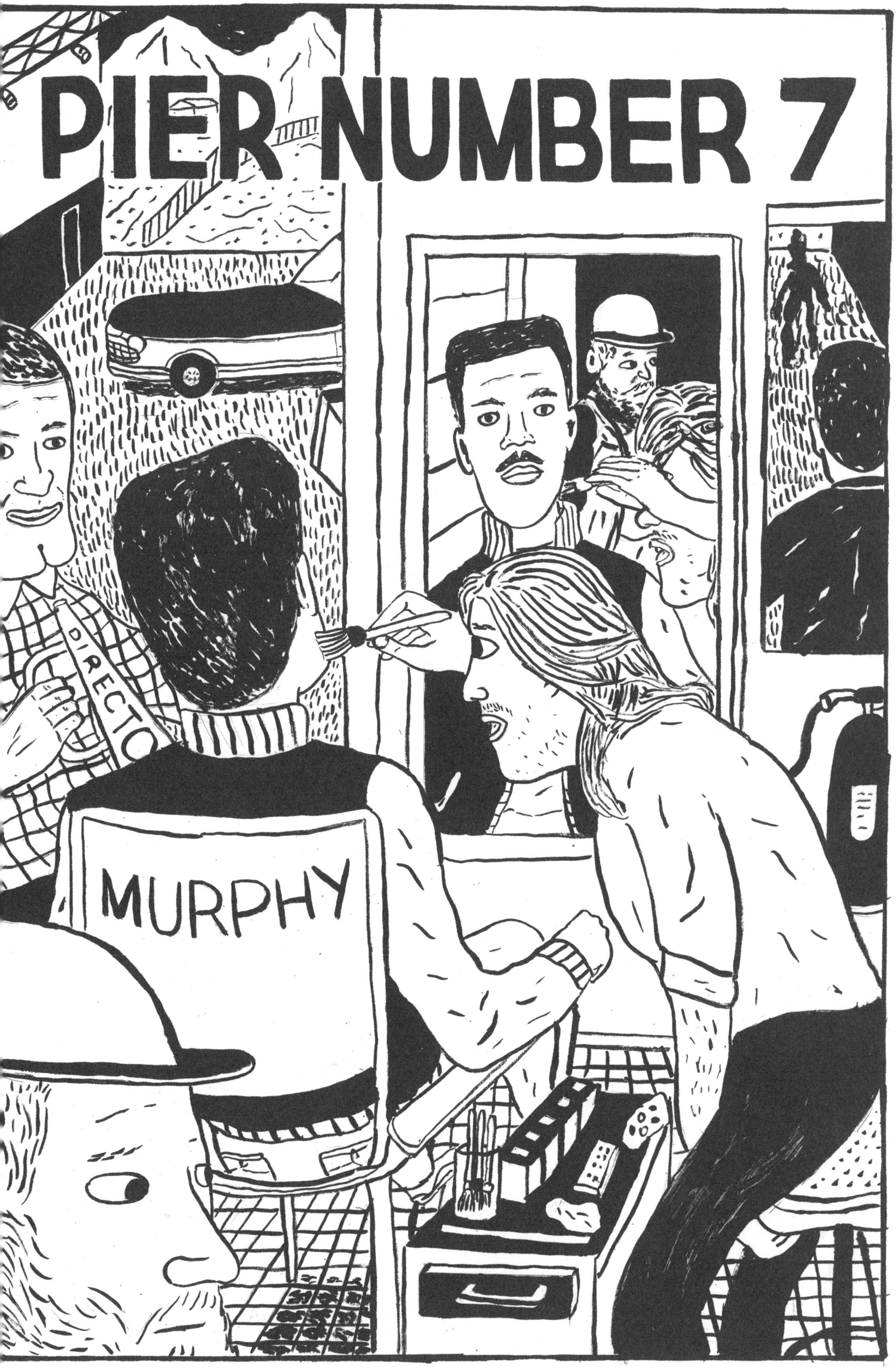
PIER NUMBER 7
DIRECTO
MURPHY

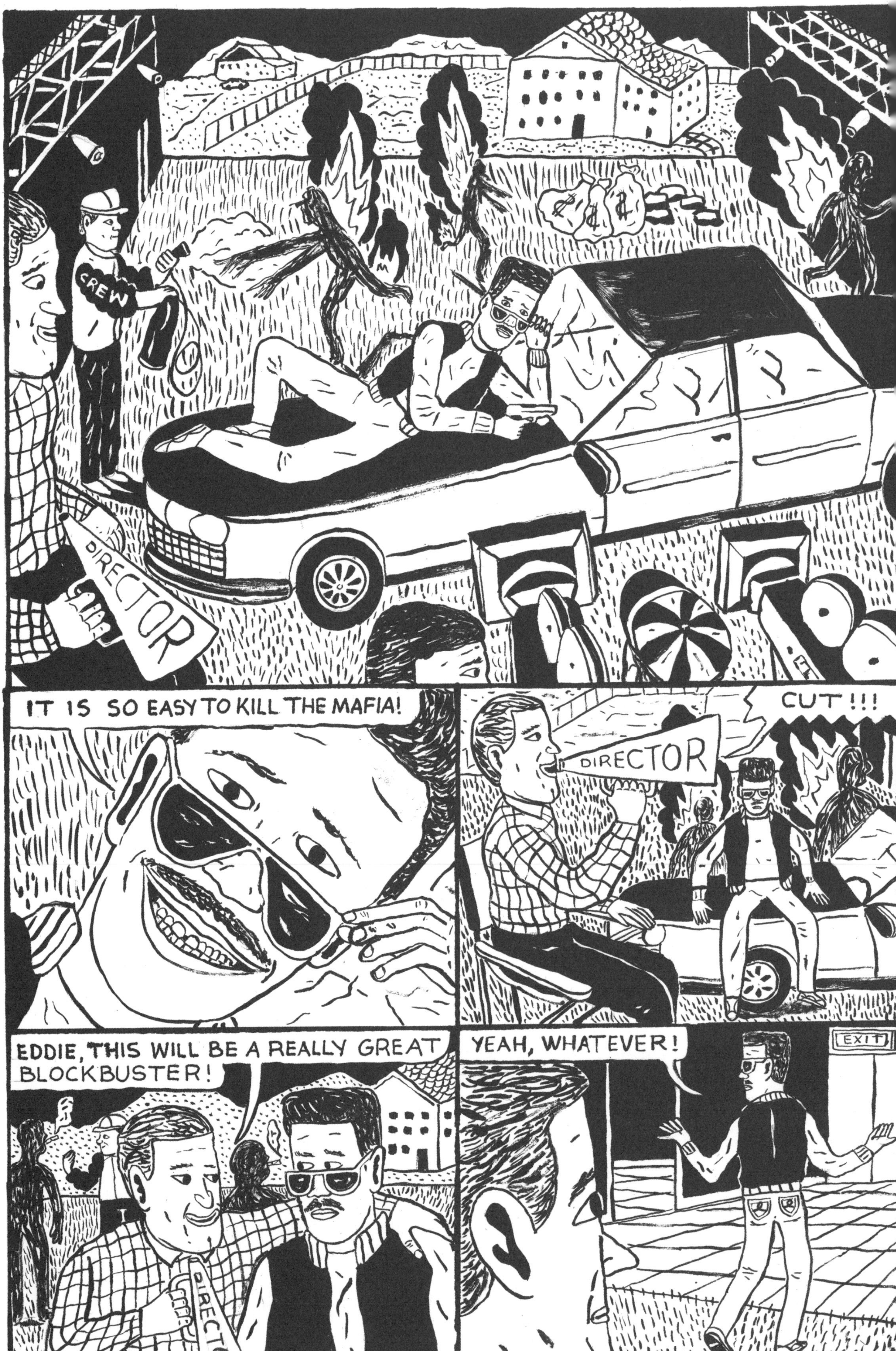
CREW
DIRECTOR
IT IS SO EASY TO KILL THE MAFIA!
CUT!!!
DIRECTOR
EDDIE, THIS WILL BE A REALLY GREAT BLOCKBUSTER!
DIRECTO
YEAH, WHATEVER!
EXIT

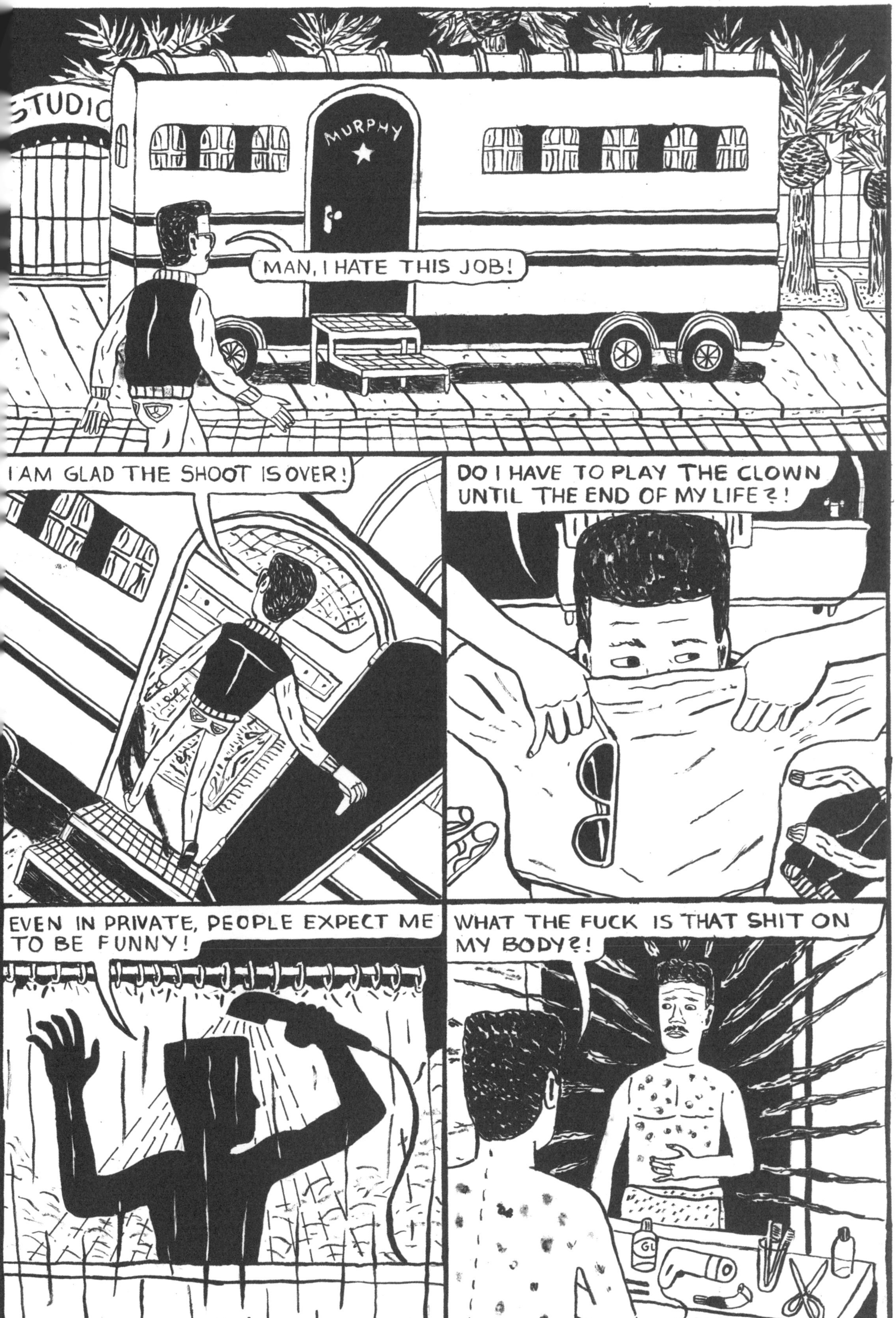
STUDIO
MURPHY
MAN, I HATE THIS JOB!
I AM GLAD THE SHOOT IS OVER!
DO I HAVE TO PLAY THE CLOWN UNTIL THE END OF MY LIFE?!
EVEN IN PRIVATE, PEOPLE EXPECT ME TO BE FUNNY!
WHAT THE FUCK IS THAT SHIT ON MY BODY?!

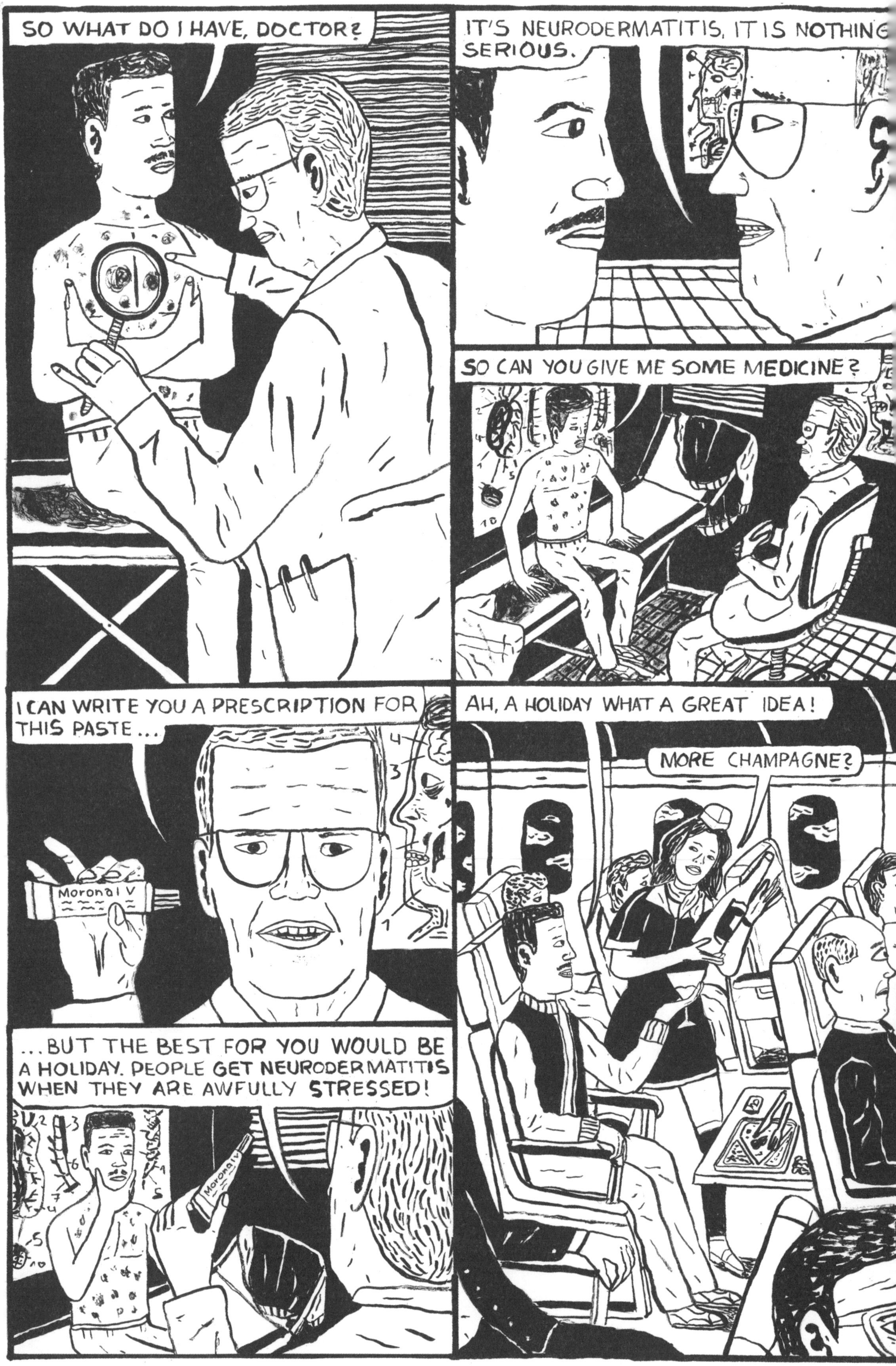

SO WHAT DO I HAVE, DOCTOR?
IT'S NEURODERMATITIS, IT IS NOTHING SERIOUS.
SO CAN YOU GIVE ME SOME MEDICINE?
I CAN WRITE YOU A PRESCRIPTION FOR THIS PASTE...
Moronal V
...BUT THE BEST FOR YOU WOULD BE A HOLIDAY. PEOPLE GET NEURODERMATITIS WHEN THEY ARE AWFULLY STRESSED!
AH, A HOLIDAY WHAT A GREAT IDEA!
MORE CHAMPAGNE?

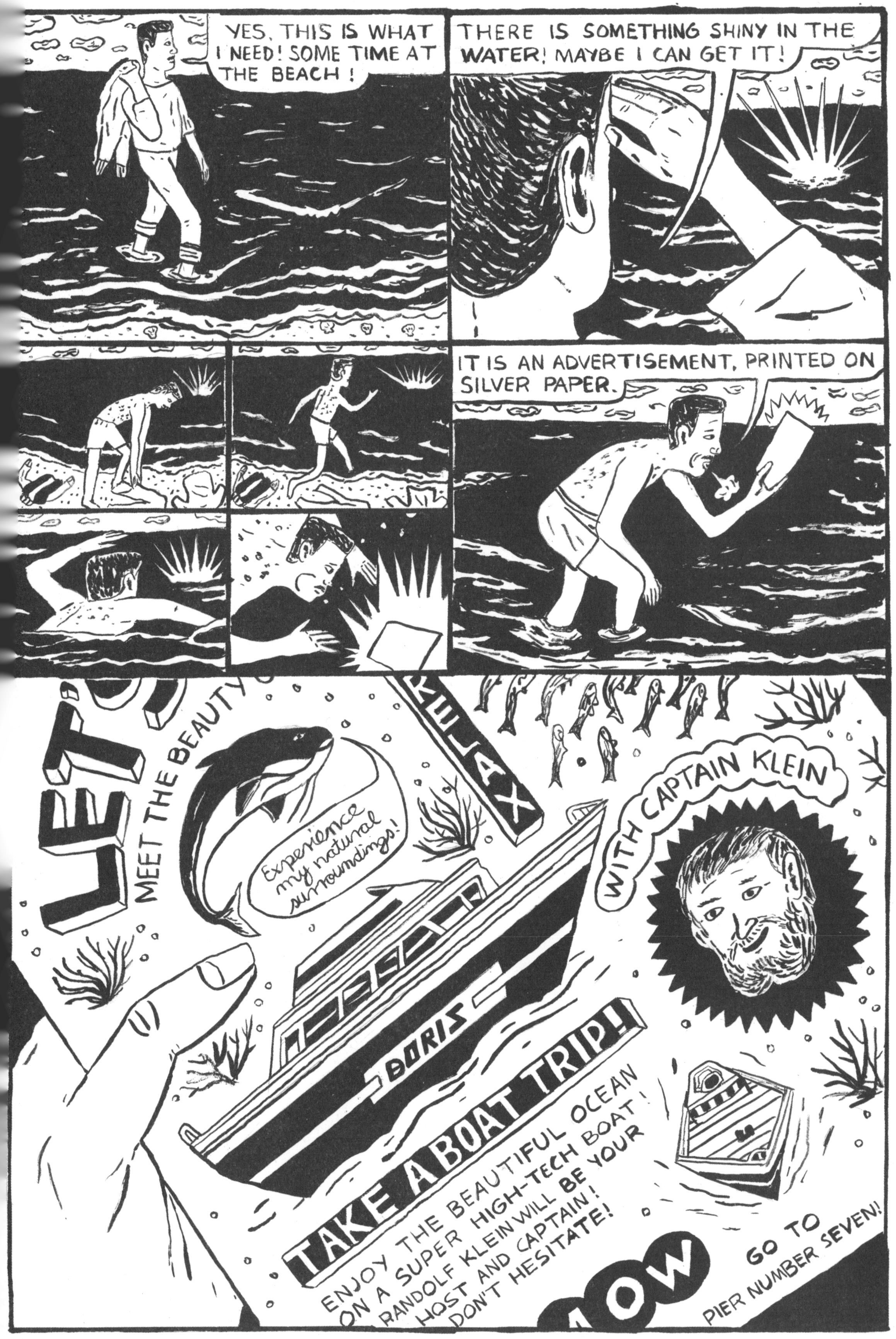
YES, THIS IS WHAT I NEED! SOME TIME AT THE BEACH!
THERE IS SOMETHING SHINY IN THE WATER! MAYBE I CAN GET IT!
IT IS AN ADVERTISEMENT, PRINTED ON SILVER PAPER.
LET
MEET THE BEAUTY
RELAX
Experience my natural surroundings!
WITH CAPTAIN KLEIN
DORIS
TAKE A BOAT TRIP!
ENJOY THE BEAUTIFUL OCEAN ON A SUPER HIGH-TECH BOAT! RANDOLF KLEIN WILL BE YOUR HOST AND CAPTAIN! DON'T HESITATE!
OW
GO TO PIER NUMBER SEVEN!

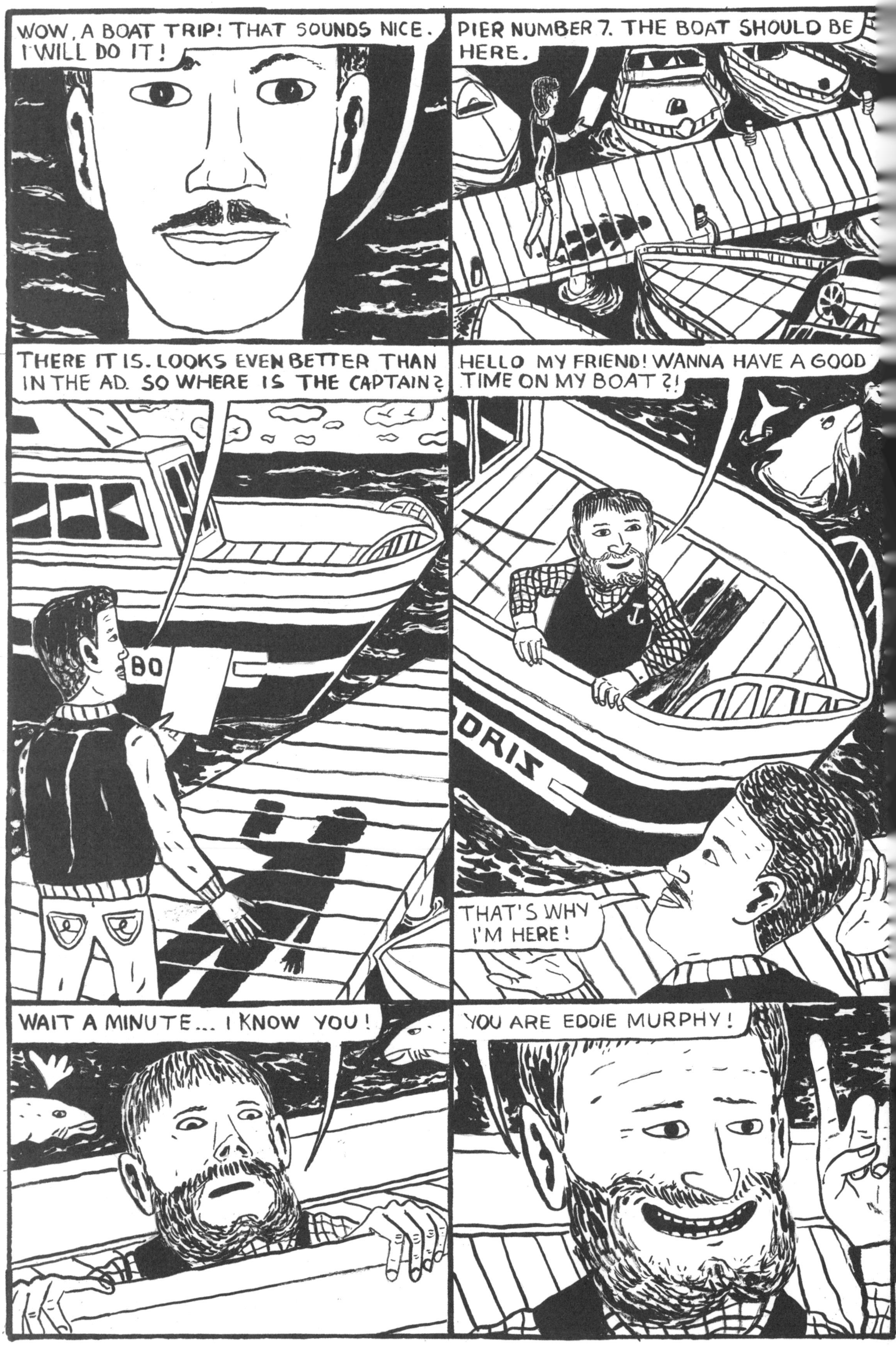
WOW, A BOAT TRIP! THAT SOUNDS NICE. I WILL DO IT!
PIER NUMBER 7. THE BOAT SHOULD BE HERE.
THERE IT IS. LOOKS EVEN BETTER THAN IN THE AD. SO WHERE IS THE CAPTAIN?
BO
HELLO MY FRIEND! WANNA HAVE A GOOD TIME ON MY BOAT?!
DORIS
THAT'S WHY I'M HERE!
WAIT A MINUTE... I KNOW YOU!
YOU ARE EDDIE MURPHY!

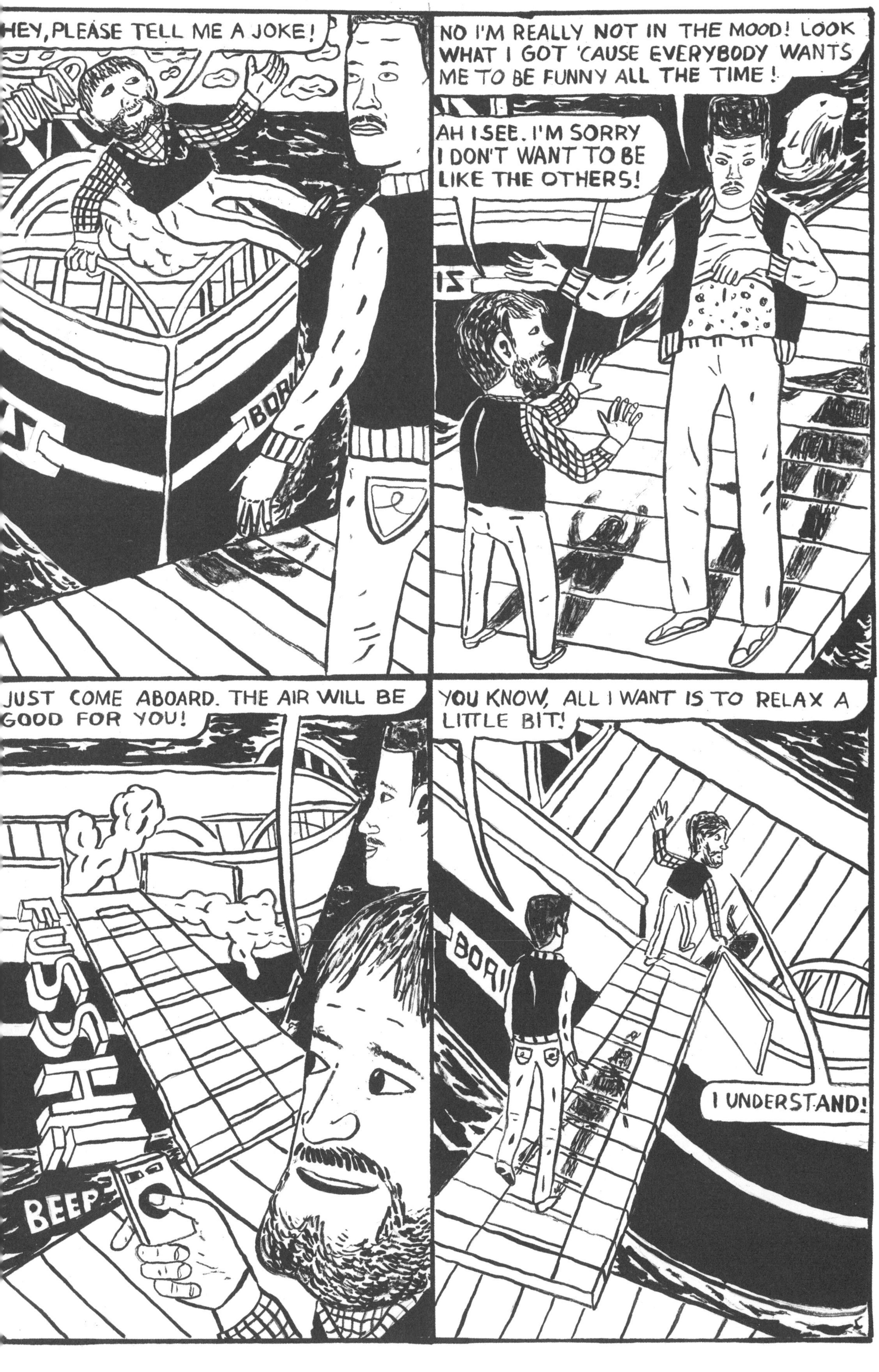
HEY, PLEASE TELL ME A JOKE!
NO I'M REALLY NOT IN THE MOOD! LOOK WHAT I GOT 'CAUSE EVERYBODY WANTS ME TO BE FUNNY ALL THE TIME!
AH I SEE. I'M SORRY I DON'T WANT TO BE LIKE THE OTHERS!
JUST COME ABOARD. THE AIR WILL BE GOOD FOR YOU!
FLUSH
BEEP
YOU KNOW, ALL I WANT IS TO RELAX A LITTLE BIT!
I UNDERSTAND!

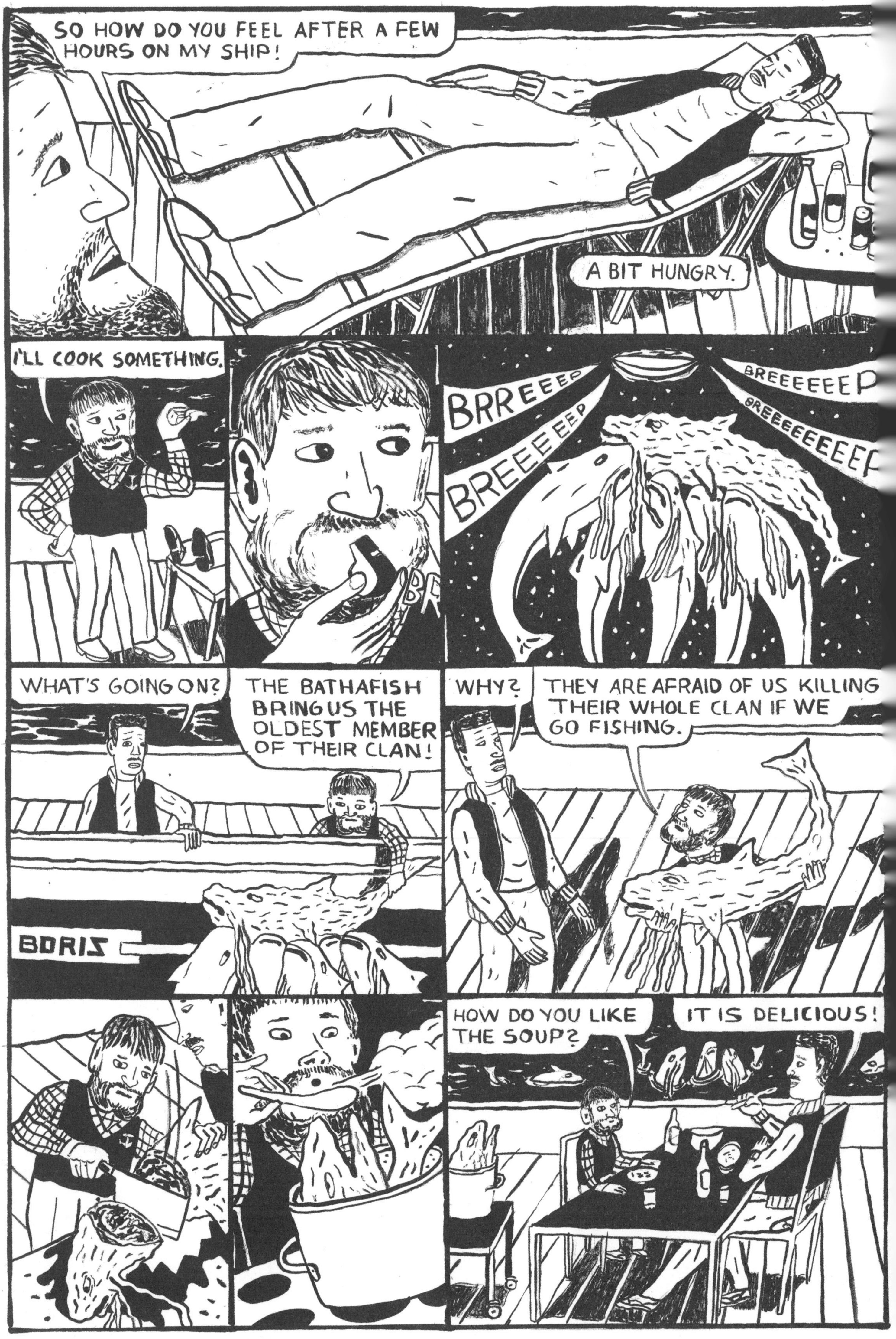
SO HOW DO YOU FEEL AFTER A FEW HOURS ON MY SHIP!
A BIT HUNGRY.
I'LL COOK SOMETHING.
BRREEEEP
BREEEEEP
BREEEEEEEP
BREEEEEEEEEP
WHAT'S GOING ON?
THE BATHAFISH BRING US THE OLDEST MEMBER OF THEIR CLAN!
BORIS
WHY?
THEY ARE AFRAID OF US KILLING THEIR WHOLE CLAN IF WE GO FISHING.
HOW DO YOU LIKE THE SOUP?
IT IS DELICIOUS!

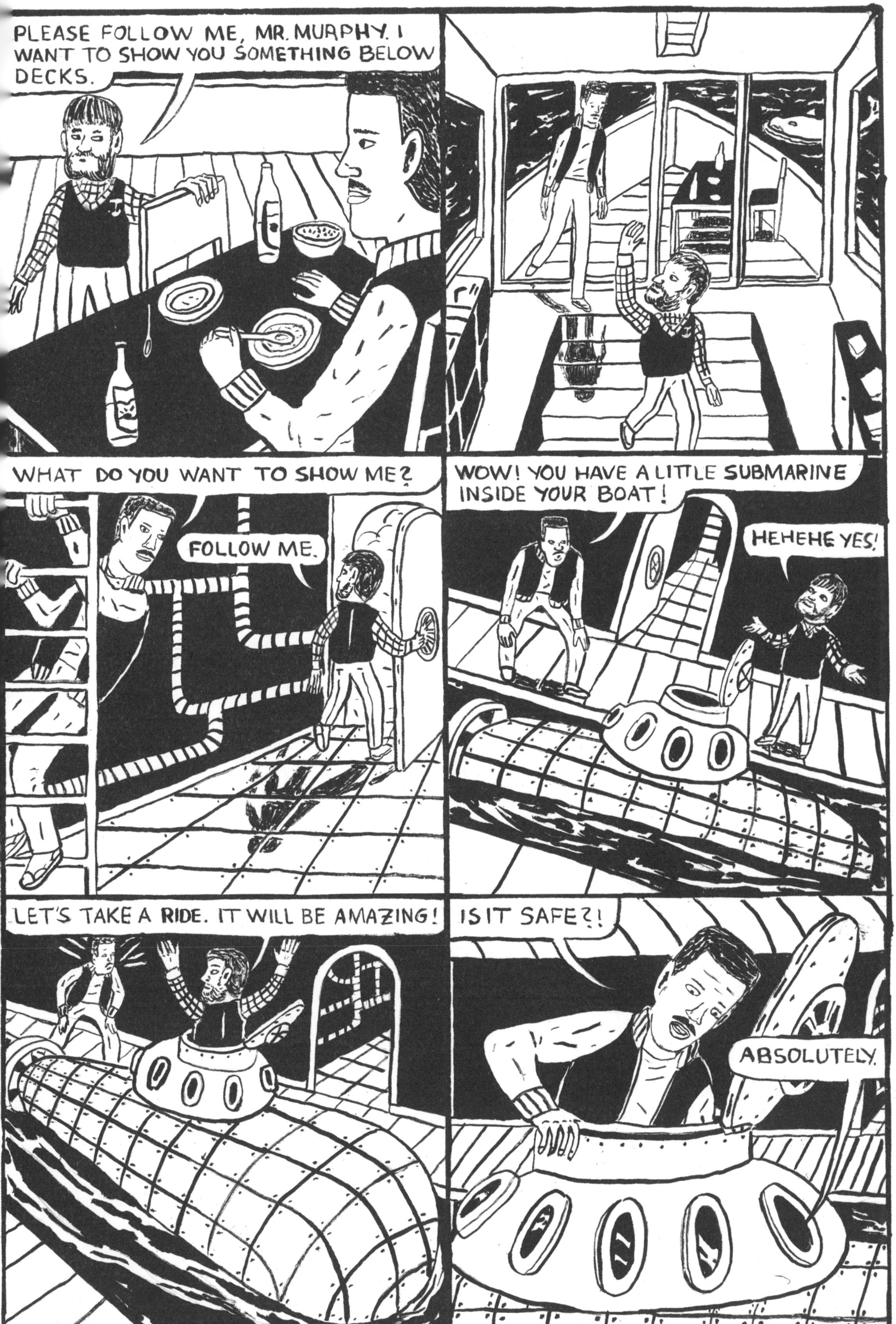
PLEASE FOLLOW ME, MR. MURPHY. I WANT TO SHOW YOU SOMETHING BELOW DECKS.
WHAT DO YOU WANT TO SHOW ME?
FOLLOW ME.
WOW! YOU HAVE A LITTLE SUBMARINE INSIDE YOUR BOAT!
HEHEHE YES!
LET'S TAKE A RIDE. IT WILL BE AMAZING!
IS IT SAFE?!
ABSOLUTELY.

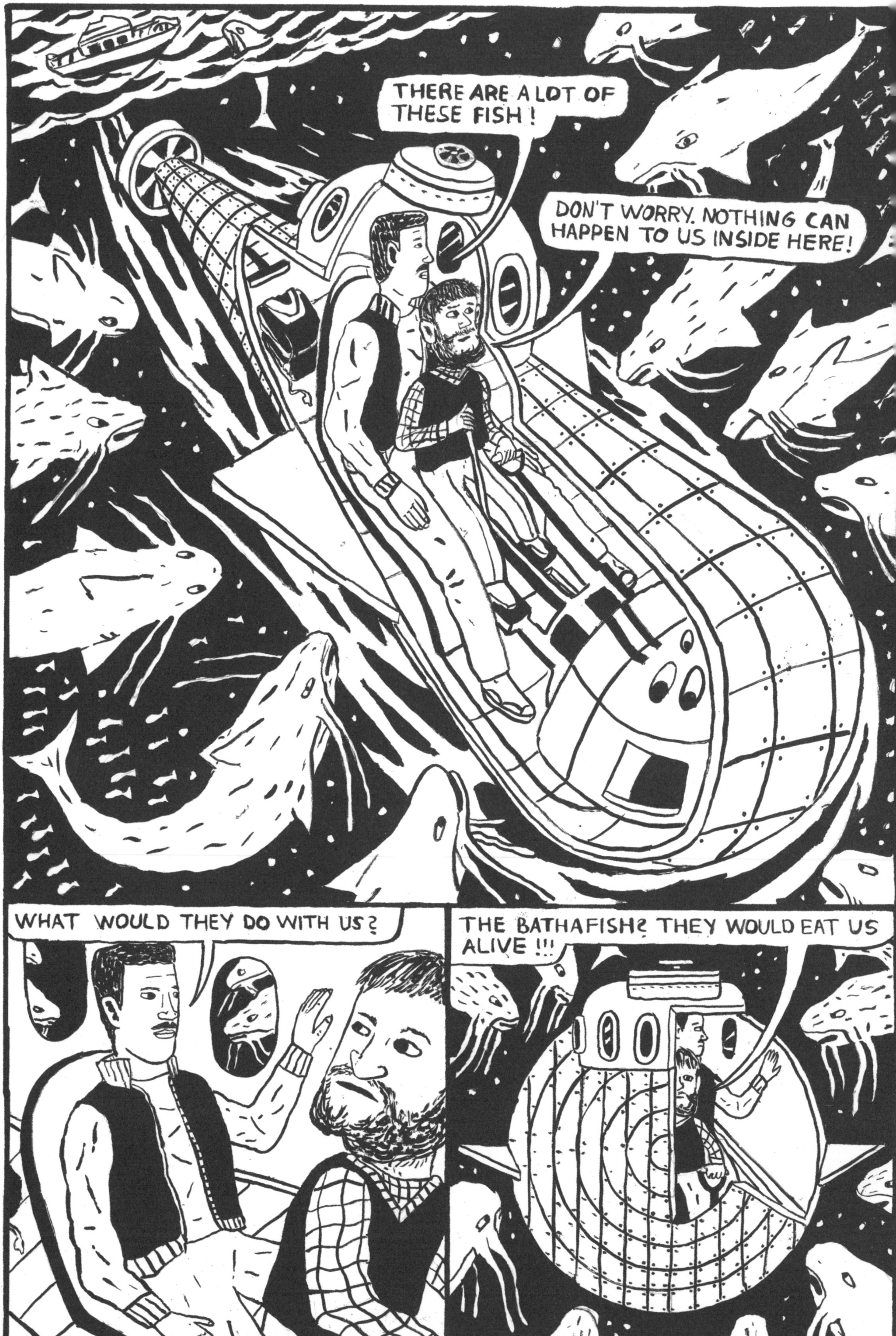
THERE ARE A LOT OF THESE FISH !
DON'T WORRY. NOTHING CAN HAPPEN TO US INSIDE HERE!
WHAT WOULD THEY DO WITH US?
THE BATHAFISH? THEY WOULD EAT US ALIVE !!!

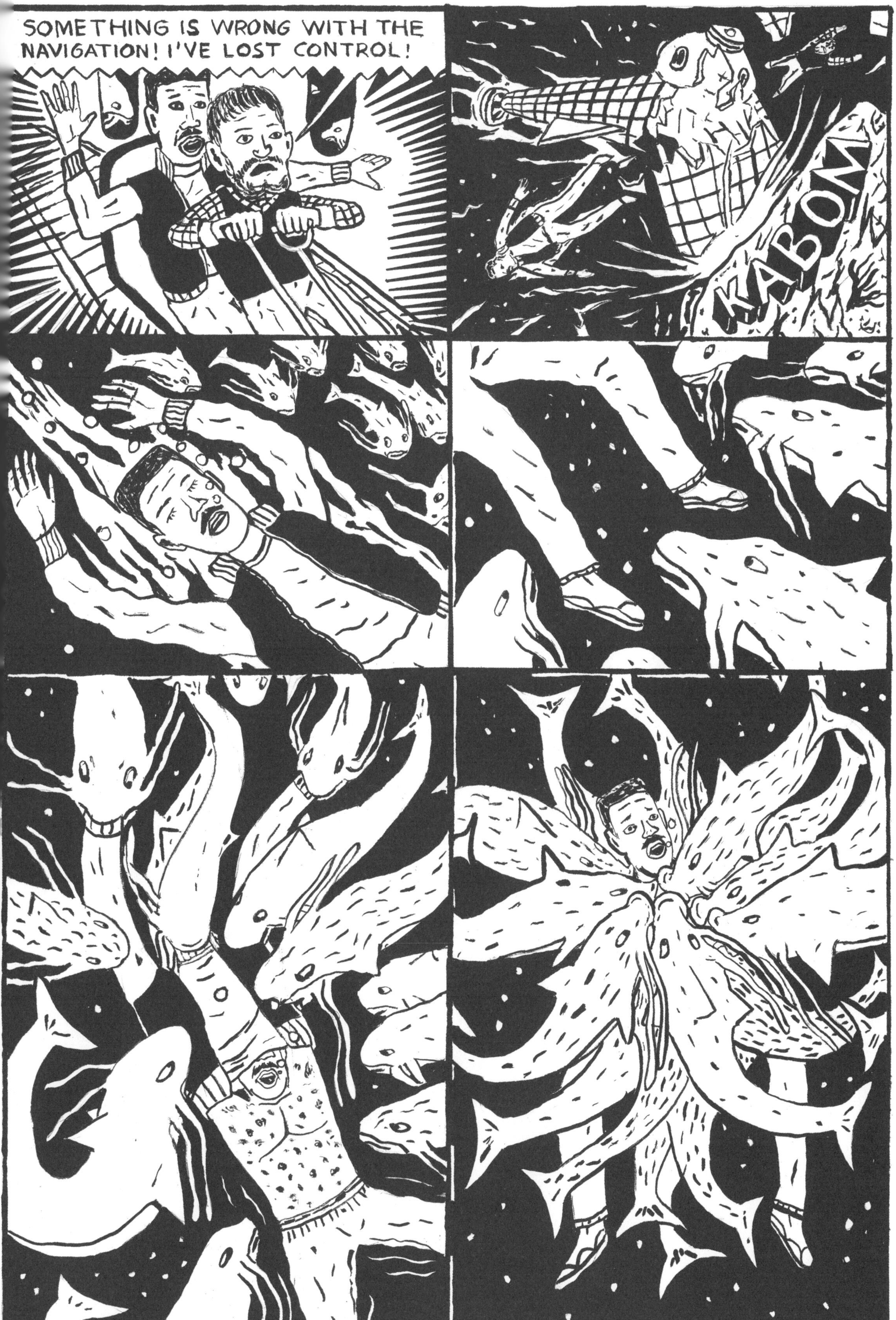
SOMETHING IS WRONG WITH THE NAVIGATION! I'VE LOST CONTROL!
KABOOM

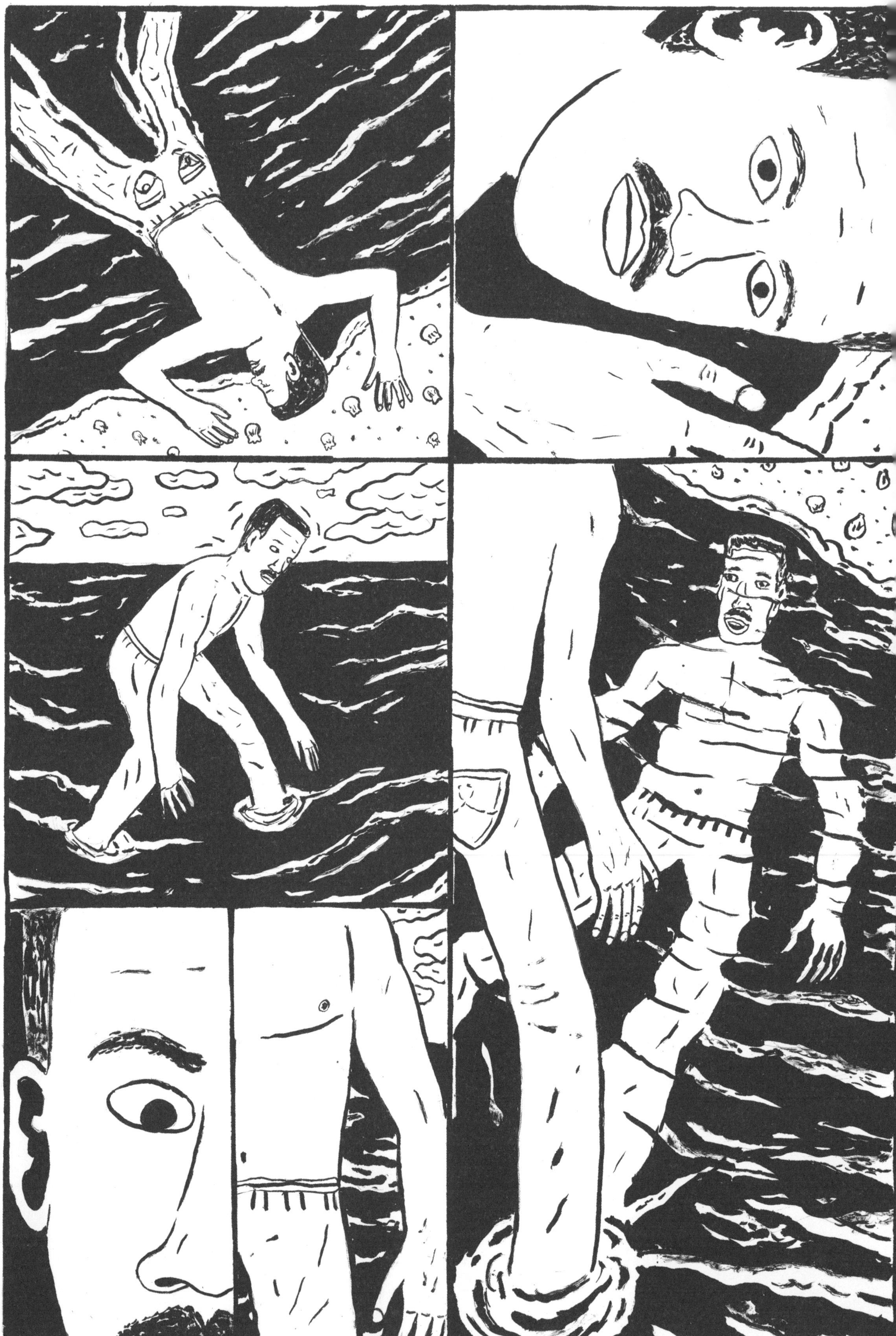

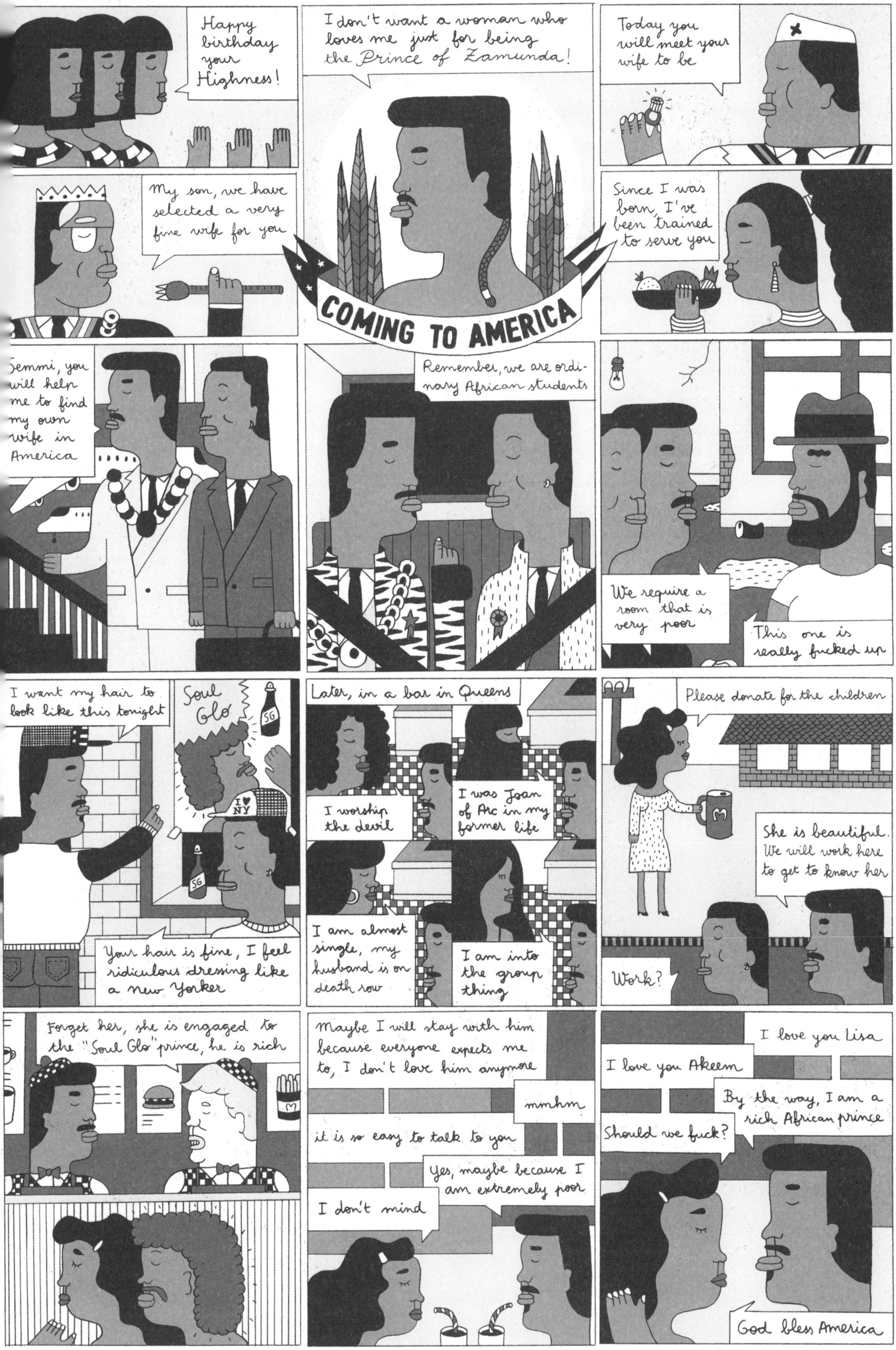
Happy birthday your Highness!
I don't want a woman who loves me just for being the Prince of Zamunda!
Today you will meet your wife to be
My son, we have selected a very fine wife for you
COMING TO AMERICA
Since I was born, I've been trained to serve you
Semmi, you will help me to find my own wife in America
Remember, we are ordinary African students
We require a room that is very poor
This one is really fucked up
I want my hair to look like this tonight
Soul Glo
SG
I ♥ NY
SG
Your hair is fine, I feel ridiculous dressing like a New Yorker
Later, in a bar in Queens
I worship the devil
I was Joan of Arc in my former life
I am almost single, my husband is on death row
I am into the group thing
Please donate for the children
M
She is beautiful. We will work here to get to know her
Work?
Forget her, she is engaged to the "Soul Glo" prince, he is rich
M
Maybe I will stay with him because everyone expects me to, I don't love him anymore
mmhm
it is so easy to talk to you
Yes, maybe because I am extremely poor
I don't mind
I love you Lisa
I love you Akeem
By the way, I am a rich African prince
Should we fuck?
God bless America

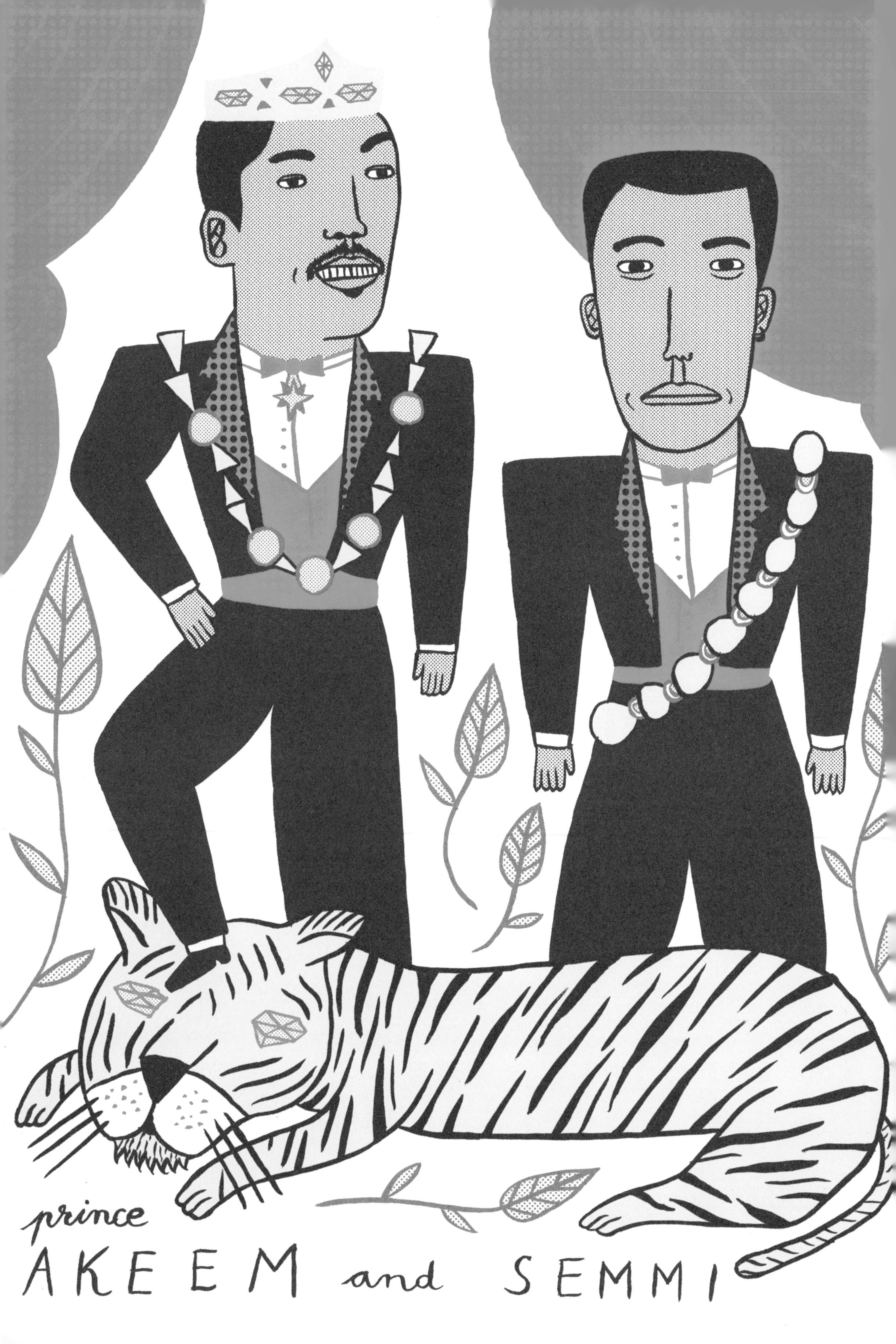
prince
AKEEM and SEMMI

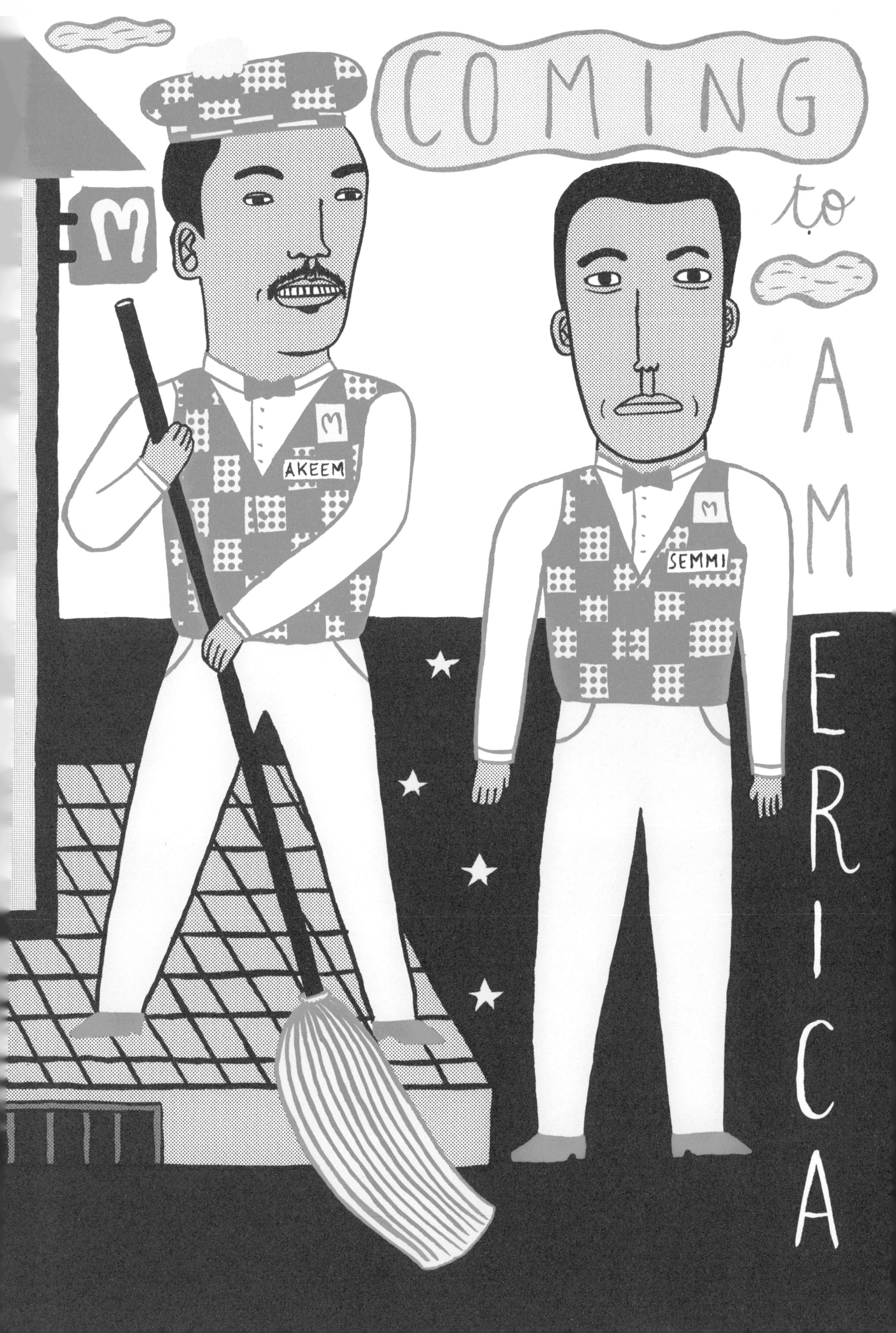
COMING
to
AMERICA
M
AKEEM
M
SEMMI
M

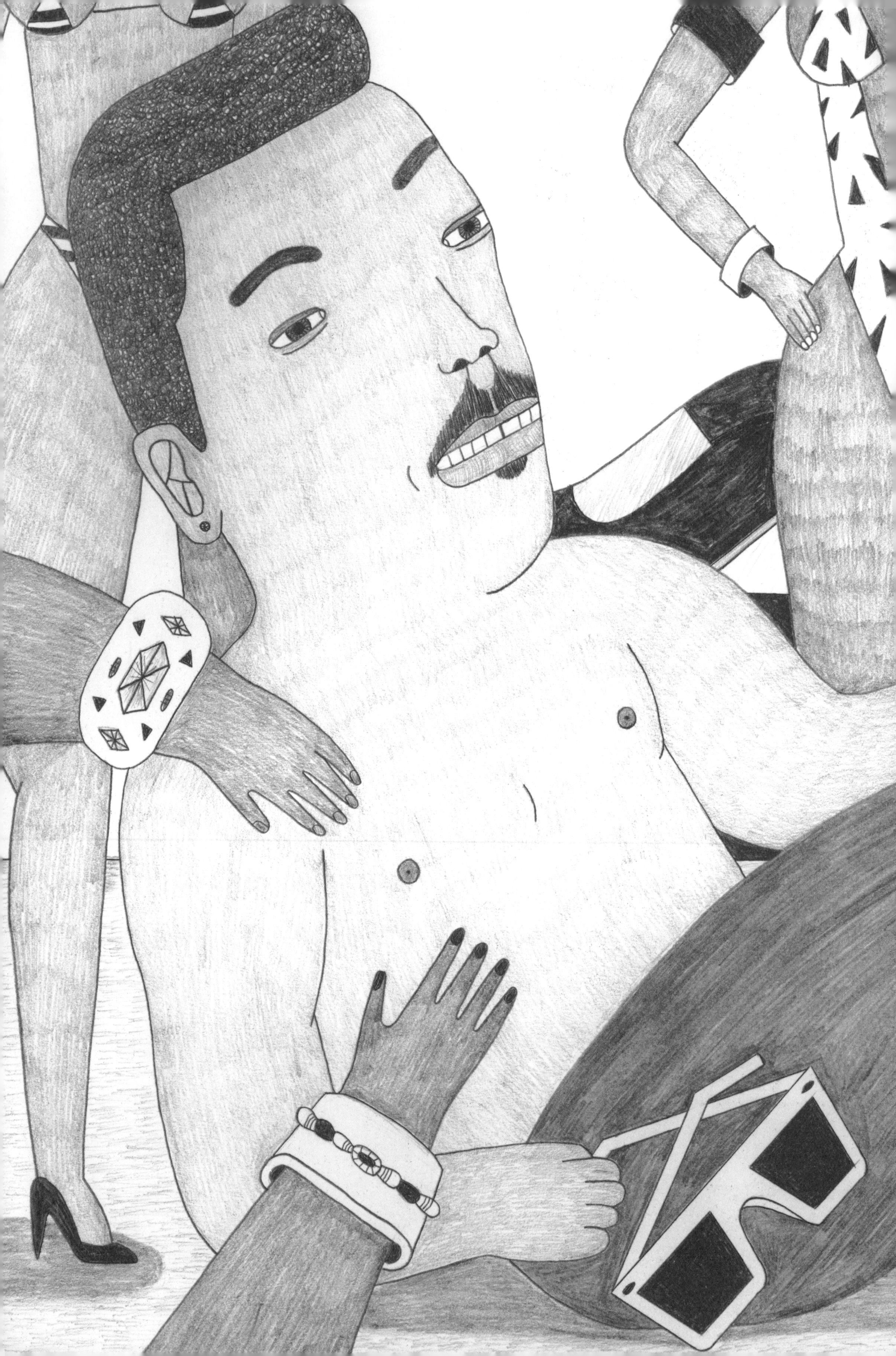

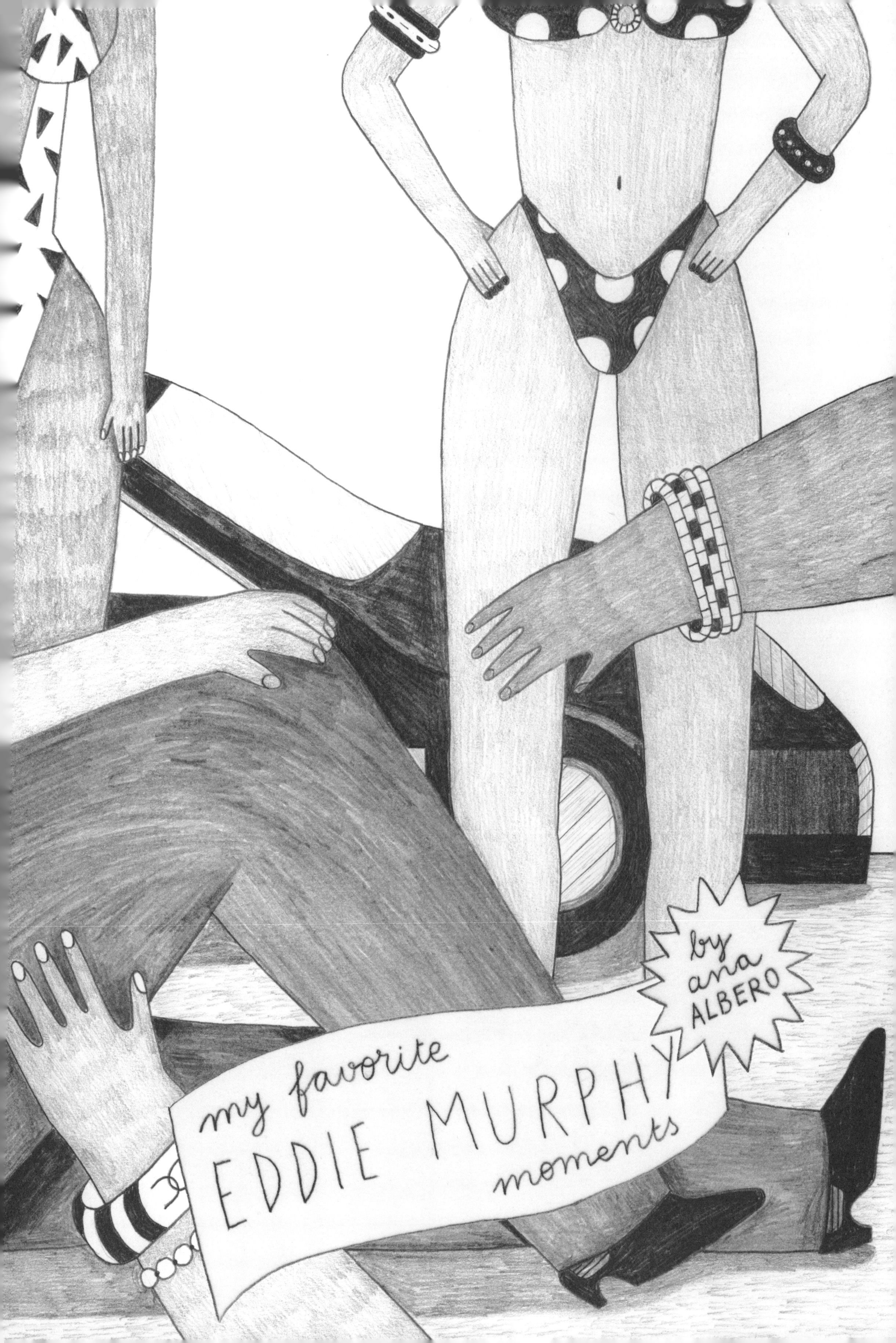

by ana ALBERO
my favorite
EDDIE MURPHY
moments

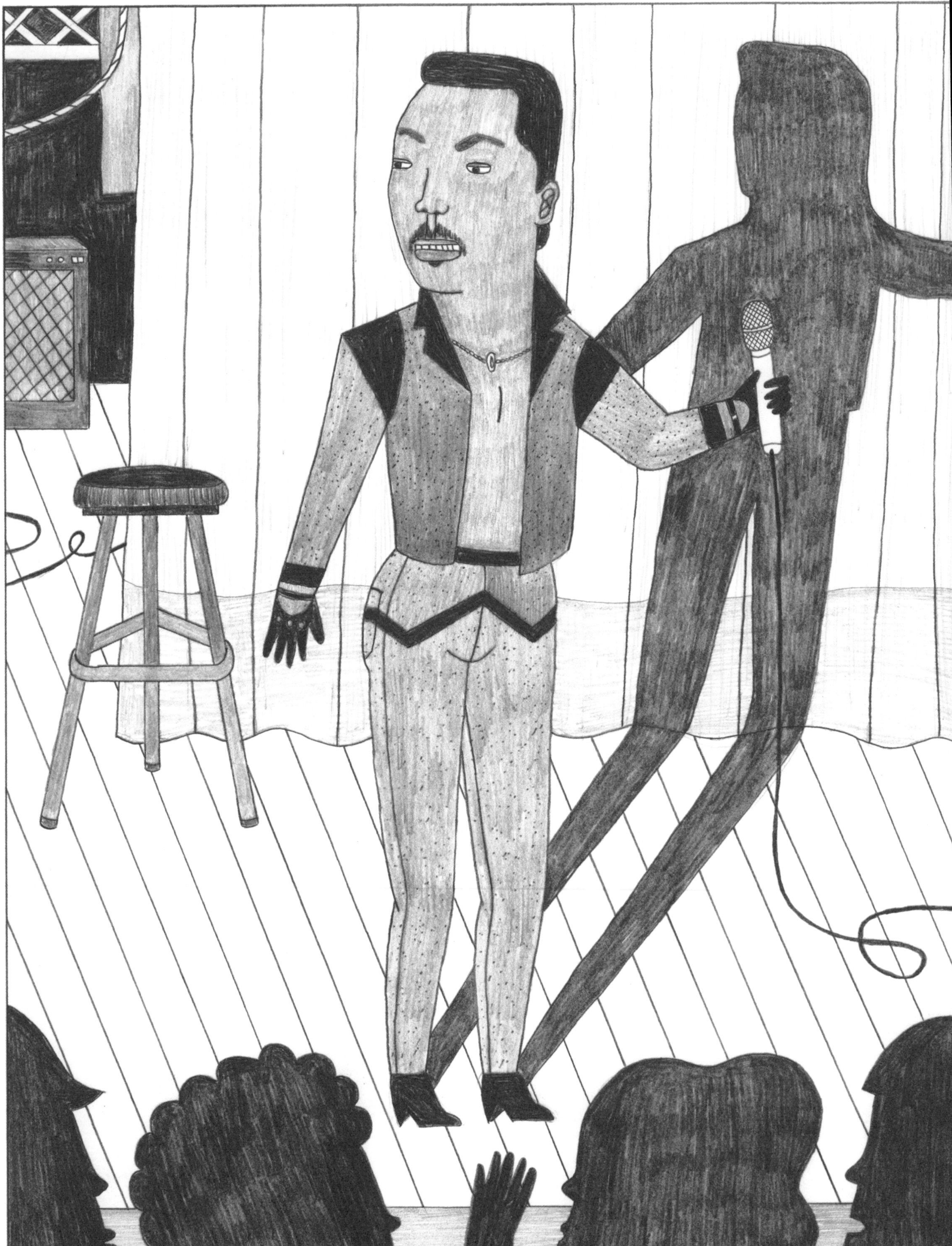

I LOVE THE TIGHT LEATHER OUTFITS MURPHY WAS WEARING IN THE 80'S AT HIS STAND-UP COMEDY SHOWS. IN 1983 HE RELEASED HIS SHOW "DELIRIOUS" ON TELEVISION. IT WAS A MAJOR SUCCESS. "RAW" FOLLOWED IN 1987. IT CONTAINS THE MOST USES OF THE WORD "FUCK" IN AN 80'S FILM.

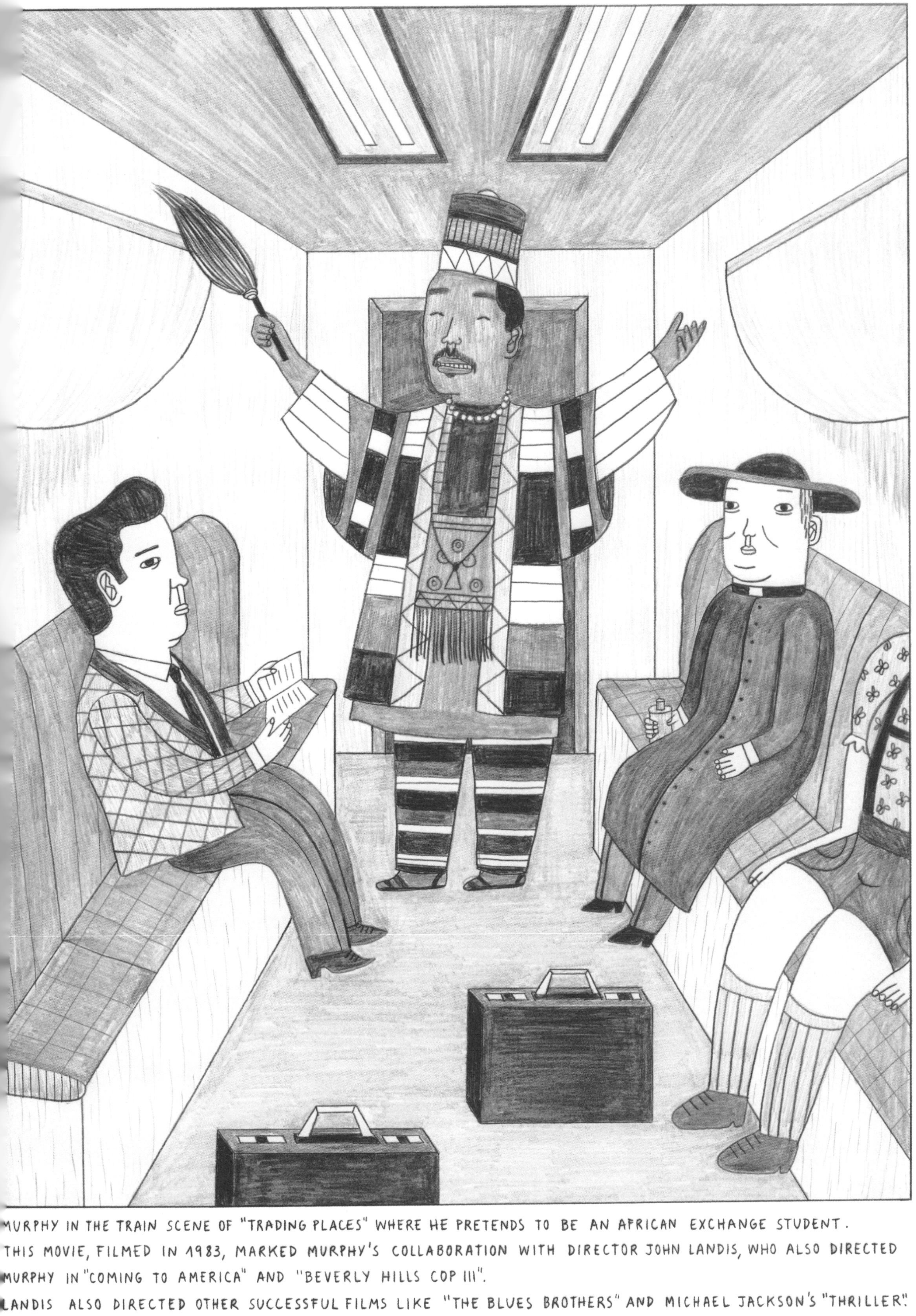

MURPHY IN THE TRAIN SCENE OF "TRADING PLACES" WHERE HE PRETENDS TO BE AN AFRICAN EXCHANGE STUDENT.
THIS MOVIE, FILMED IN 1983, MARKED MURPHY'S COLLABORATION WITH DIRECTOR JOHN LANDIS, WHO ALSO DIRECTED MURPHY IN "COMING TO AMERICA" AND "BEVERLY HILLS COP III".
LANDIS ALSO DIRECTED OTHER SUCCESSFUL FILMS LIKE "THE BLUES BROTHERS" AND MICHAEL JACKSON'S "THRILLER".

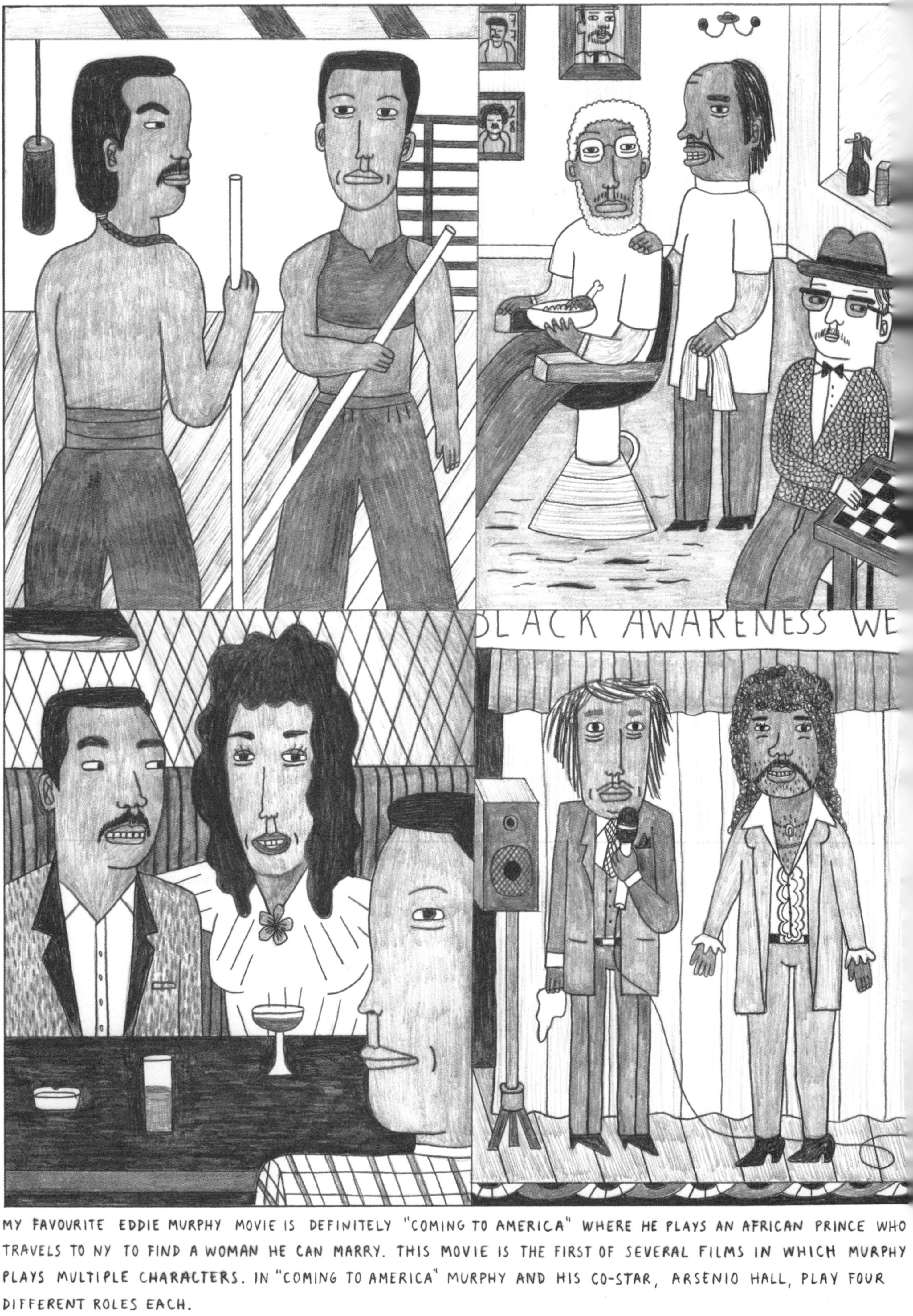
BLACK AWARENESS WE

MY FAVOURITE EDDIE MURPHY MOVIE IS DEFINITELY "COMING TO AMERICA" WHERE HE PLAYS AN AFRICAN PRINCE WHO TRAVELS TO NY TO FIND A WOMAN HE CAN MARRY. THIS MOVIE IS THE FIRST OF SEVERAL FILMS IN WHICH MURPHY PLAYS MULTIPLE CHARACTERS. IN "COMING TO AMERICA" MURPHY AND HIS CO-STAR, ARSENIO HALL, PLAY FOUR DIFFERENT ROLES EACH.

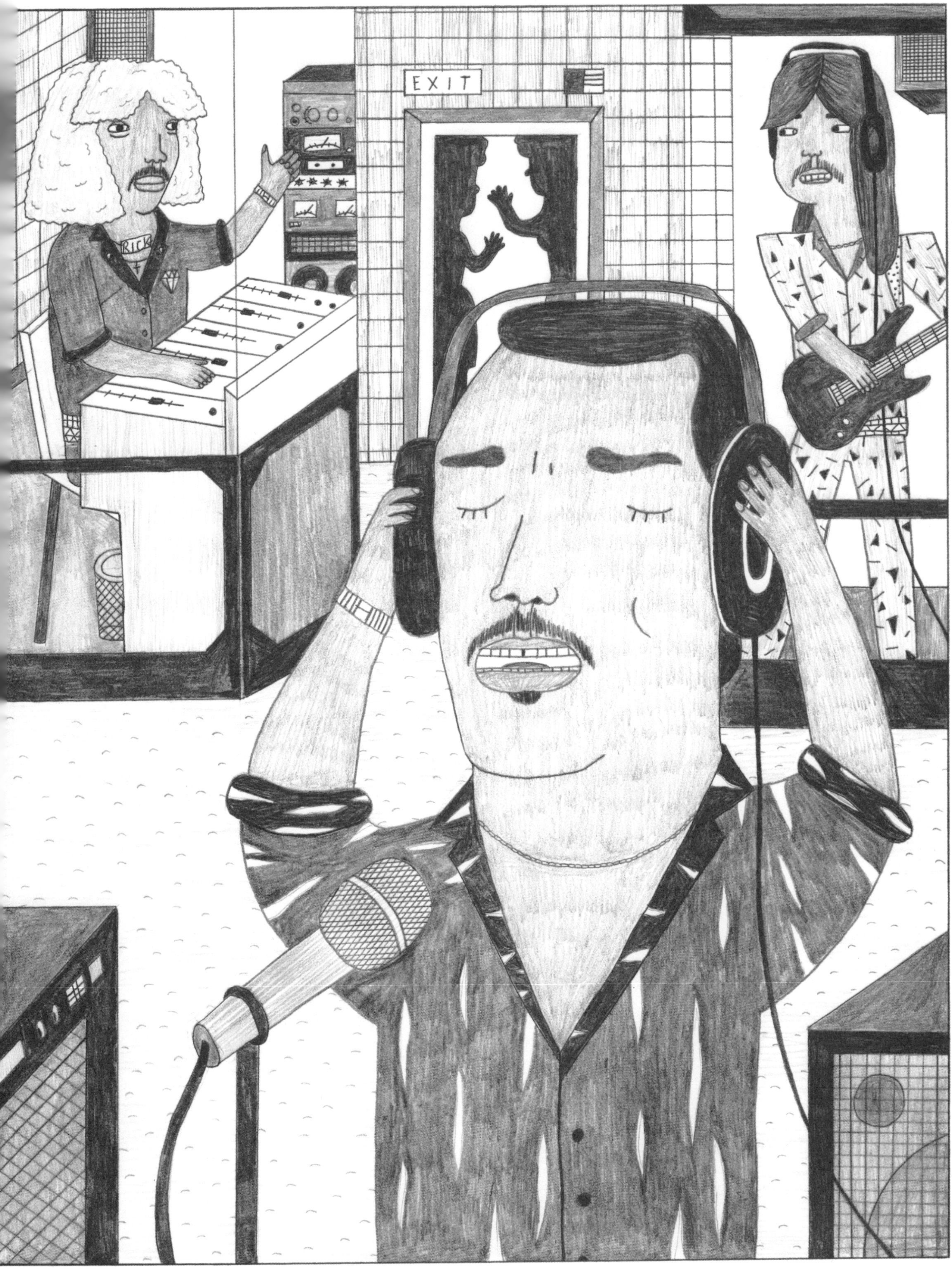
EXIT
RICK

I LOVE MURPHY'S MUSIC VIDEO "PARTY ALL THE TIME" WHERE HE APPEARS RECORDING HIS SINGLE. YOU CAN ALSO SEE SINGER RICK JAMES AND HIS AMAZING HAIRSTYLE. IN 1981, JAMES WROTE THE HIT SONG "SUPERFREAK" AND NINE YEARS LATER MC HAMMER SAMPLED IT IN "U CAN'T TOUCH THIS". "PARTY ALL THE TIME" IS CONSIDERED ONE OF THE WORST SONGS OF ALL TIME.

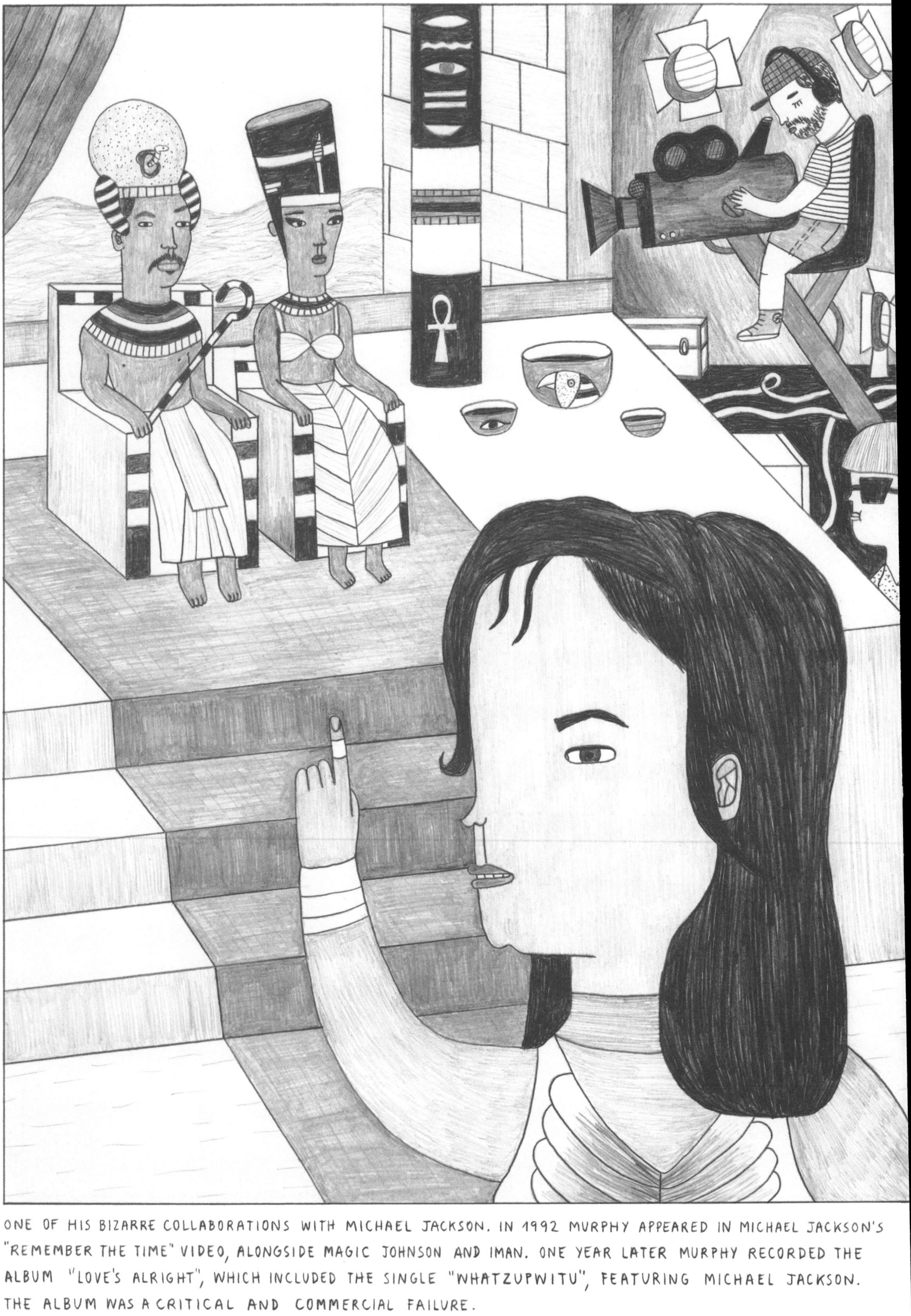

ONE OF HIS BIZARRE COLLABORATIONS WITH MICHAEL JACKSON. IN 1992 MURPHY APPEARED IN MICHAEL JACKSON'S "REMEMBER THE TIME" VIDEO, ALONGSIDE MAGIC JOHNSON AND IMAN. ONE YEAR LATER MURPHY RECORDED THE ALBUM "LOVE'S ALRIGHT", WHICH INCLUDED THE SINGLE "WHATZUPWITU", FEATURING MICHAEL JACKSON. THE ALBUM WAS A CRITICAL AND COMMERCIAL FAILURE.

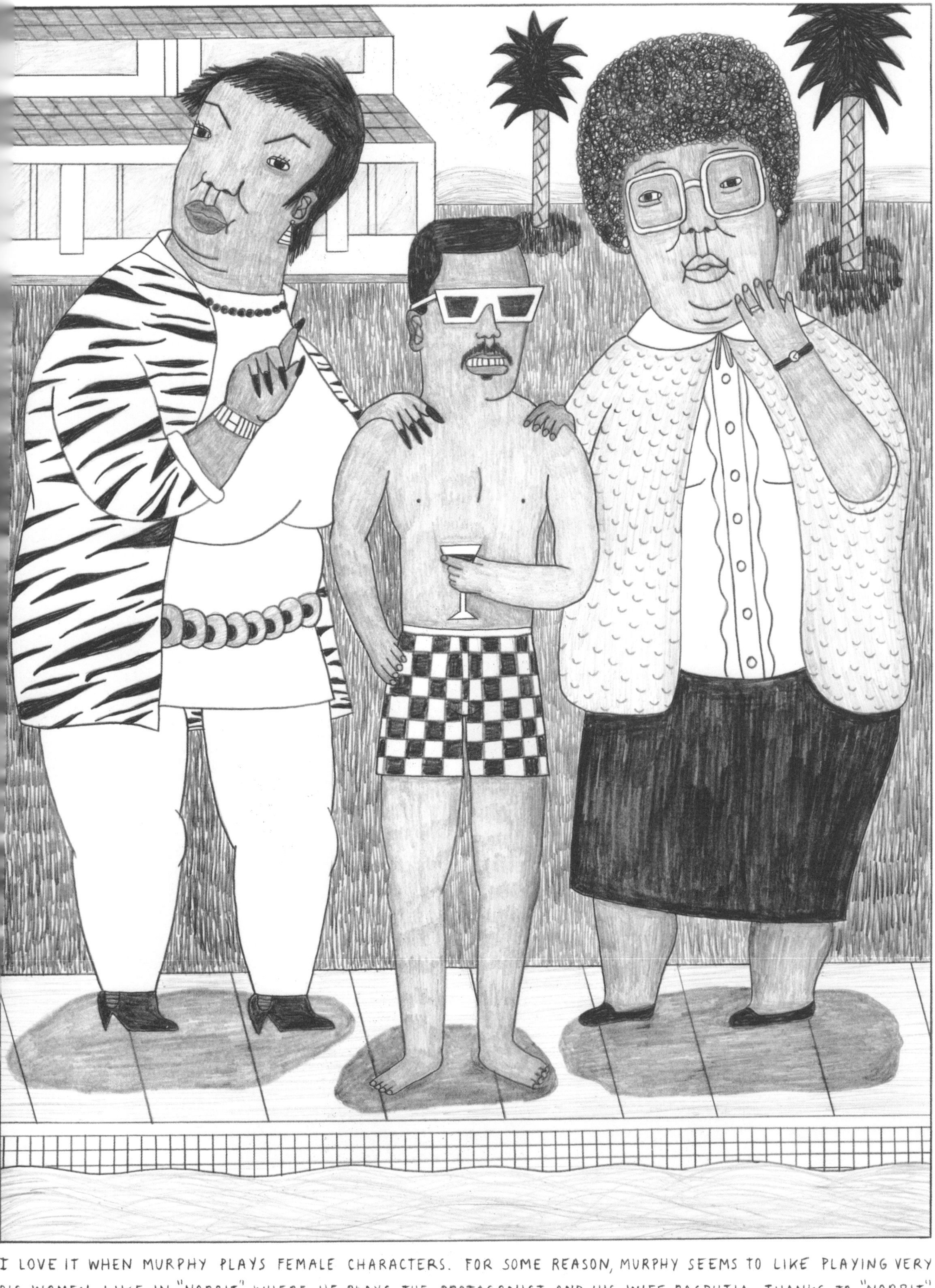

I LOVE IT WHEN MURPHY PLAYS FEMALE CHARACTERS. FOR SOME REASON, MURPHY SEEMS TO LIKE PLAYING VERY BIG WOMEN. LIKE IN "NORBIT", WHERE HE PLAYS THE PROTAGONIST AND HIS WIFE RASPUTIA. THANKS TO "NORBIT" MURPHY WAS NOMINATED FOR WORST ACTOR AND WORST SUPPORTING ACTRESS, BECOMING THE FIRST PERSON EVER TO WIN A RAZZIE AWARD IN BOTH MALE AND FEMALE ACTING CATEGORIES IN ONE YEAR.

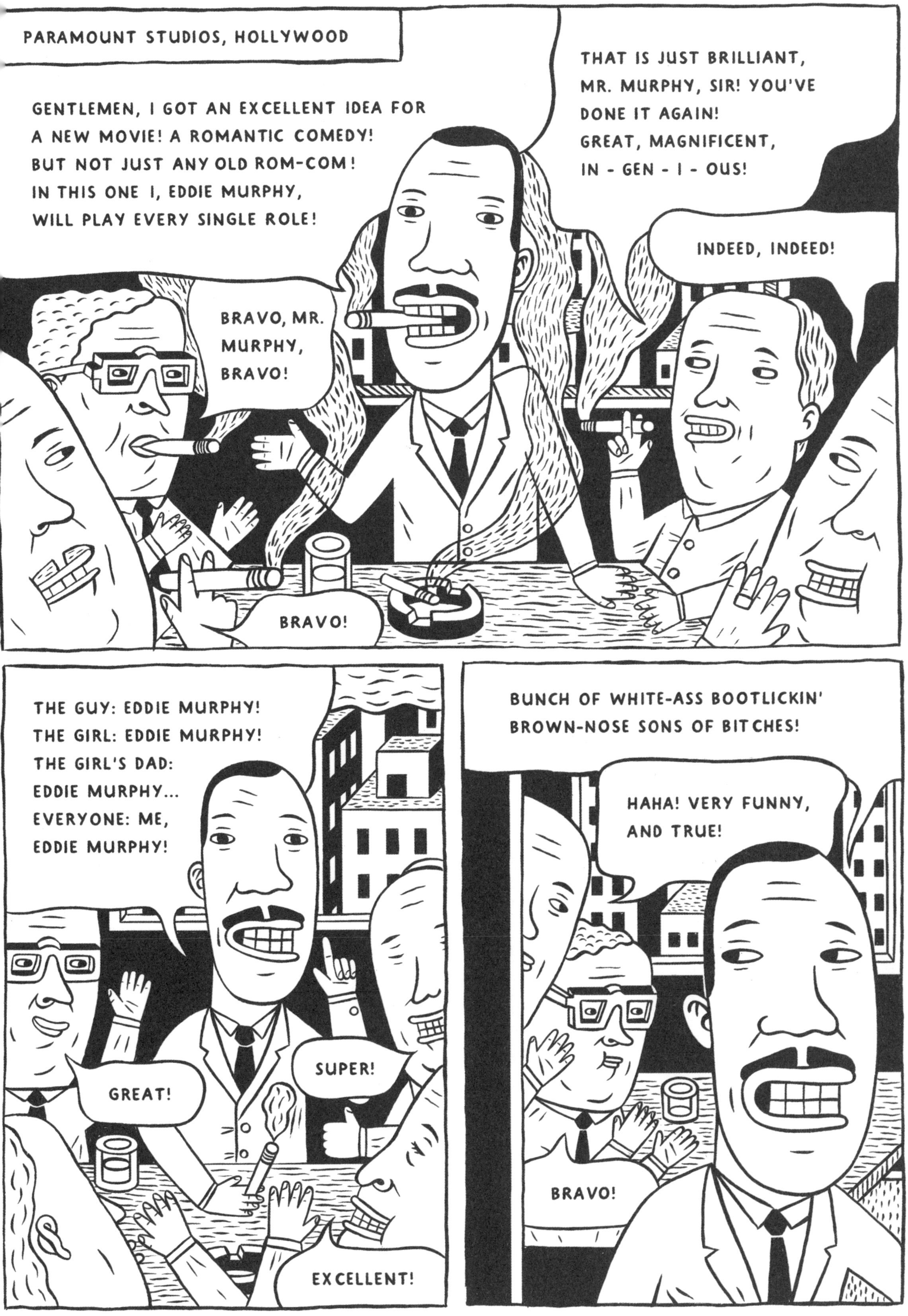
PARAMOUNT STUDIOS, HOLLYWOOD
GENTLEMEN, I GOT AN EXCELLENT IDEA FOR A NEW MOVIE! A ROMANTIC COMEDY! BUT NOT JUST ANY OLD ROM-COM! IN THIS ONE I, EDDIE MURPHY, WILL PLAY EVERY SINGLE ROLE!
THAT IS JUST BRILLIANT, MR. MURPHY, SIR! YOU'VE DONE IT AGAIN! GREAT, MAGNIFICENT, IN - GEN - I - OUS!
INDEED, INDEED!
BRAVO, MR. MURPHY, BRAVO!
BRAVO!
THE GUY: EDDIE MURPHY! THE GIRL: EDDIE MURPHY! THE GIRL'S DAD: EDDIE MURPHY... EVERYONE: ME, EDDIE MURPHY!
SUPER!
GREAT!
EXCELLENT!
BUNCH OF WHITE-ASS BOOTLICKIN' BROWN-NOSE SONS OF BITCHES!
HAHA! VERY FUNNY, AND TRUE!
BRAVO!

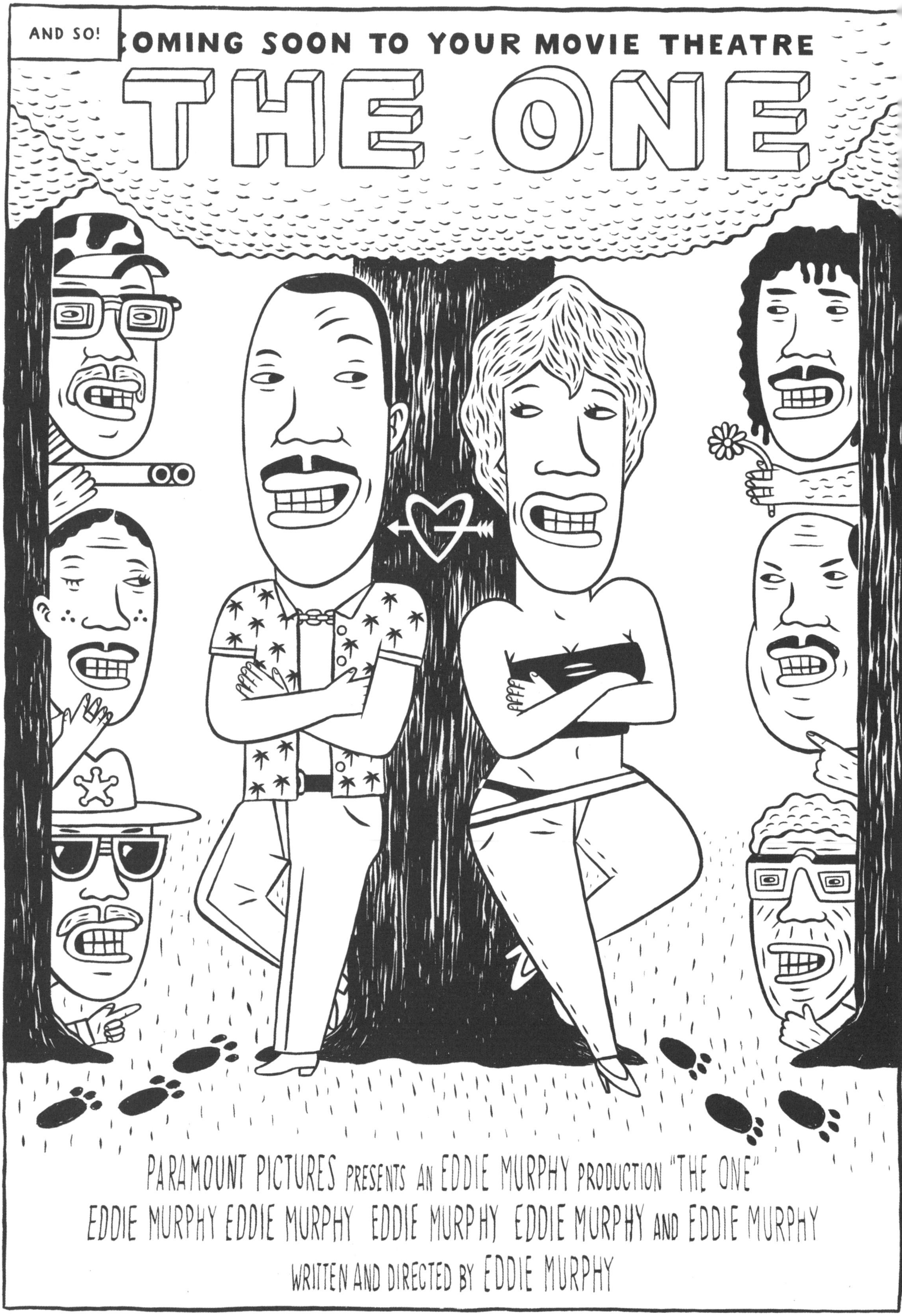
AND SO!
COMING SOON TO YOUR MOVIE THEATRE
THE ONE
PARAMOUNT PICTURES PRESENTS AN EDDIE MURPHY PRODUCTION "THE ONE"
EDDIE MURPHY EDDIE MURPHY EDDIE MURPHY EDDIE MURPHY AND EDDIE MURPHY
WRITTEN AND DIRECTED BY EDDIE MURPHY

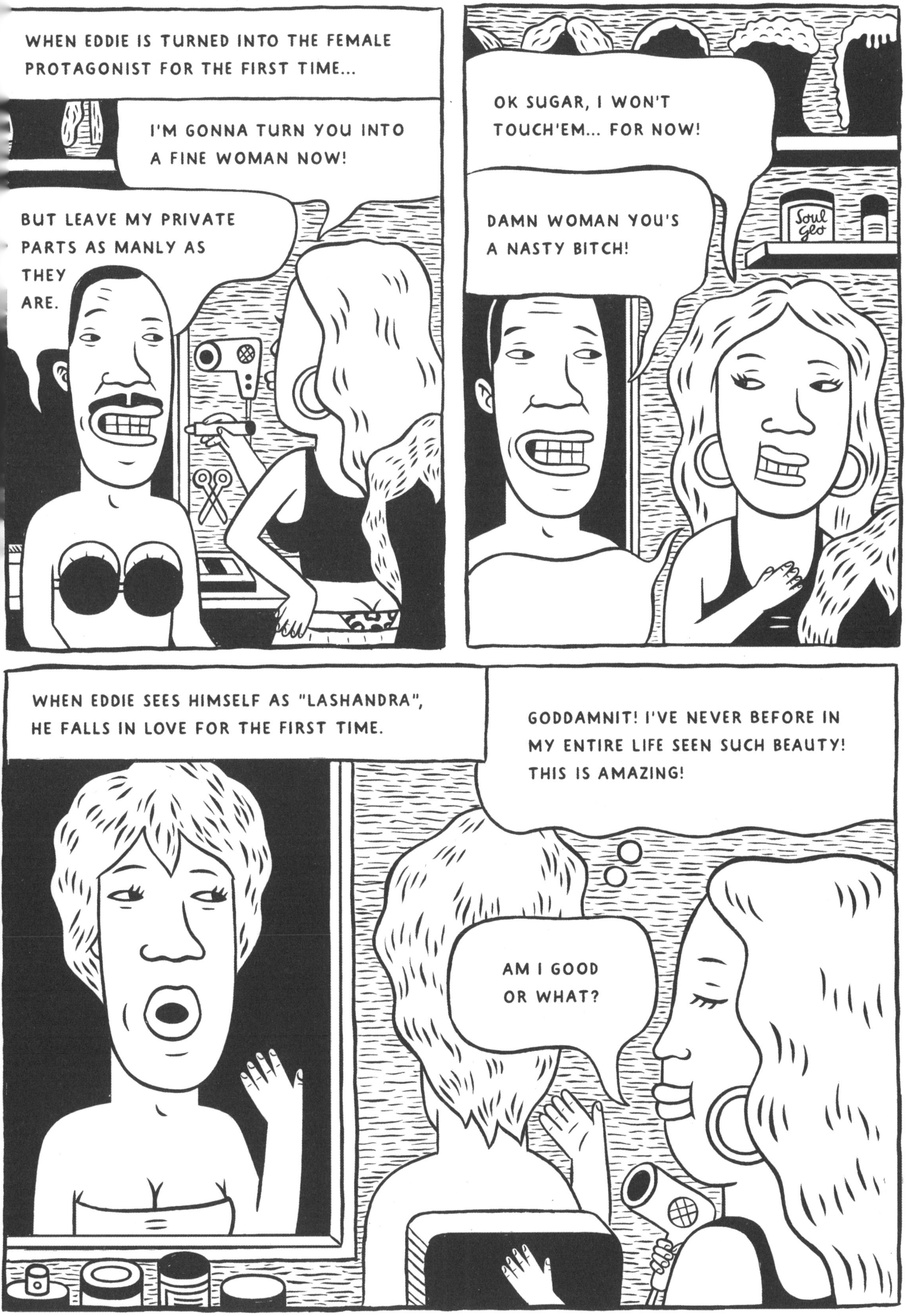
WHEN EDDIE IS TURNED INTO THE FEMALE PROTAGONIST FOR THE FIRST TIME...
I'M GONNA TURN YOU INTO A FINE WOMAN NOW!
BUT LEAVE MY PRIVATE PARTS AS MANLY AS THEY ARE.
OK SUGAR, I WON'T TOUCH'EM... FOR NOW!
DAMN WOMAN YOU'S A NASTY BITCH!
Soul Glo
WHEN EDDIE SEES HIMSELF AS "LASHANDRA", HE FALLS IN LOVE FOR THE FIRST TIME.
GODDAMNIT! I'VE NEVER BEFORE IN MY ENTIRE LIFE SEEN SUCH BEAUTY! THIS IS AMAZING!
AM I GOOD OR WHAT?

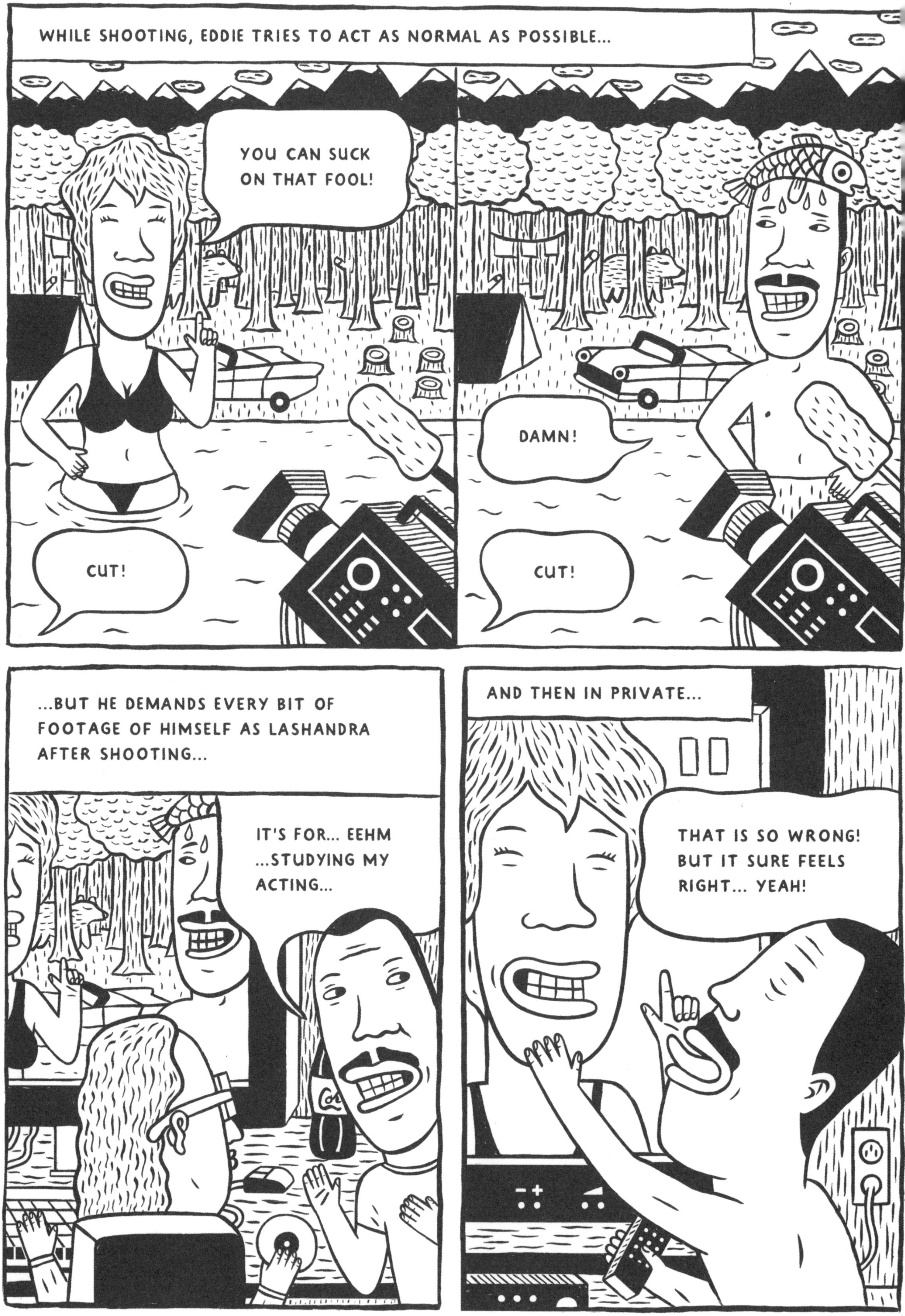
WHILE SHOOTING, EDDIE TRIES TO ACT AS NORMAL AS POSSIBLE...
YOU CAN SUCK ON THAT FOOL!
CUT!
DAMN!
CUT!
...BUT HE DEMANDS EVERY BIT OF FOOTAGE OF HIMSELF AS LASHANDRA AFTER SHOOTING...
IT'S FOR... EEHM ...STUDYING MY ACTING...
AND THEN IN PRIVATE...
THAT IS SO WRONG! BUT IT SURE FEELS RIGHT... YEAH!

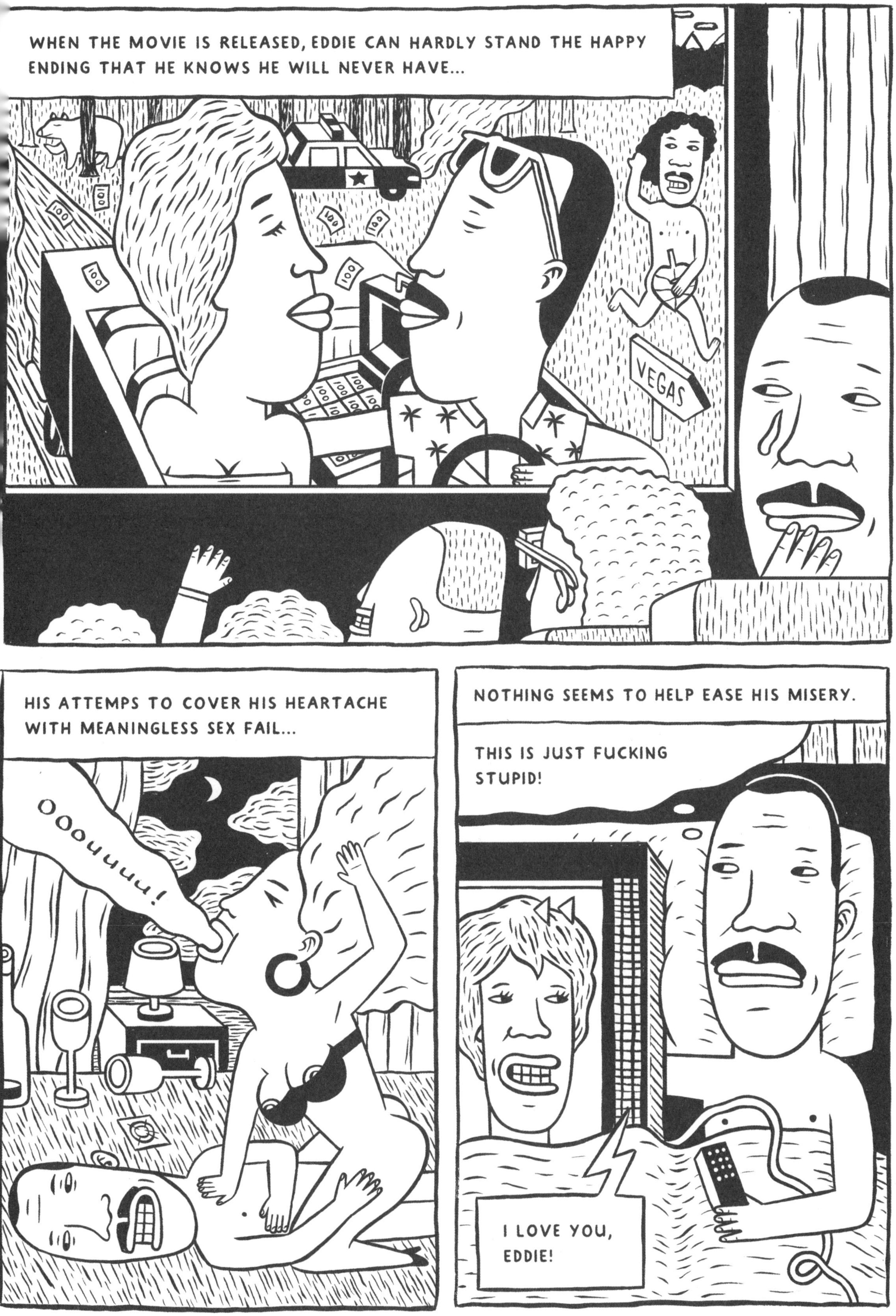
WHEN THE MOVIE IS RELEASED, EDDIE CAN HARDLY STAND THE HAPPY ENDING THAT HE KNOWS HE WILL NEVER HAVE...
VEGAS
HIS ATTEMPS TO COVER HIS HEARTACHE WITH MEANINGLESS SEX FAIL...
OOohhhh!
NOTHING SEEMS TO HELP EASE HIS MISERY.
THIS IS JUST FUCKING STUPID!
I LOVE YOU, EDDIE!

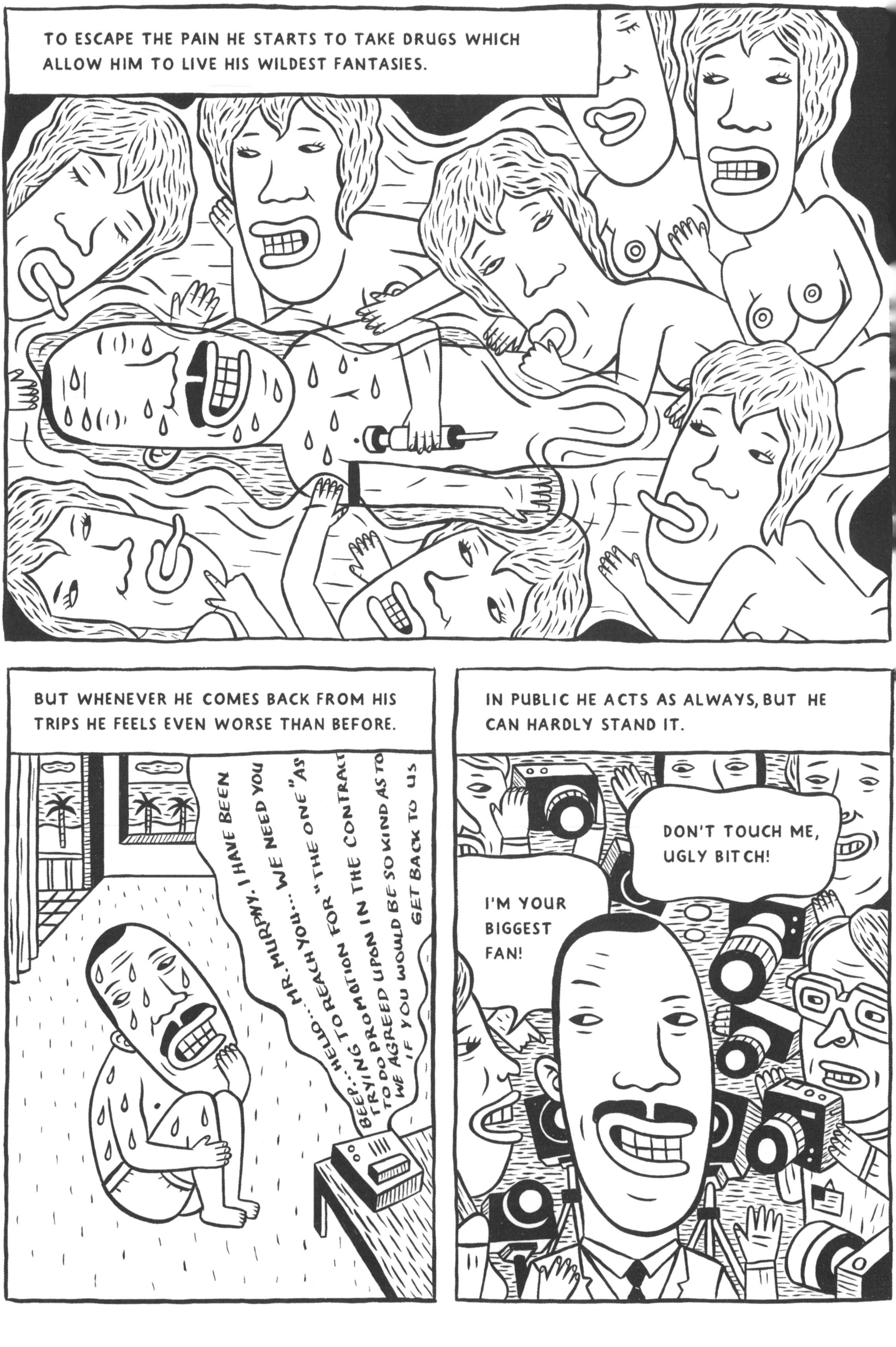
TO ESCAPE THE PAIN HE STARTS TO TAKE DRUGS WHICH ALLOW HIM TO LIVE HIS WILDEST FANTASIES.
BUT WHENEVER HE COMES BACK FROM HIS TRIPS HE FEELS EVEN WORSE THAN BEFORE.
BEEP... HELLO... MR. MURPHY. I HAVE BEEN TRYING TO REACH YOU... WE NEED YOU TO DO PROMOTION FOR "THE ONE" AS WE AGREED UPON IN THE CONTRACT IF YOU WOULD BE SO KIND AS TO GET BACK TO US
IN PUBLIC HE ACTS AS ALWAYS, BUT HE CAN HARDLY STAND IT.
I'M YOUR BIGGEST FAN!
DON'T TOUCH ME, UGLY BITCH!

SOON OTHER CHARACTERS, EDDIE DRESSED UP AS IN HIS PREVIOUS MOVIES, START TO HAUNT HIM WHEN HE IS ON DRUGS...

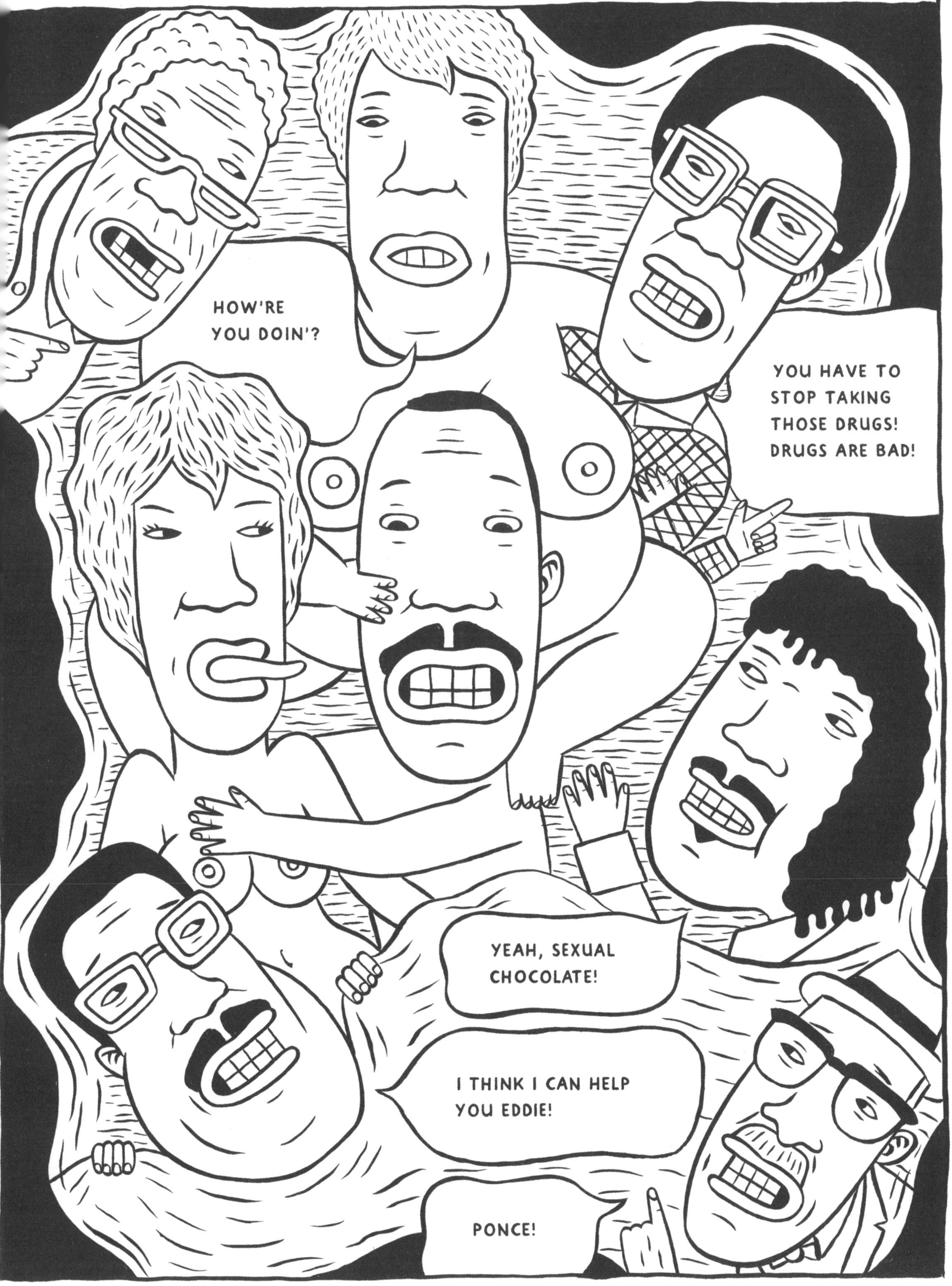

HOW'RE YOU DOIN'?
YOU HAVE TO STOP TAKING THOSE DRUGS! DRUGS ARE BAD!
YEAH, SEXUAL CHOCOLATE!
I THINK I CAN HELP YOU EDDIE!
PONCE!

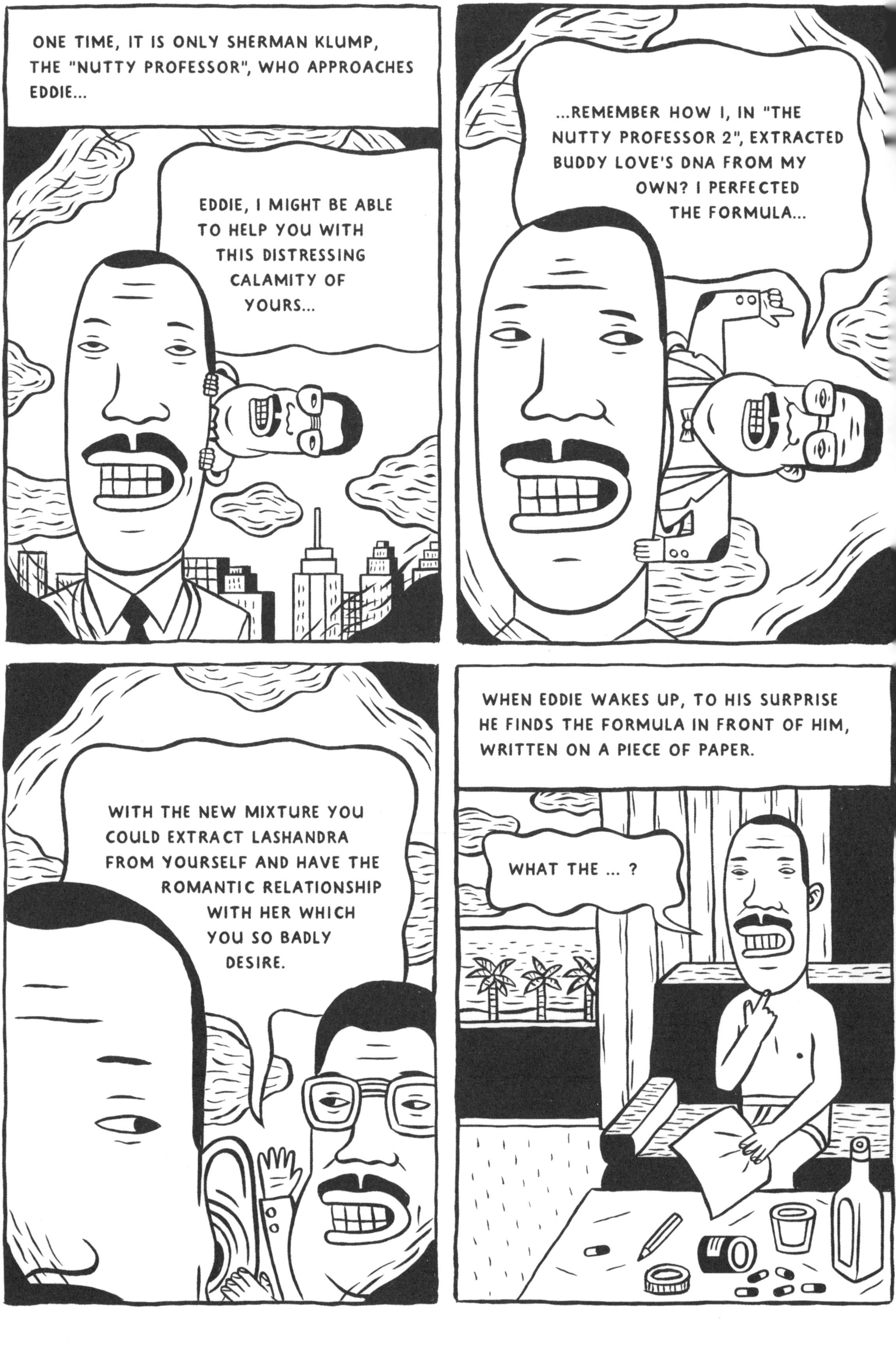
ONE TIME, IT IS ONLY SHERMAN KLUMP, THE "NUTTY PROFESSOR", WHO APPROACHES EDDIE...
EDDIE, I MIGHT BE ABLE TO HELP YOU WITH THIS DISTRESSING CALAMITY OF YOURS...
...REMEMBER HOW I, IN "THE NUTTY PROFESSOR 2", EXTRACTED BUDDY LOVE'S DNA FROM MY OWN? I PERFECTED THE FORMULA...
WITH THE NEW MIXTURE YOU COULD EXTRACT LASHANDRA FROM YOURSELF AND HAVE THE ROMANTIC RELATIONSHIP WITH HER WHICH YOU SO BADLY DESIRE.
WHEN EDDIE WAKES UP, TO HIS SURPRISE HE FINDS THE FORMULA IN FRONT OF HIM, WRITTEN ON A PIECE OF PAPER.
WHAT THE ... ?

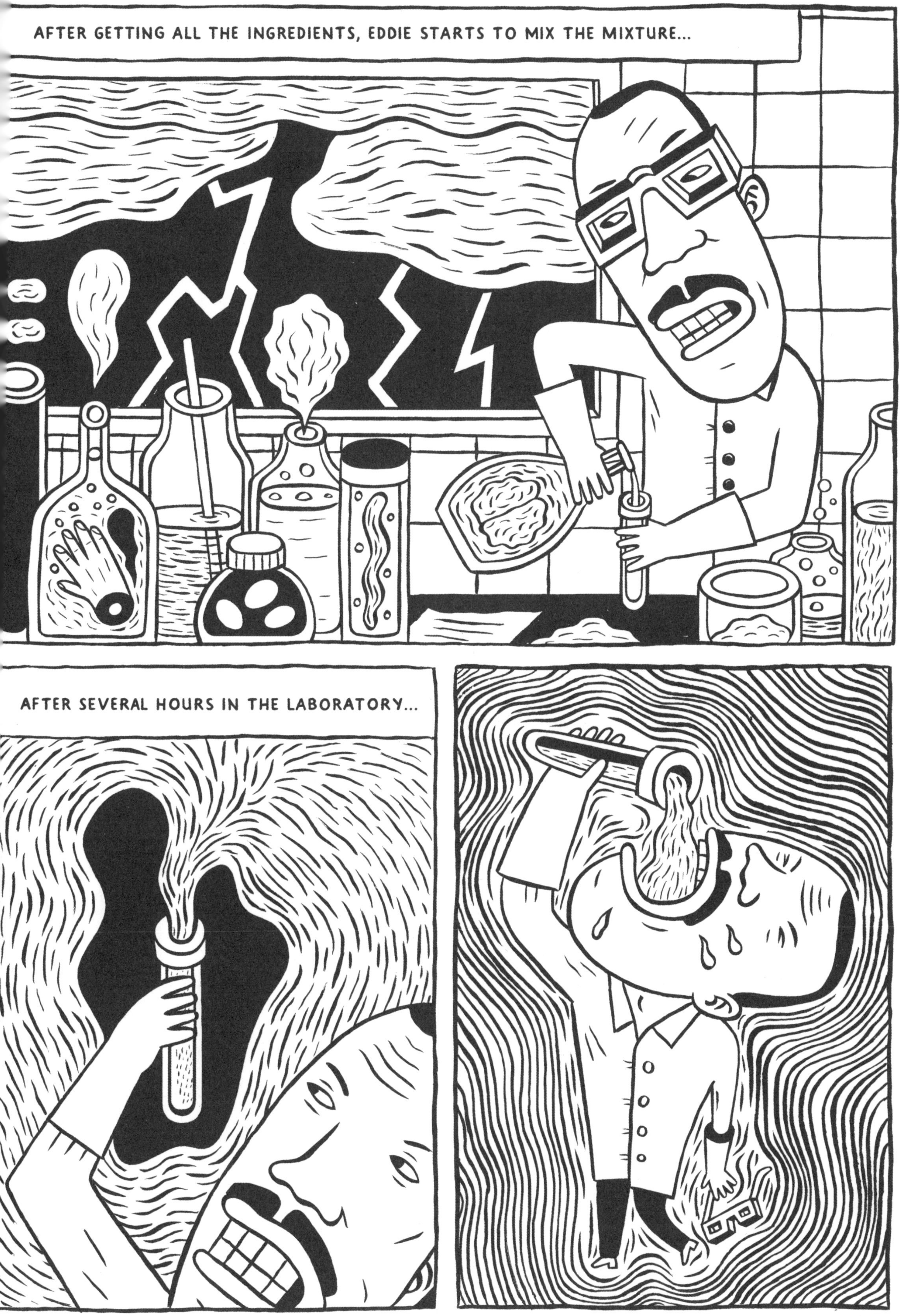
AFTER GETTING ALL THE INGREDIENTS, EDDIE STARTS TO MIX THE MIXTURE...
AFTER SEVERAL HOURS IN THE LABORATORY...

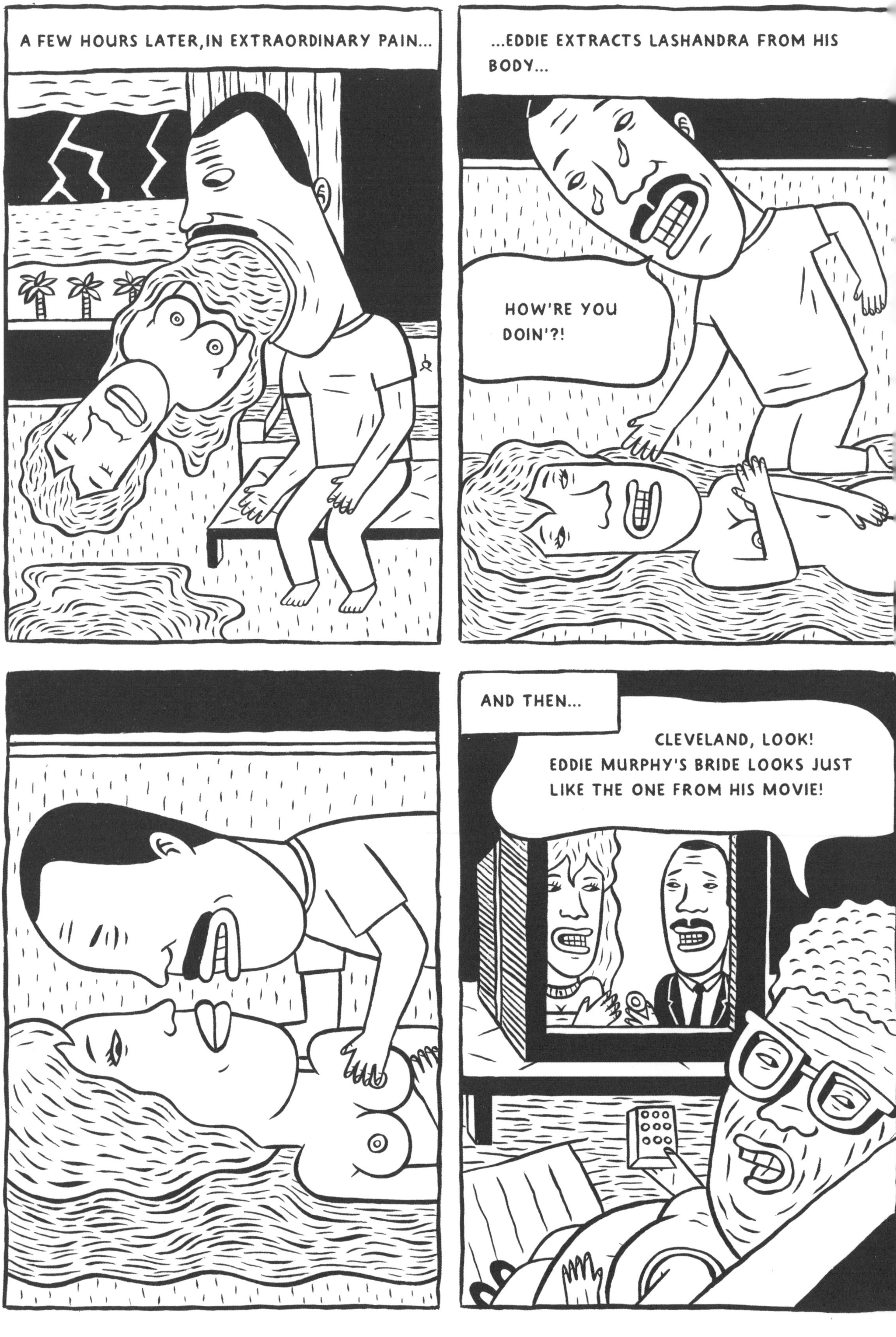
A FEW HOURS LATER, IN EXTRAORDINARY PAIN...
...EDDIE EXTRACTS LASHANDRA FROM HIS BODY...
HOW'RE YOU DOIN'?!
AND THEN...
CLEVELAND, LOOK! EDDIE MURPHY'S BRIDE LOOKS JUST LIKE THE ONE FROM HIS MOVIE!

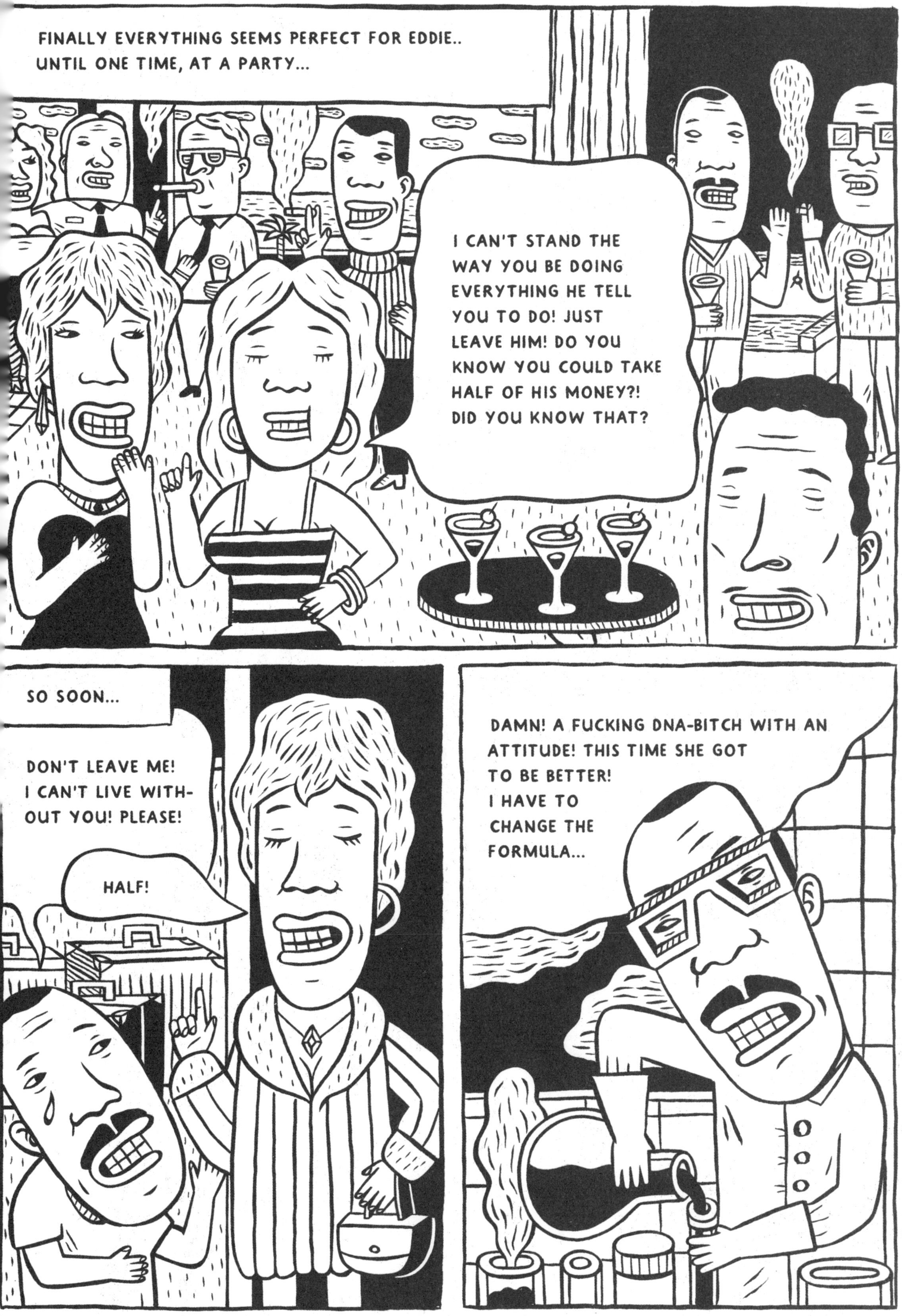
FINALLY EVERYTHING SEEMS PERFECT FOR EDDIE.. UNTIL ONE TIME, AT A PARTY...
I CAN'T STAND THE WAY YOU BE DOING EVERYTHING HE TELL YOU TO DO! JUST LEAVE HIM! DO YOU KNOW YOU COULD TAKE HALF OF HIS MONEY?! DID YOU KNOW THAT?
SO SOON...
DON'T LEAVE ME! I CAN'T LIVE WITH-OUT YOU! PLEASE!
HALF!
DAMN! A FUCKING DNA-BITCH WITH AN ATTITUDE! THIS TIME SHE GOT TO BE BETTER! I HAVE TO CHANGE THE FORMULA...

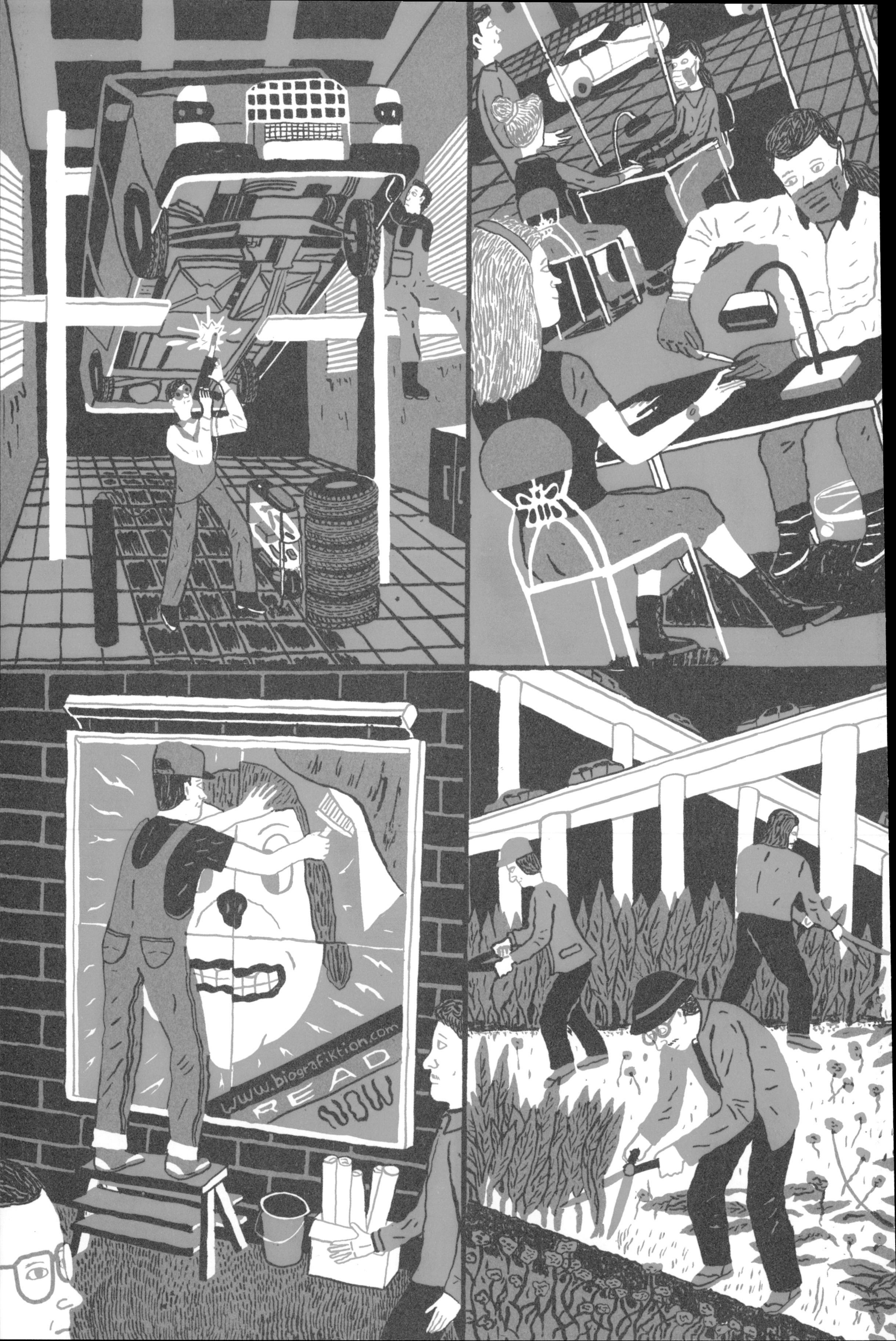
www.biografiktion.com
READ
NOW

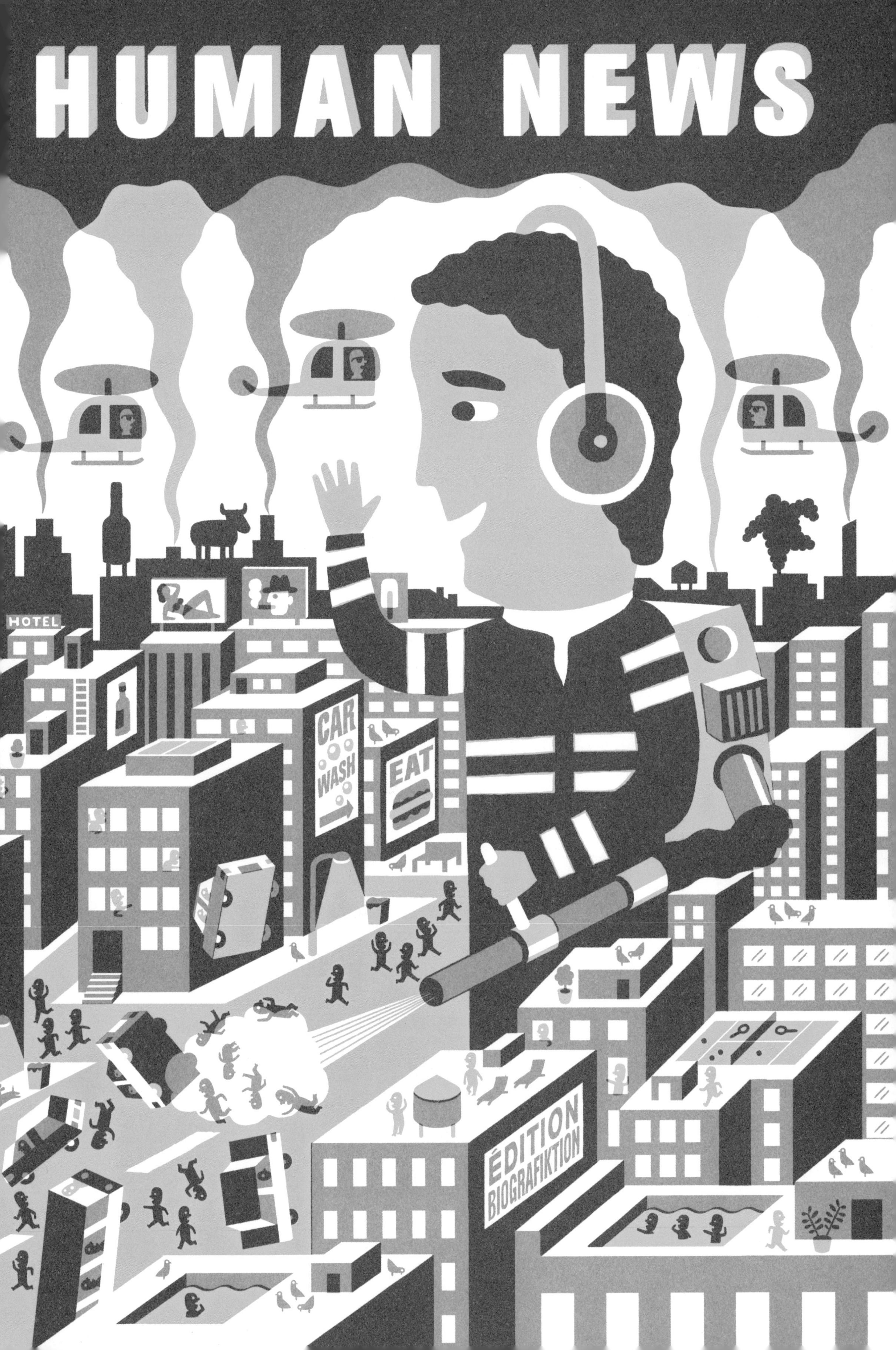
HUMAN NEWS
HOTEL
CAR WASH
EAT
ÉDITION BIOGRAFIKTION

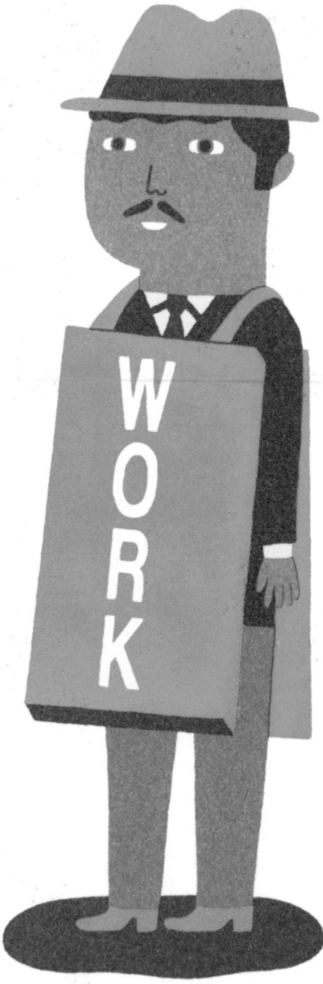
WORK

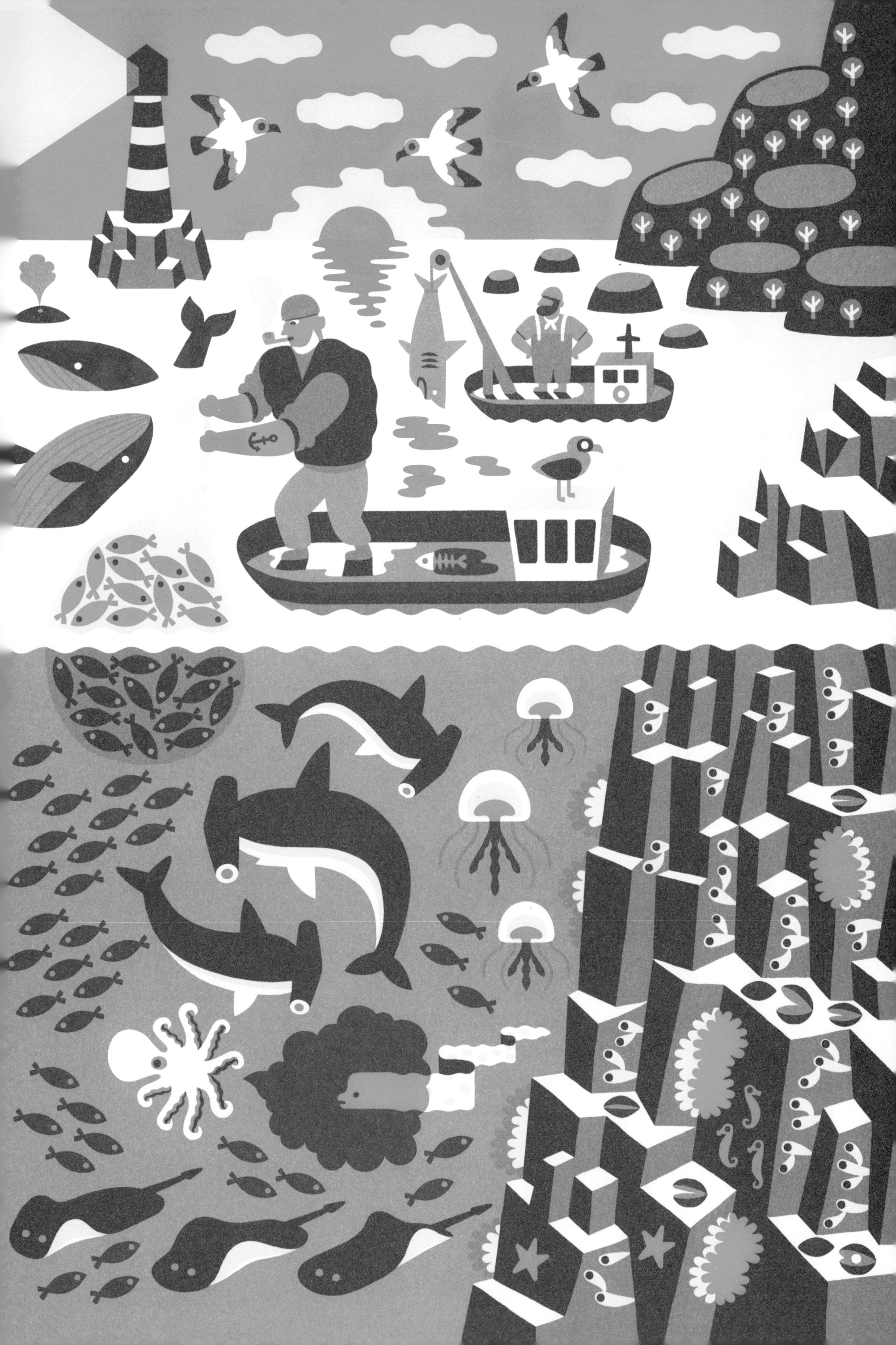

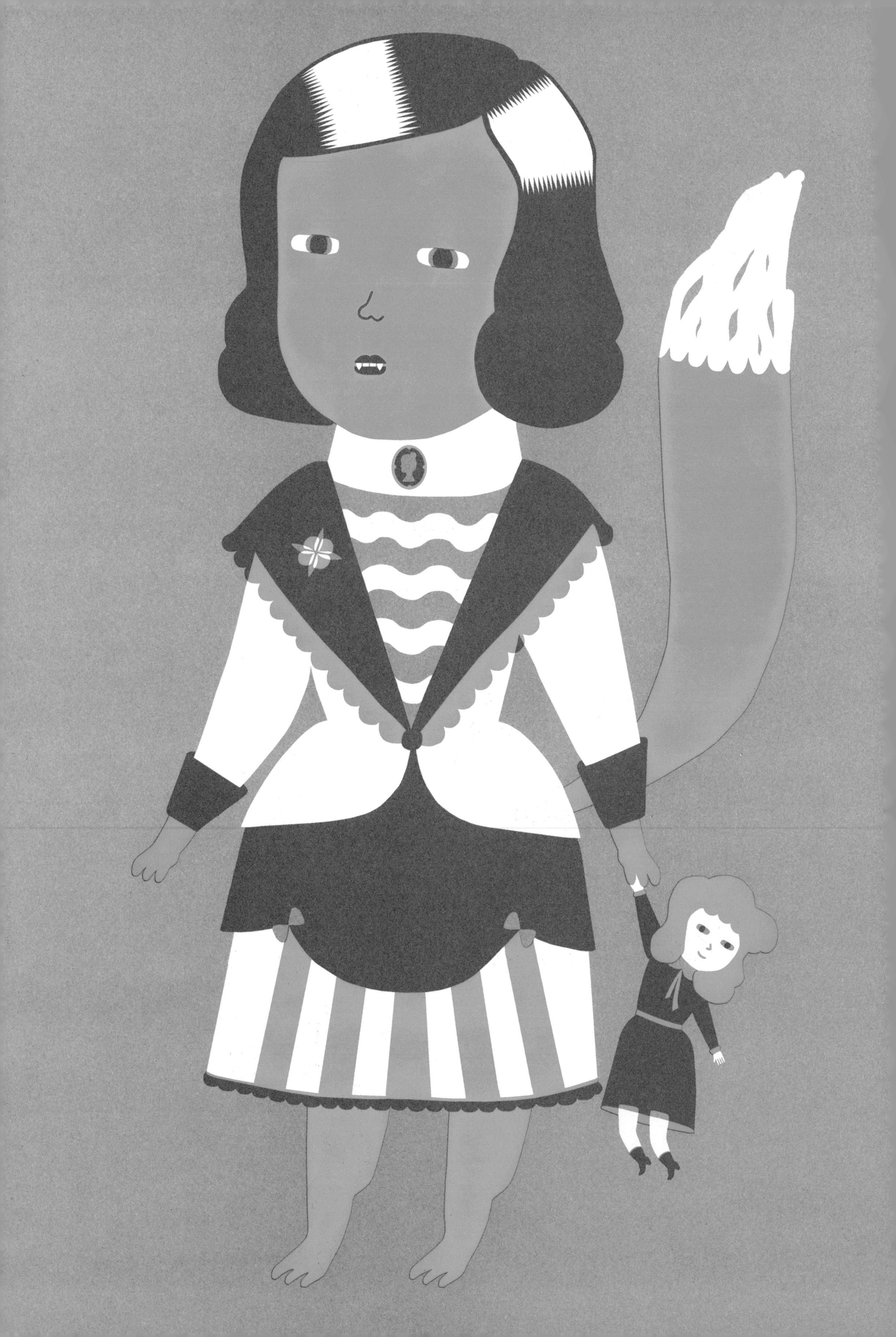

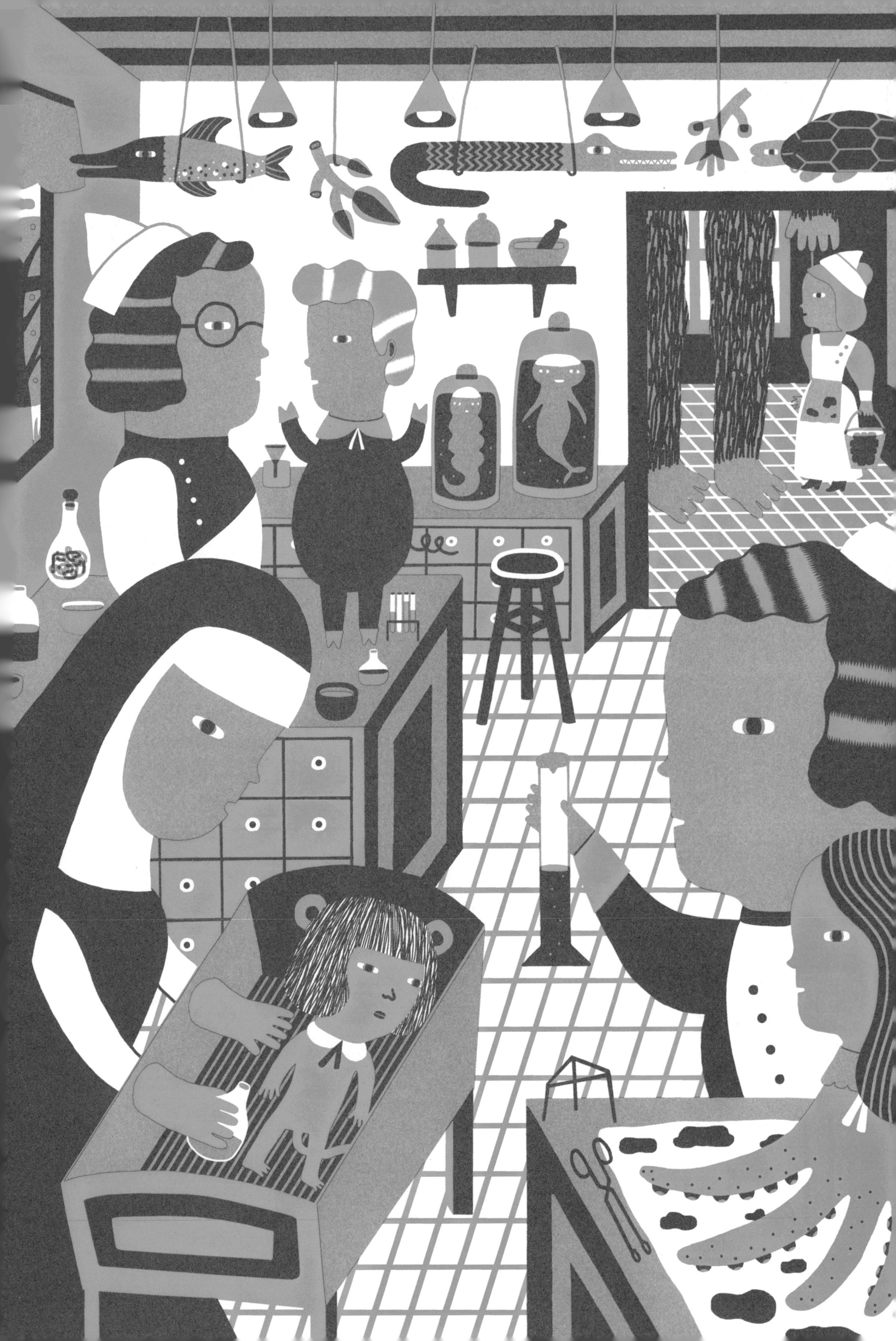

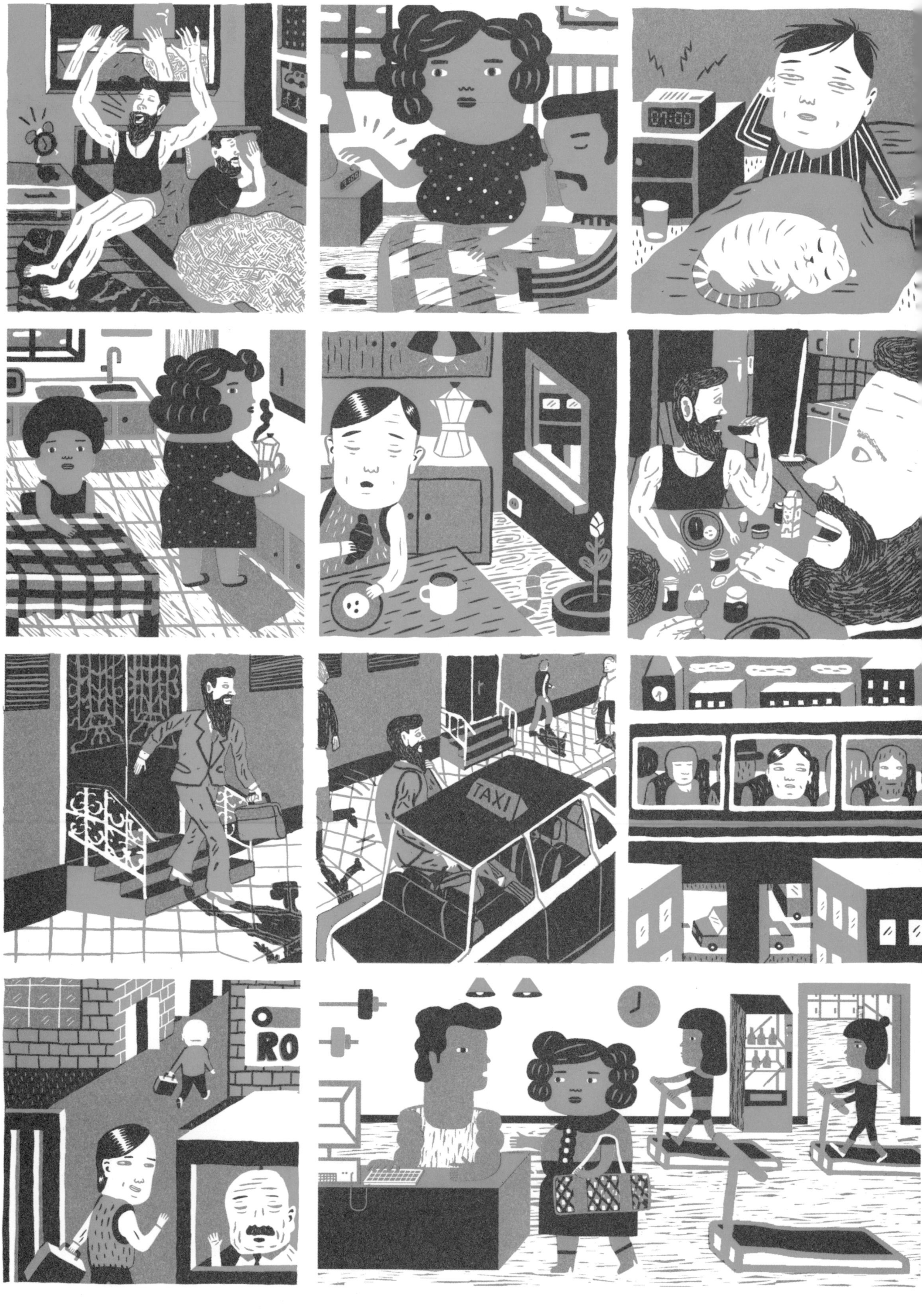
07:00
TAXI
RO

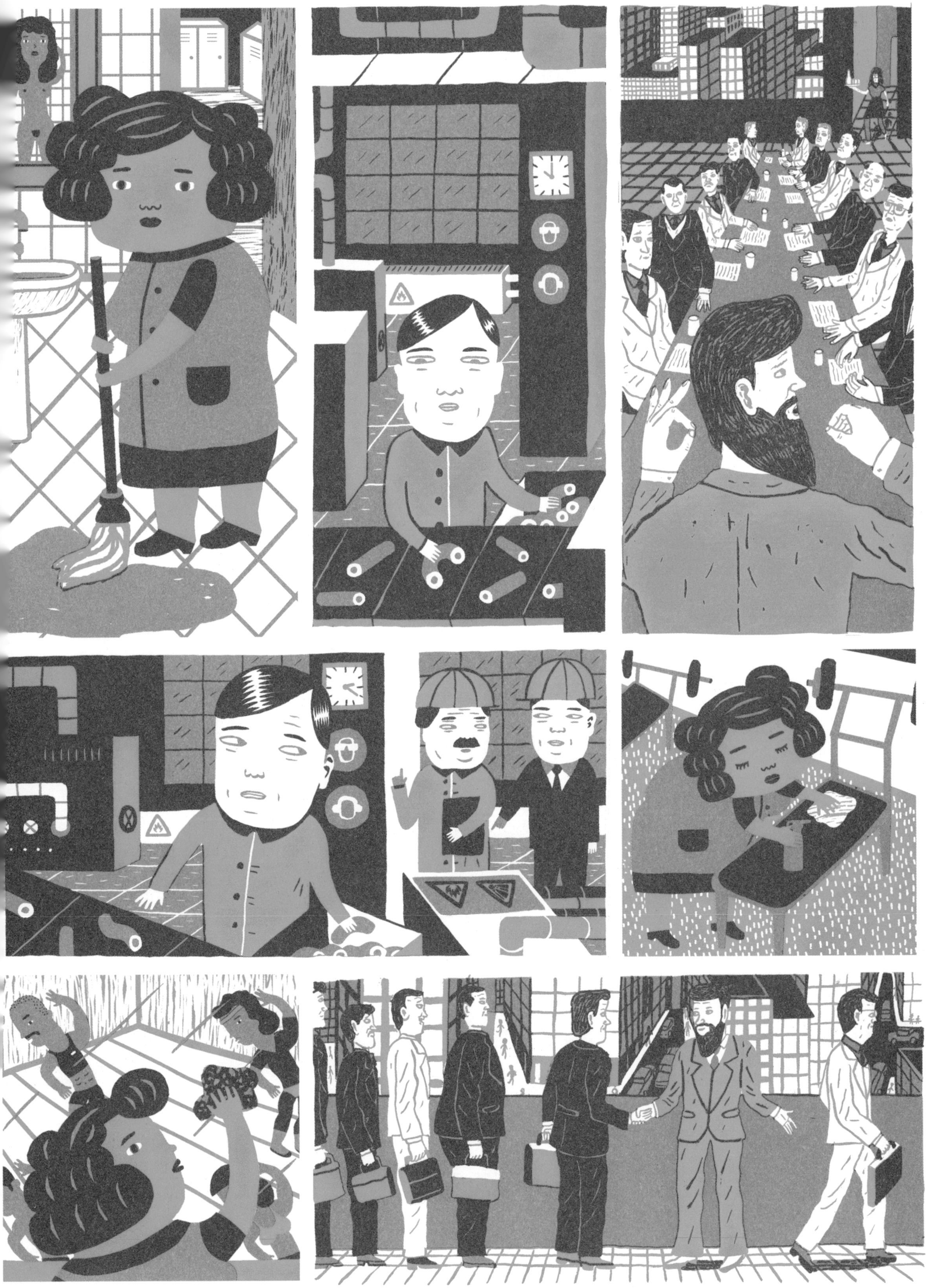

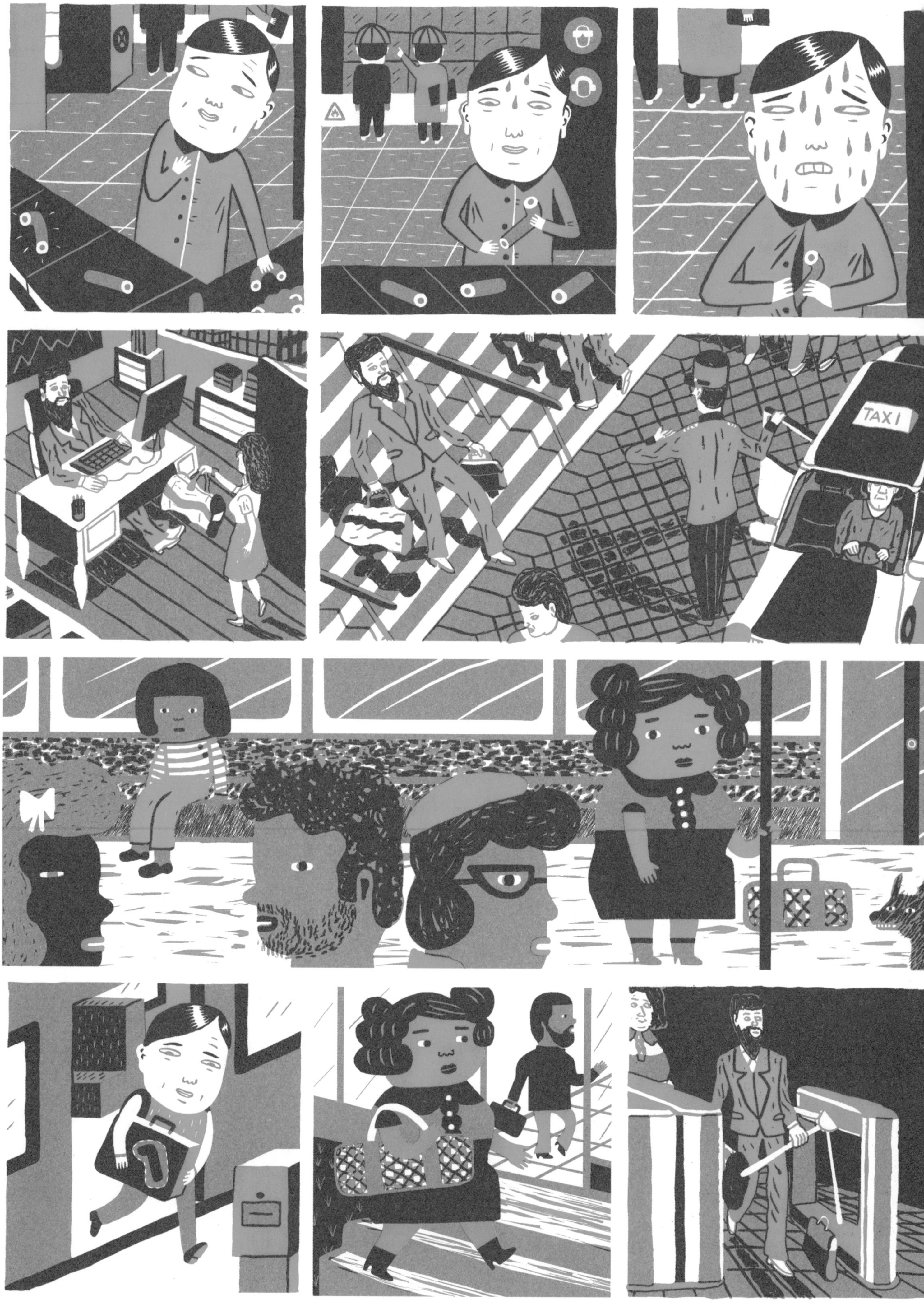
TAXI

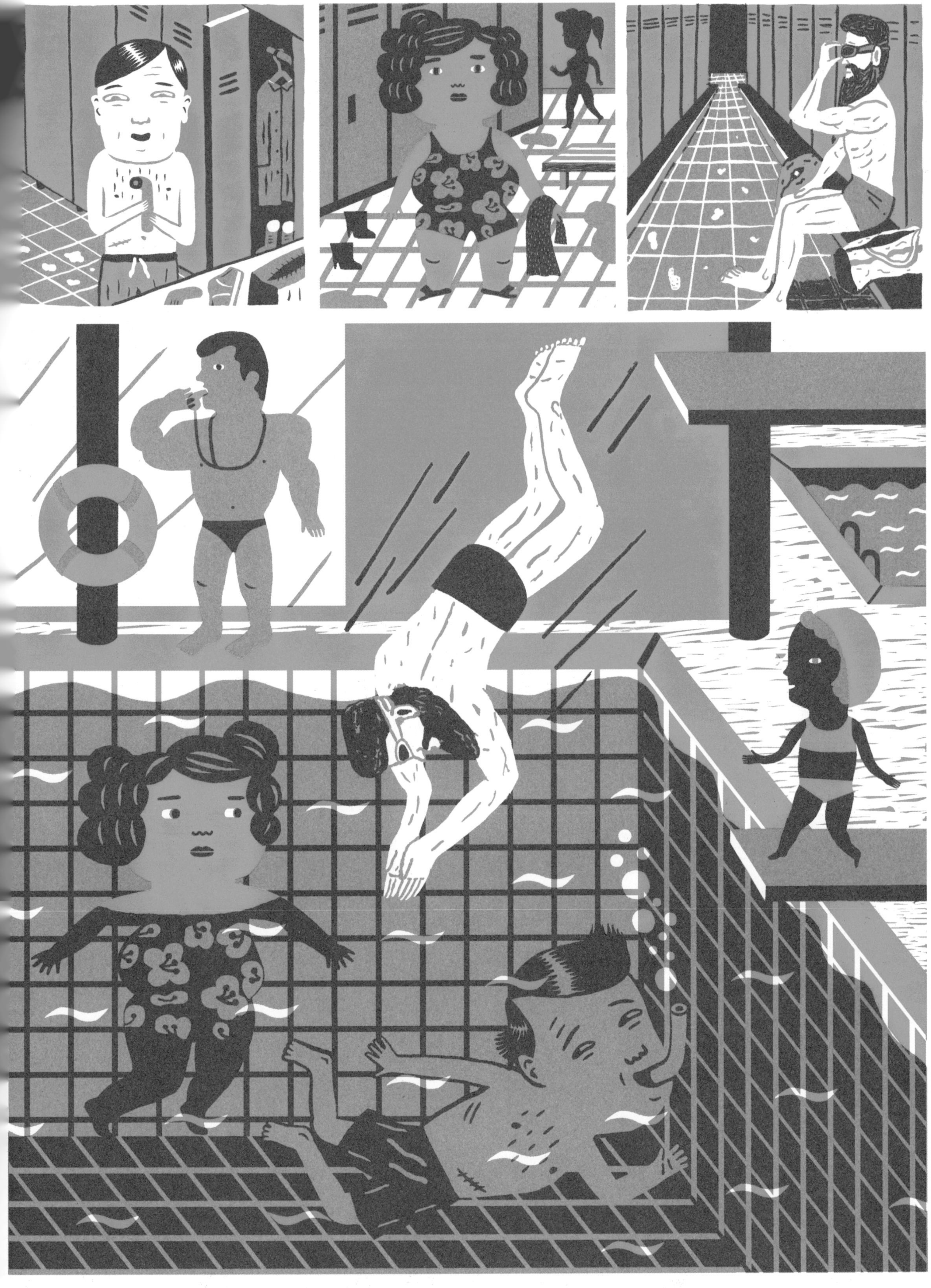

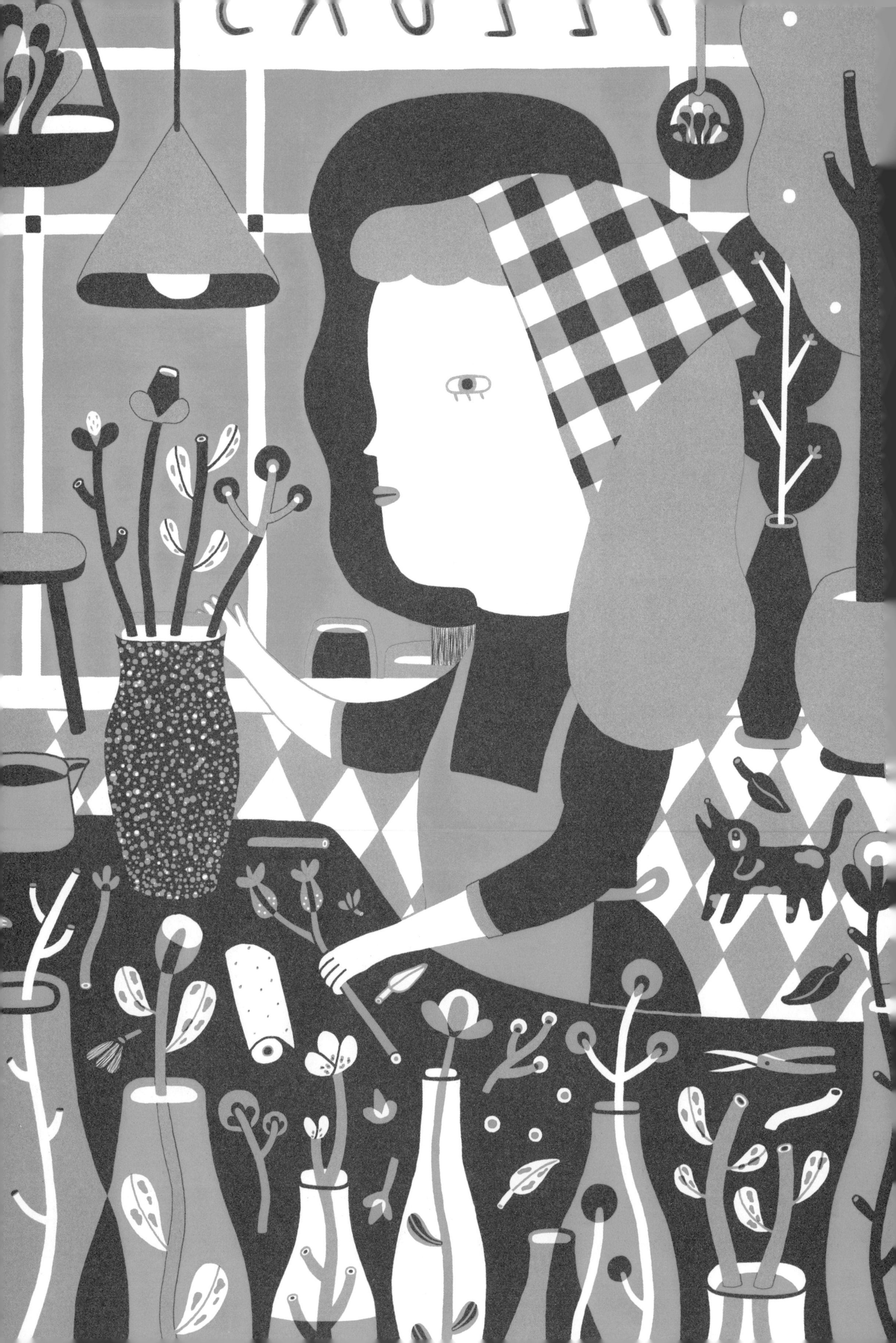

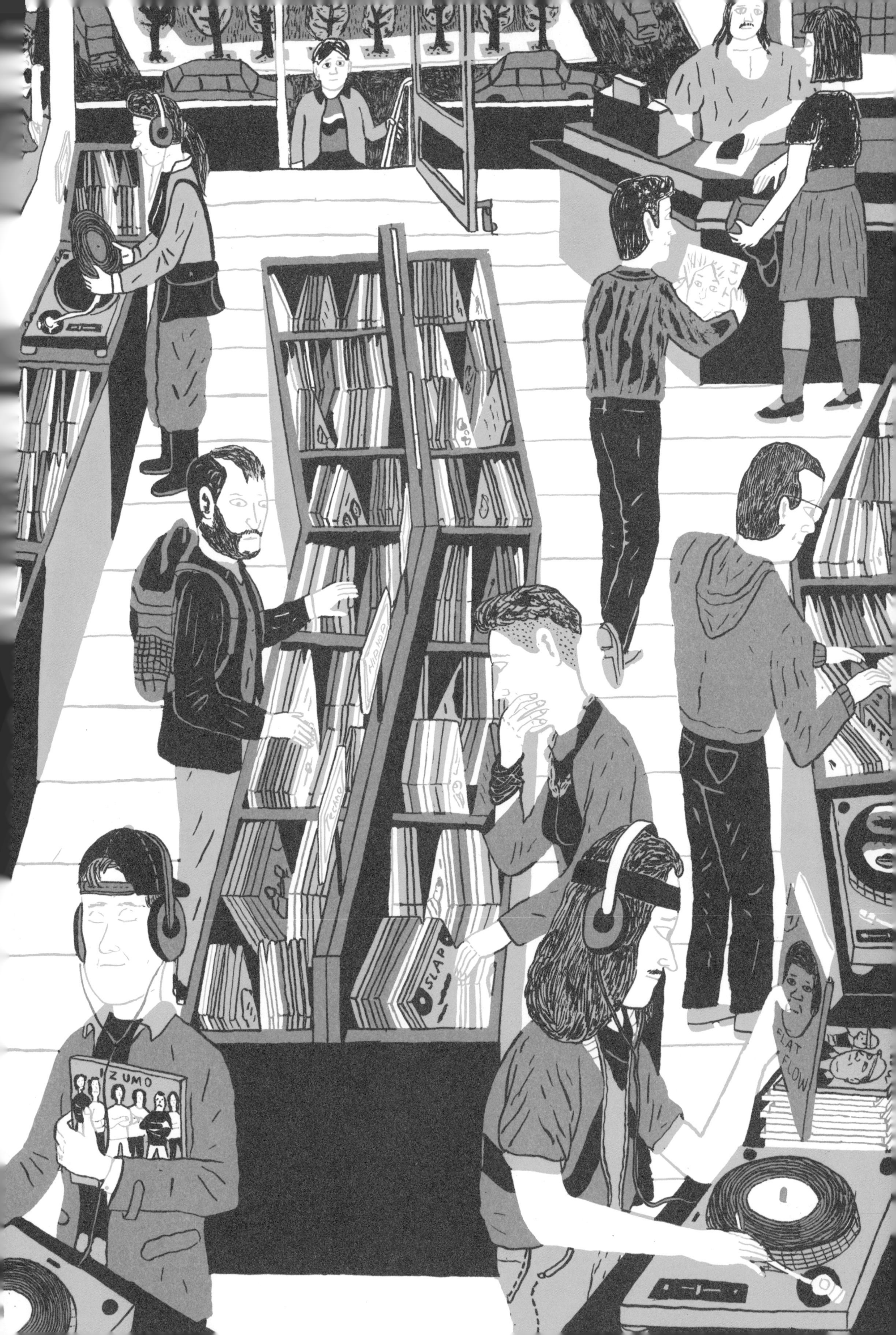
HIP HOP
TECHNO
IZUMO
SLAP
FLAT
FLOW

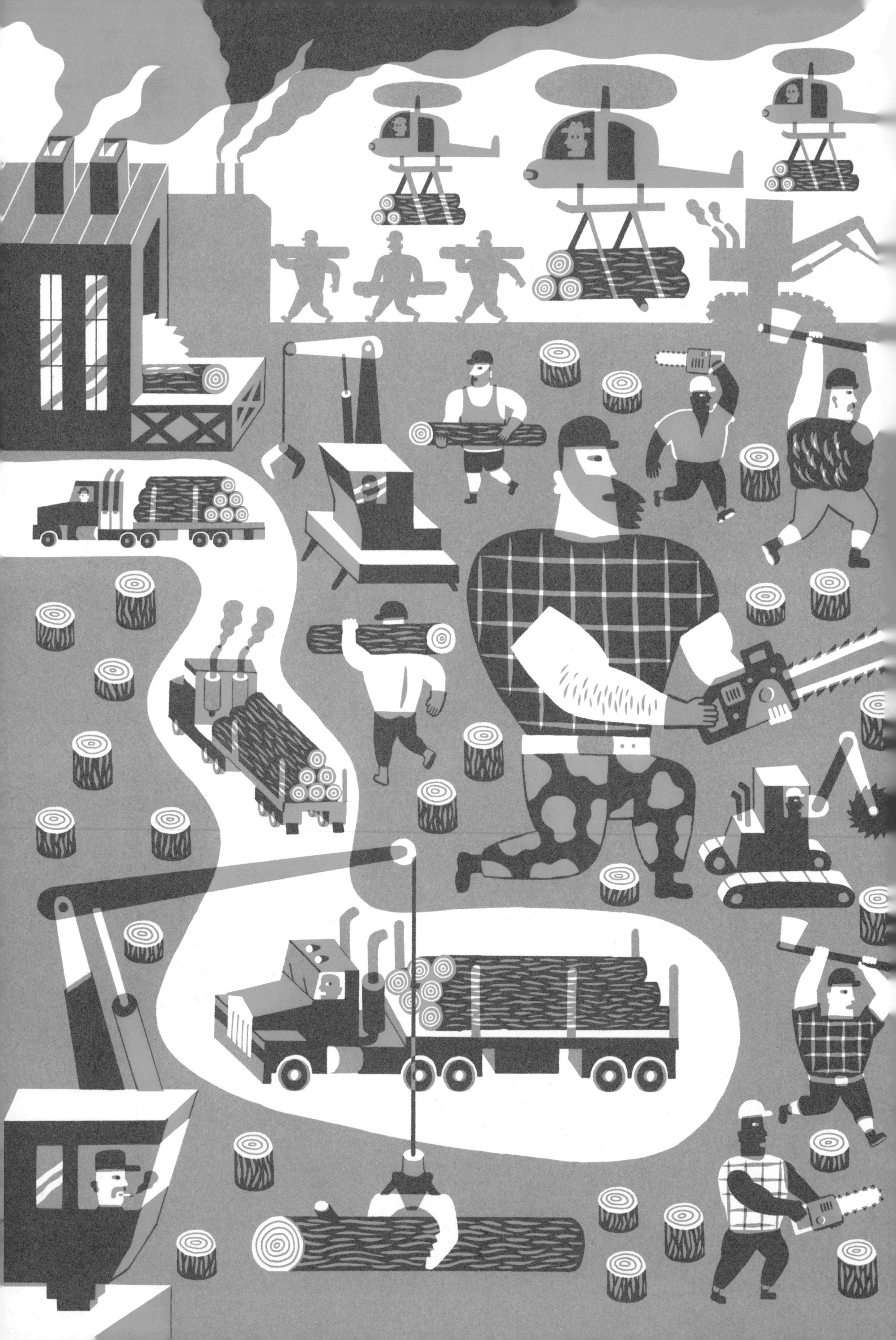

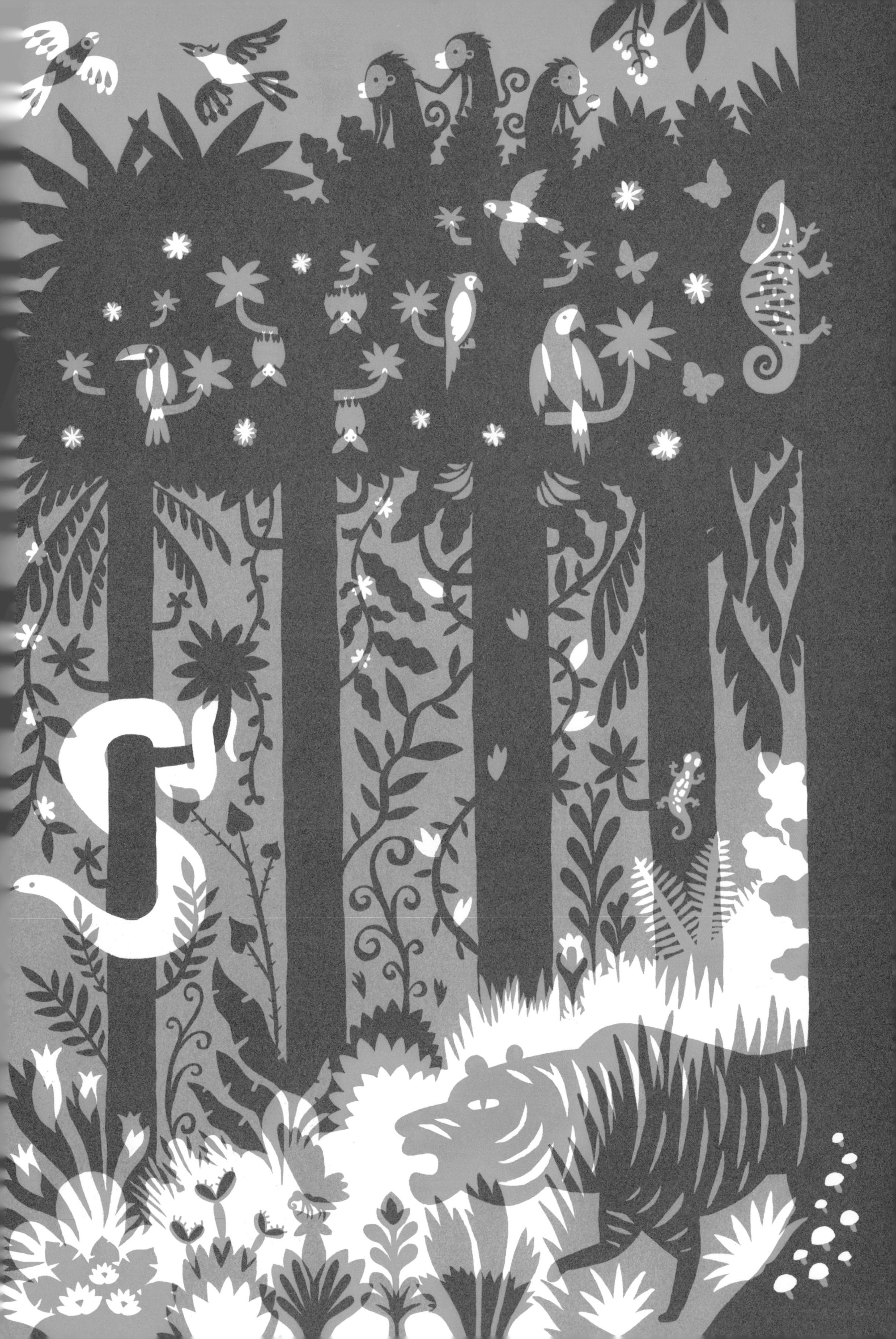

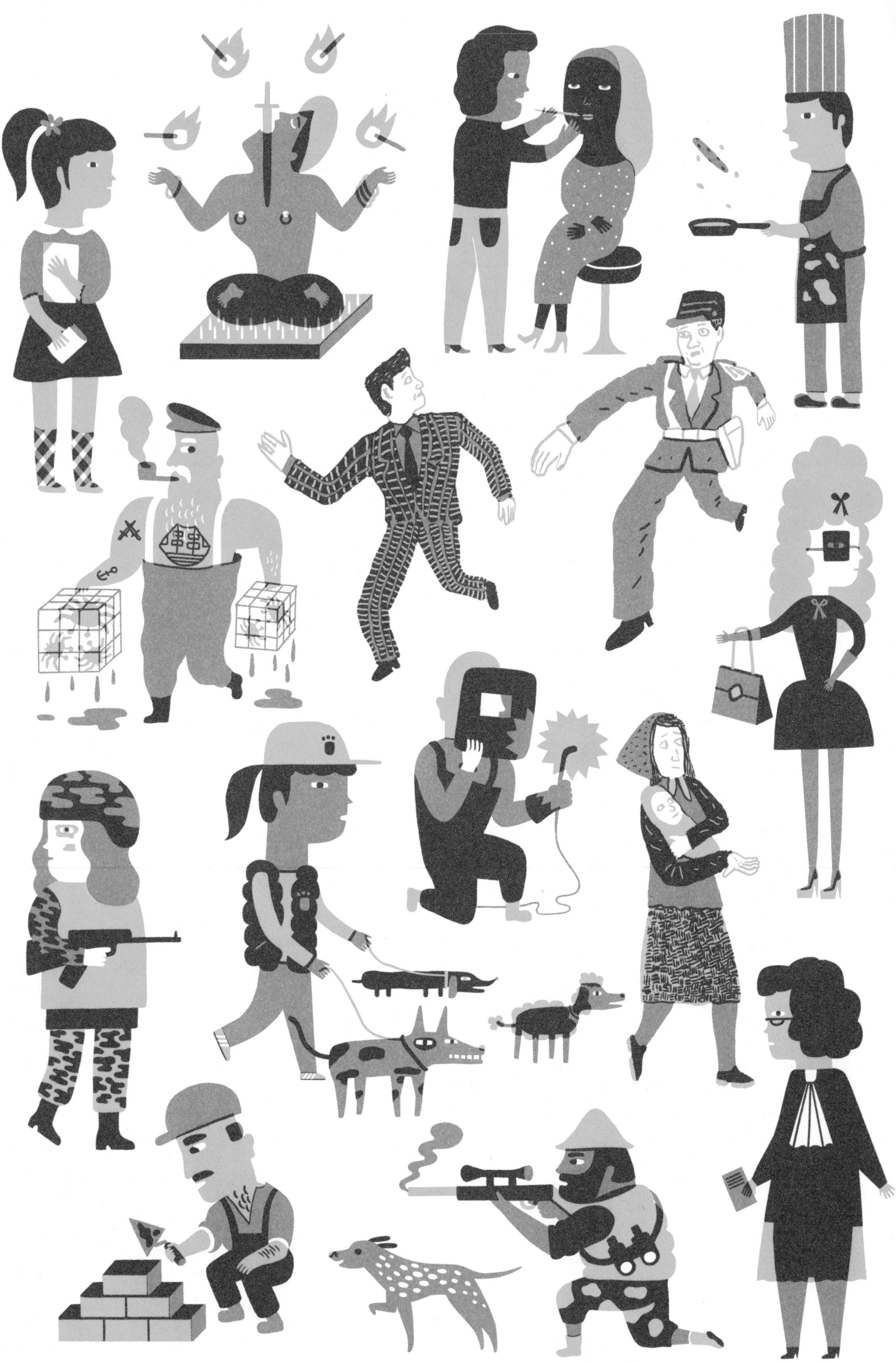

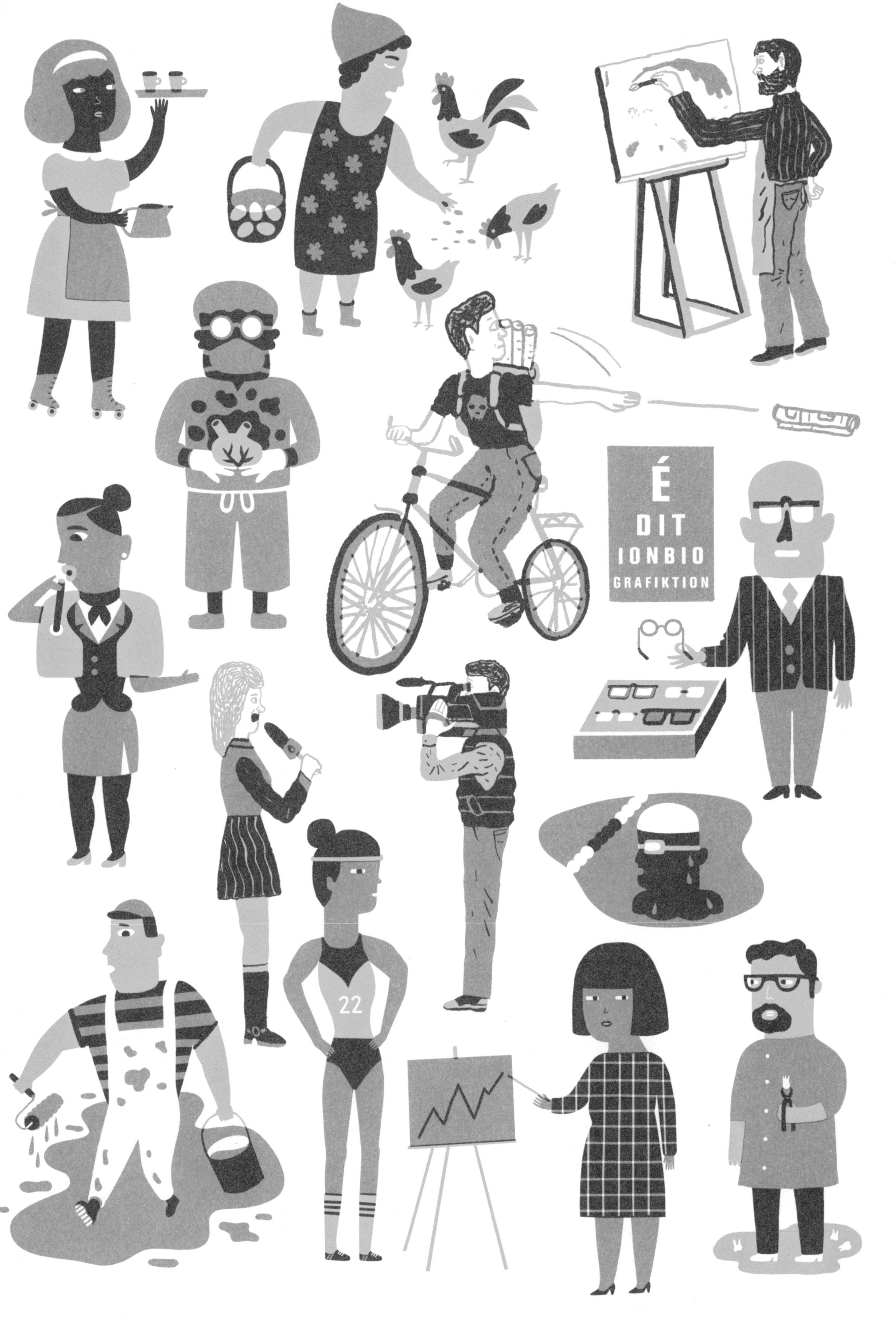
É
DIT
IONBIO
GRAFIKTION
22

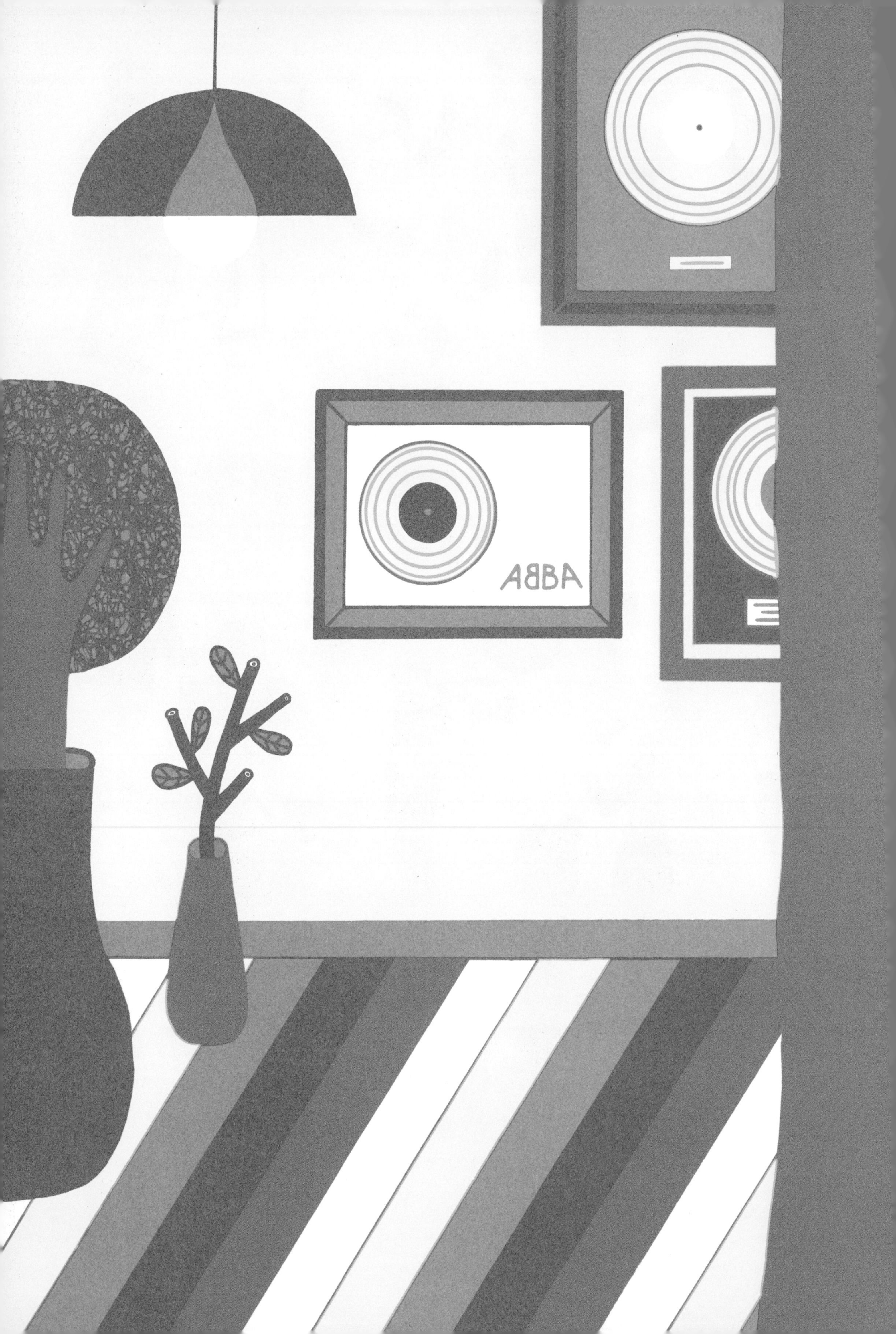
ABBA

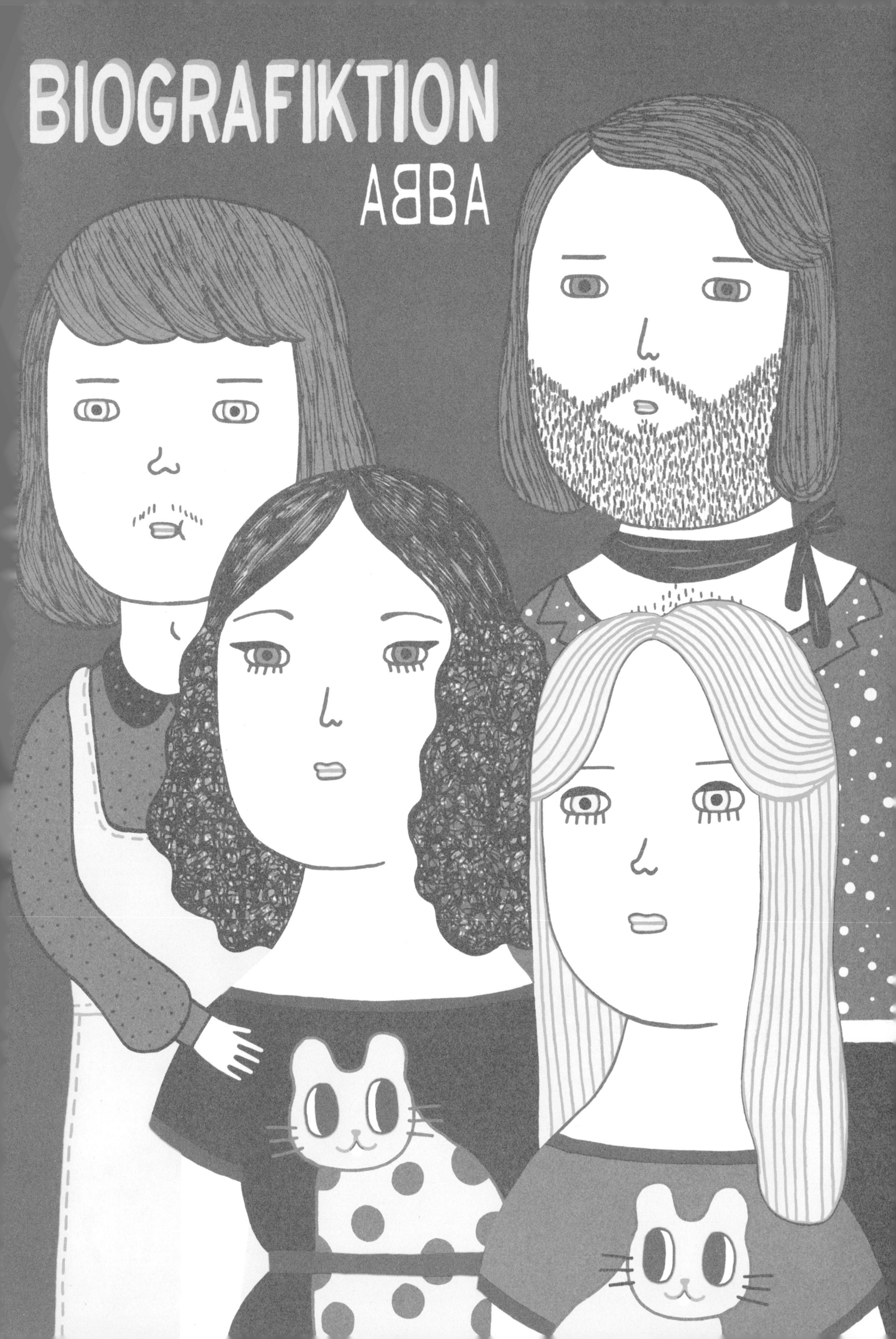
BIOGRAFIKTION
ABBA

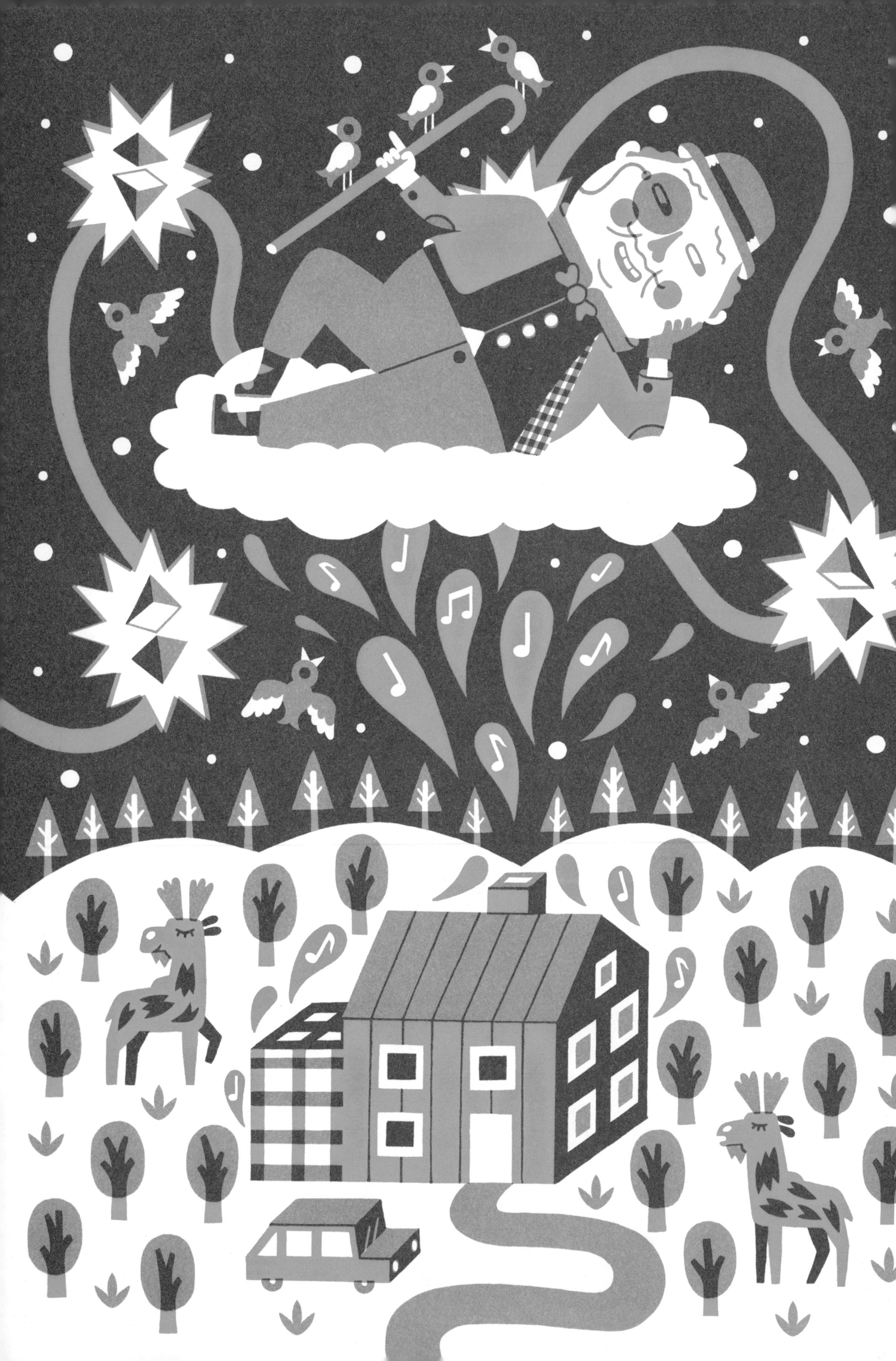

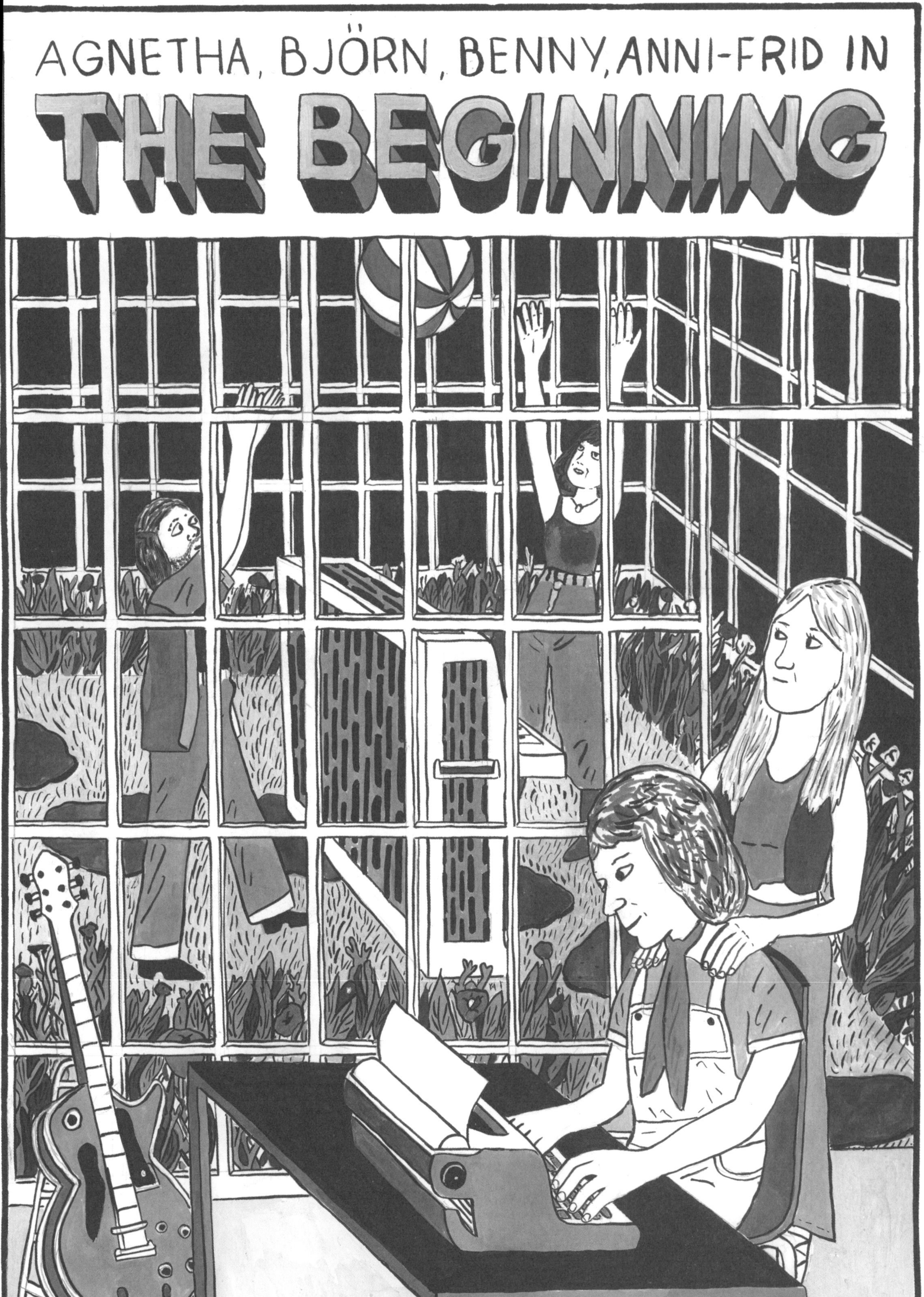
AGNETHA, BJÖRN, BENNY, ANNI-FRID IN
THE BEGINNING

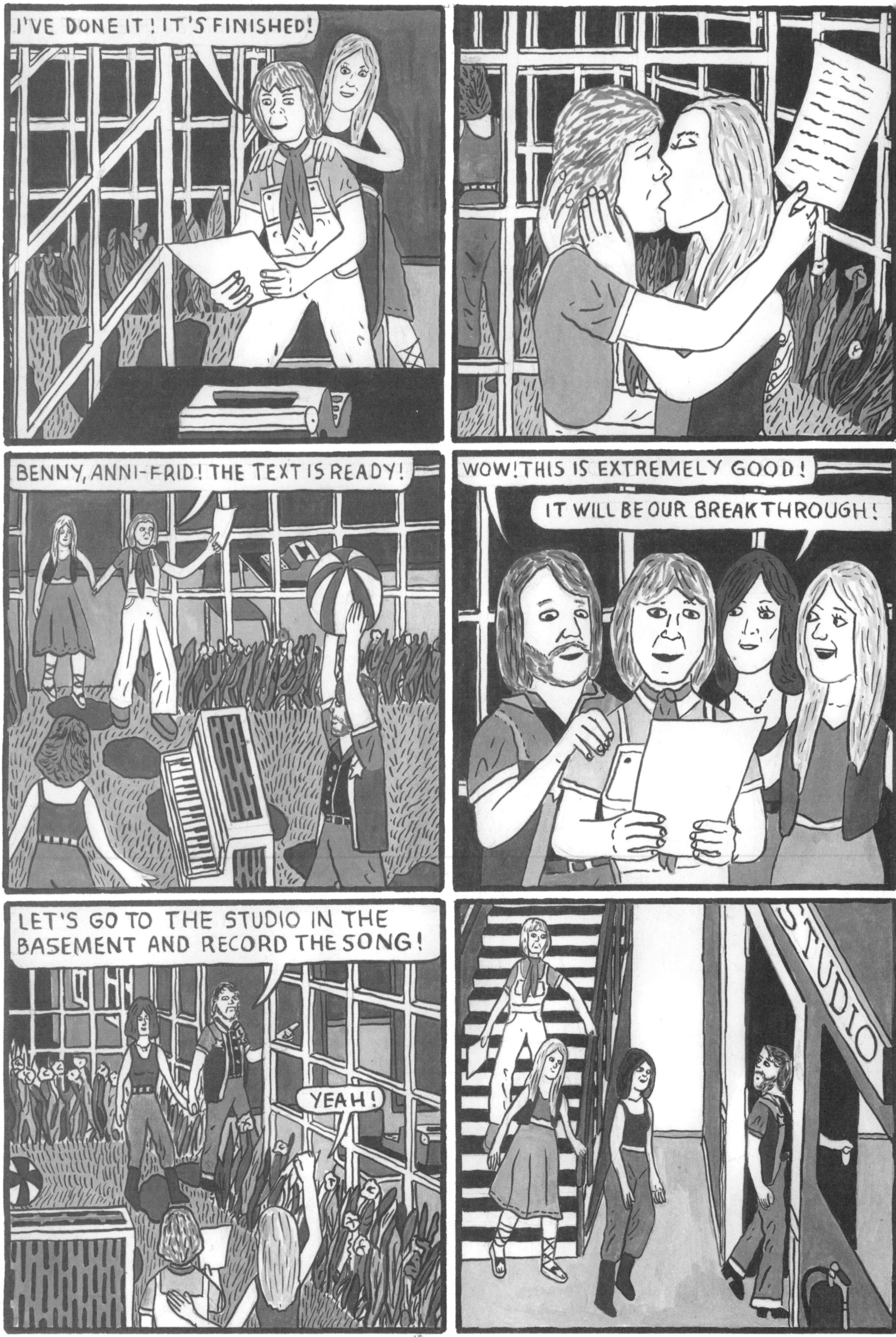
I'VE DONE IT! IT'S FINISHED!
BENNY, ANNI-FRID! THE TEXT IS READY!
WOW! THIS IS EXTREMELY GOOD!
IT WILL BE OUR BREAKTHROUGH!
LET'S GO TO THE STUDIO IN THE BASEMENT AND RECORD THE SONG!
YEAH!
STUDIO

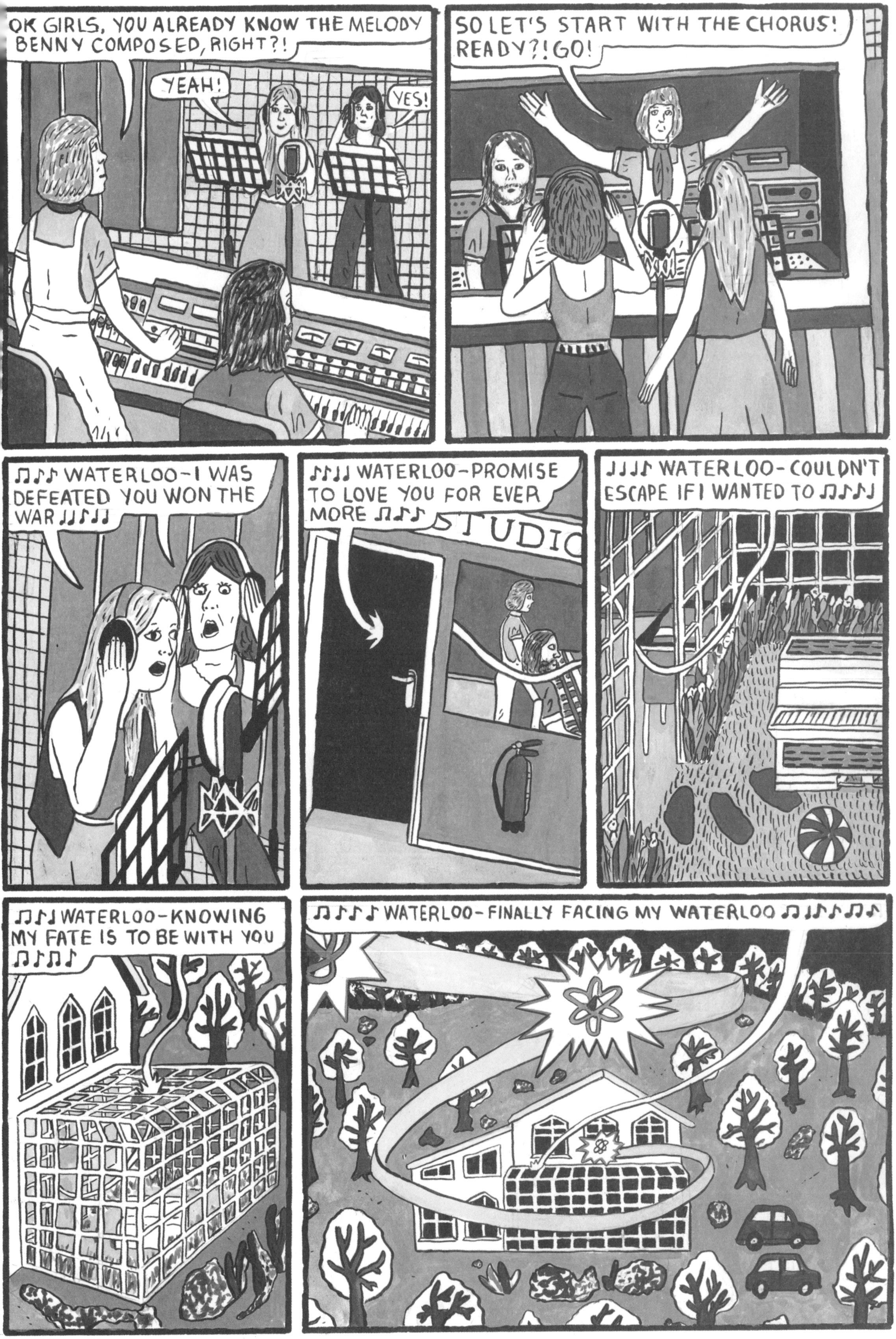
OK GIRLS, YOU ALREADY KNOW THE MELODY BENNY COMPOSED, RIGHT?!
YEAH!
YES!
SO LET'S START WITH THE CHORUS! READY?! GO!
♫♪♪ WATERLOO - I WAS DEFEATED YOU WON THE WAR ♩♩♪♩♩
♪♪♩♩ WATERLOO - PROMISE TO LOVE YOU FOR EVER MORE ♫♪♪
STUDIO
♩♩♩♪ WATERLOO - COULDN'T ESCAPE IF I WANTED TO ♫♪♪♩
♫♪♩ WATERLOO - KNOWING MY FATE IS TO BE WITH YOU ♫♪♫♪
♫♪♪♪ WATERLOO - FINALLY FACING MY WATERLOO ♫♩♪♪♫♪

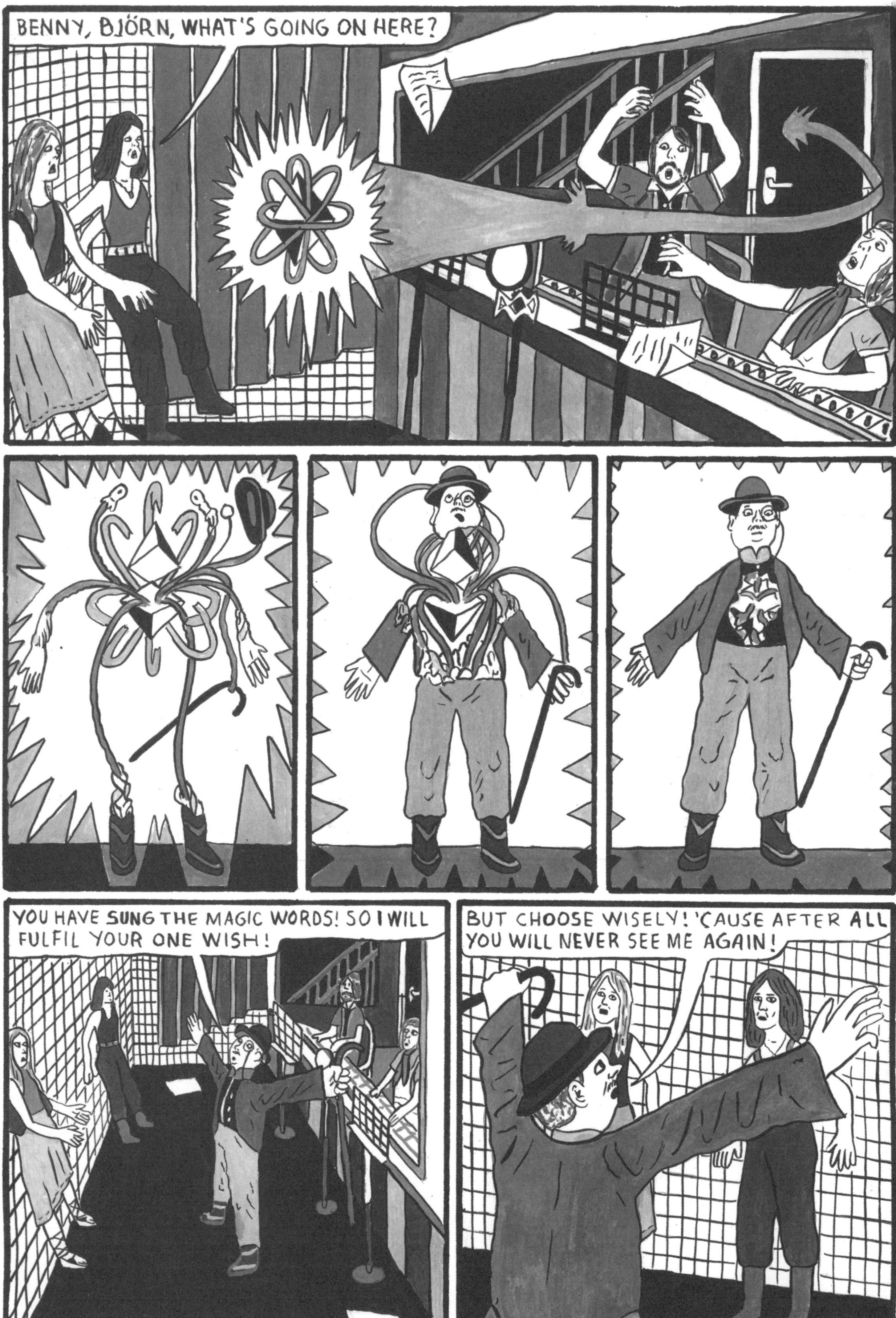
BENNY, BJÖRN, WHAT'S GOING ON HERE?
YOU HAVE SUNG THE MAGIC WORDS! SO I WILL FULFIL YOUR ONE WISH!
BUT CHOOSE WISELY! 'CAUSE AFTER ALL YOU WILL NEVER SEE ME AGAIN!

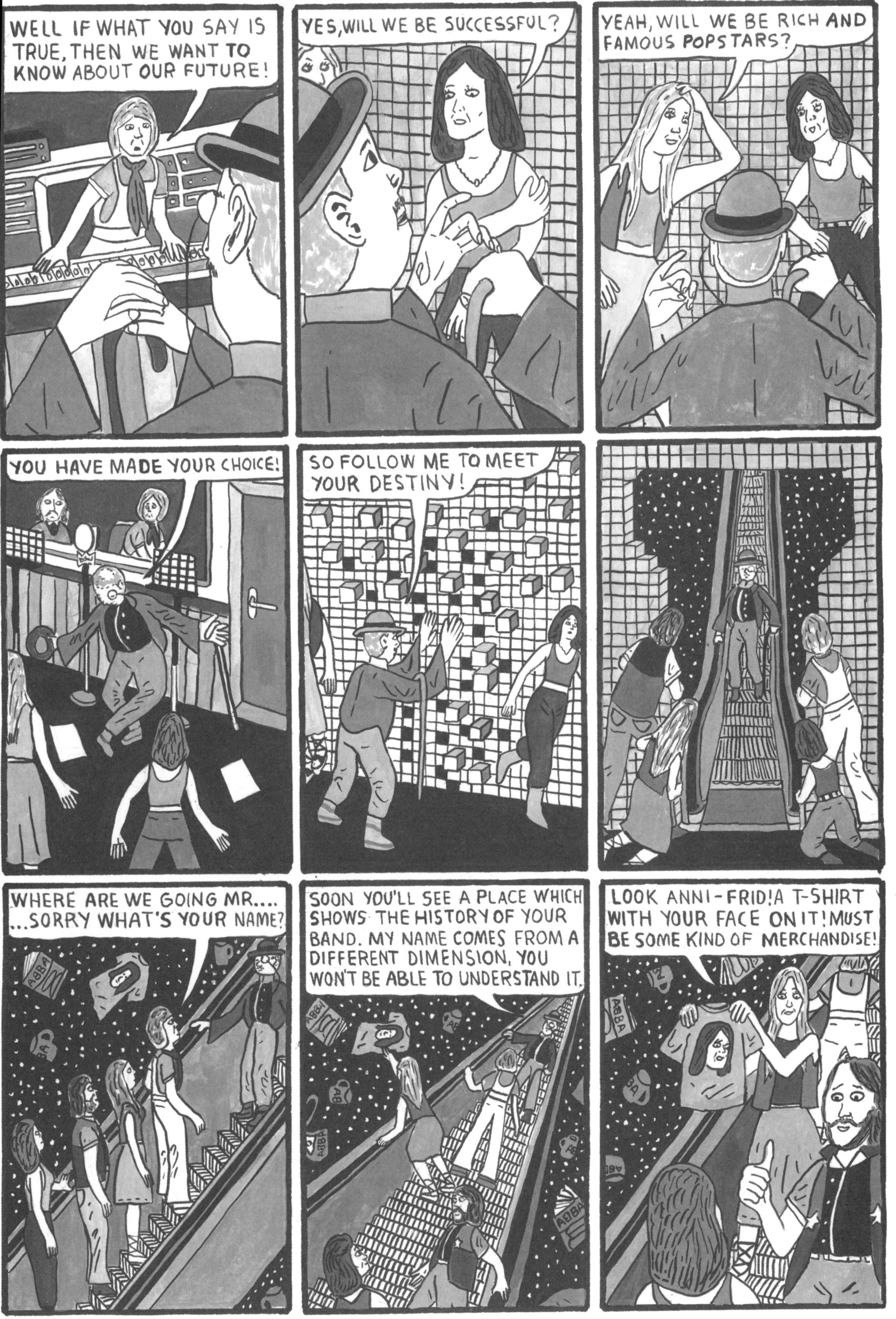
WELL IF WHAT YOU SAY IS TRUE, THEN WE WANT TO KNOW ABOUT OUR FUTURE!
YES, WILL WE BE SUCCESSFUL?
YEAH, WILL WE BE RICH AND FAMOUS POPSTARS?
YOU HAVE MADE YOUR CHOICE!
SO FOLLOW ME TO MEET YOUR DESTINY!
WHERE ARE WE GOING MR.... ...SORRY WHAT'S YOUR NAME?
SOON YOU'LL SEE A PLACE WHICH SHOWS THE HISTORY OF YOUR BAND. MY NAME COMES FROM A DIFFERENT DIMENSION, YOU WON'T BE ABLE TO UNDERSTAND IT.
LOOK ANNI-FRID! A T-SHIRT WITH YOUR FACE ON IT! MUST BE SOME KIND OF MERCHANDISE!

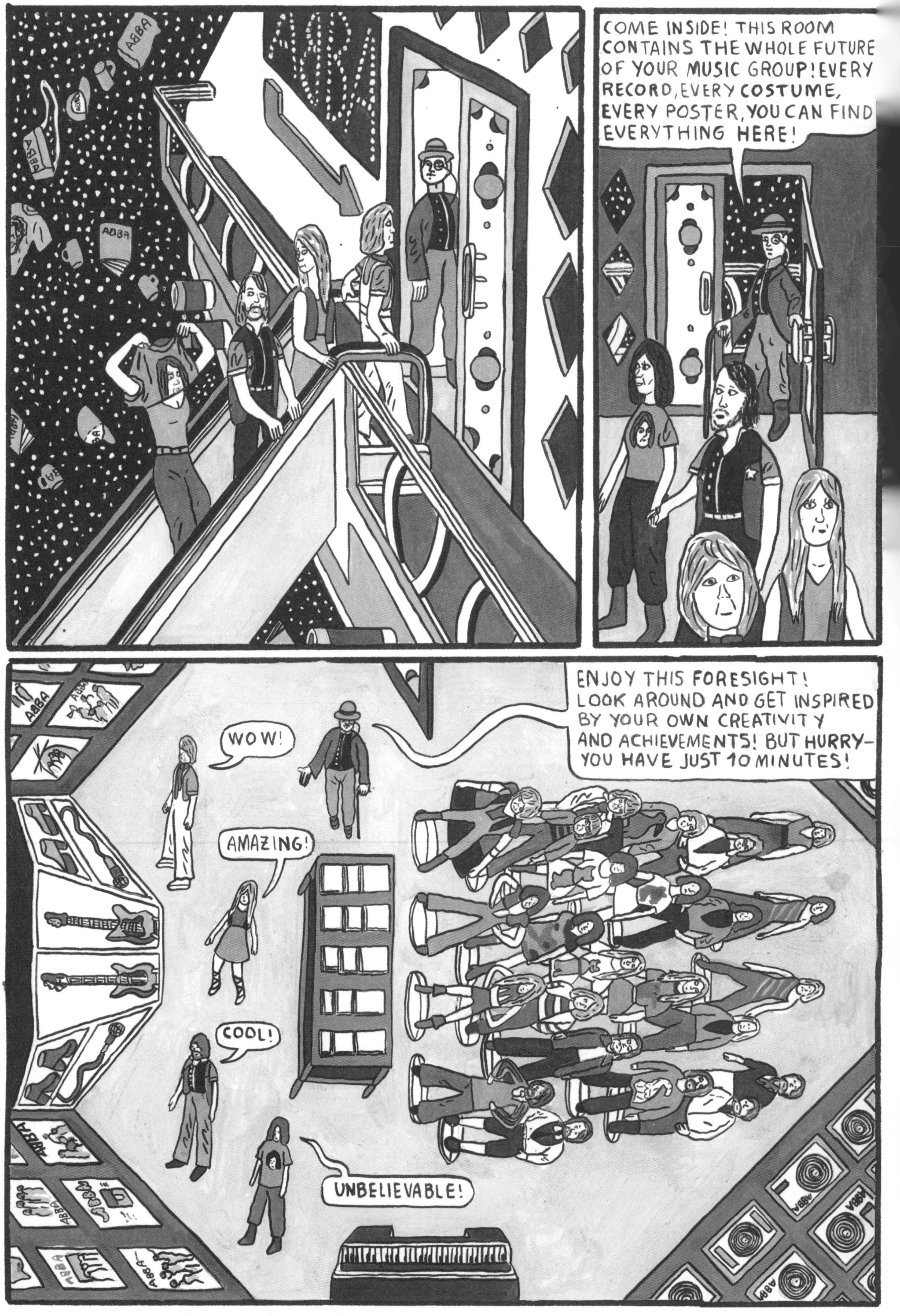
COME INSIDE! THIS ROOM CONTAINS THE WHOLE FUTURE OF YOUR MUSIC GROUP! EVERY RECORD, EVERY COSTUME, EVERY POSTER, YOU CAN FIND EVERYTHING HERE!
ENJOY THIS FORESIGHT! LOOK AROUND AND GET INSPIRED BY YOUR OWN CREATIVITY AND ACHIEVEMENTS! BUT HURRY- YOU HAVE JUST 10 MINUTES!
WOW!
AMAZING!
COOL!
UNBELIEVABLE!

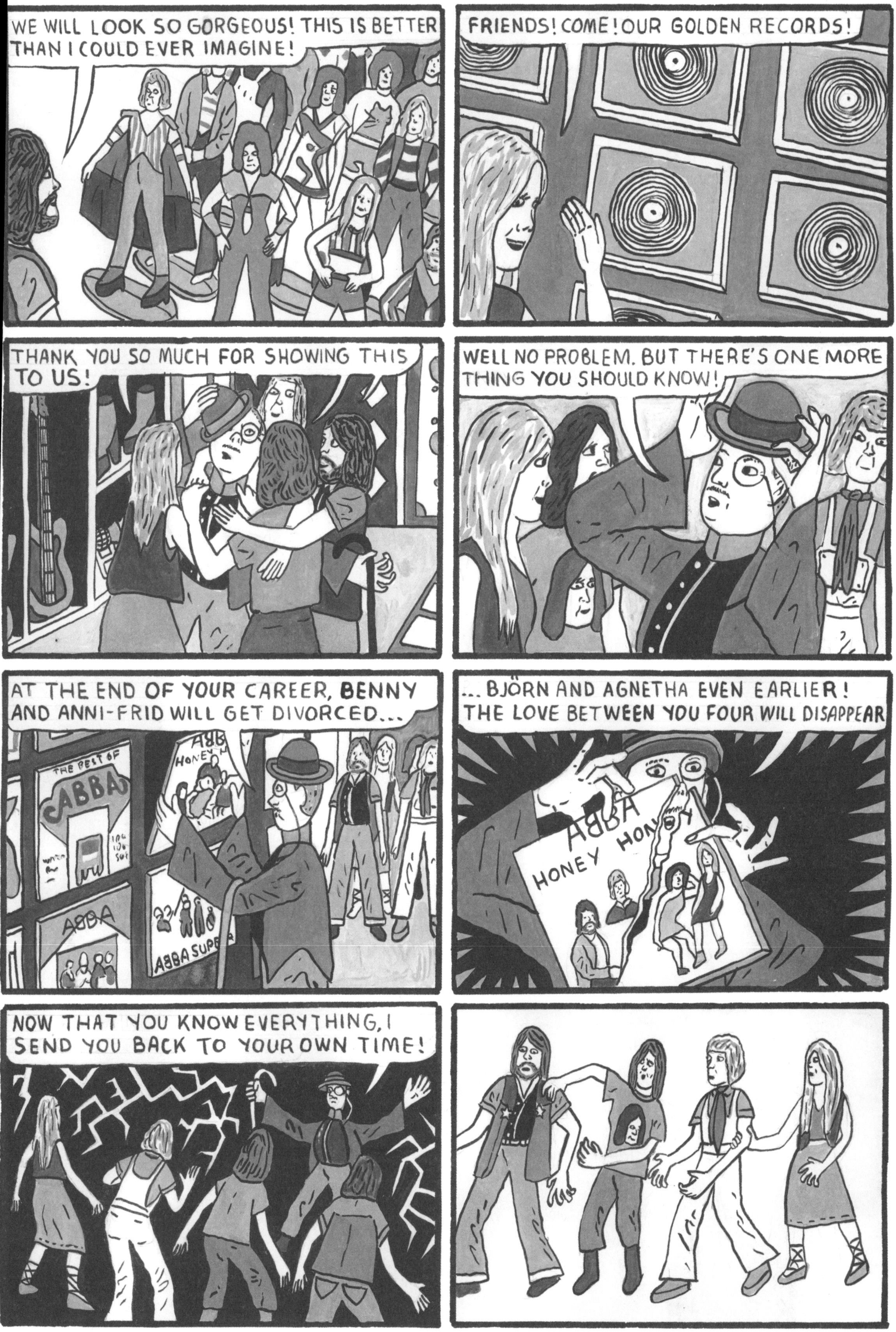
WE WILL LOOK SO GORGEOUS! THIS IS BETTER THAN I COULD EVER IMAGINE!
FRIENDS! COME! OUR GOLDEN RECORDS!
THANK YOU SO MUCH FOR SHOWING THIS TO US!
WELL NO PROBLEM. BUT THERE'S ONE MORE THING YOU SHOULD KNOW!
AT THE END OF YOUR CAREER, BENNY AND ANNI-FRID WILL GET DIVORCED...
THE BEST OF ABBA
ABBA
ABBA SUPE
... BJÖRN AND AGNETHA EVEN EARLIER! THE LOVE BETWEEN YOU FOUR WILL DISAPPEAR
ABBA
HONEY HONEY
NOW THAT YOU KNOW EVERYTHING, I SEND YOU BACK TO YOUR OWN TIME!

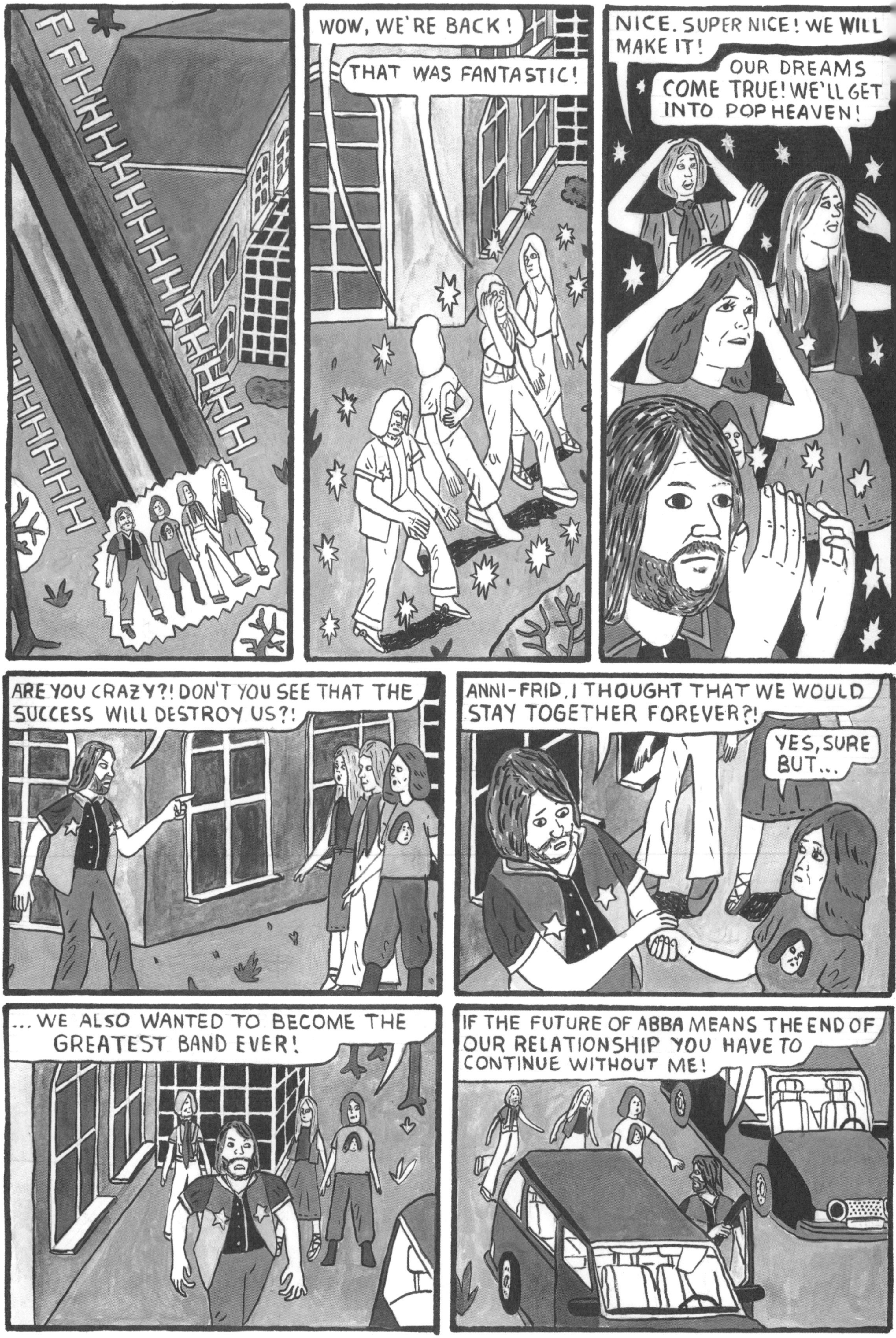
FFHHHHHHHHHHHHHH
HHHHHHHH
WOW, WE'RE BACK!
THAT WAS FANTASTIC!
NICE. SUPER NICE! WE WILL MAKE IT!
OUR DREAMS COME TRUE! WE'LL GET INTO POP HEAVEN!
ARE YOU CRAZY?! DON'T YOU SEE THAT THE SUCCESS WILL DESTROY US?!
ANNI-FRID, I THOUGHT THAT WE WOULD STAY TOGETHER FOREVER?!
YES, SURE BUT...
... WE ALSO WANTED TO BECOME THE GREATEST BAND EVER!
IF THE FUTURE OF ABBA MEANS THE END OF OUR RELATIONSHIP YOU HAVE TO CONTINUE WITHOUT ME!

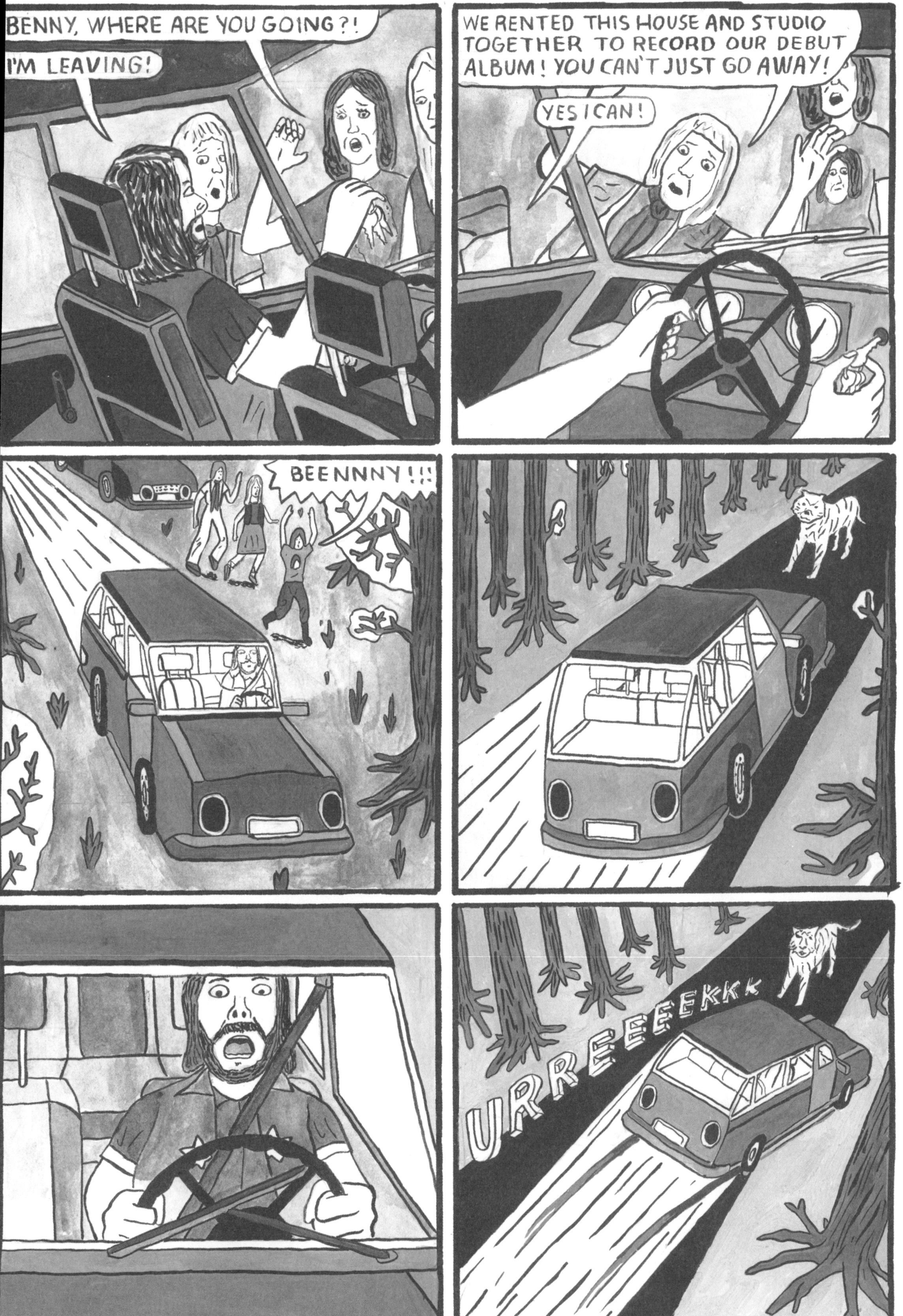
BENNY, WHERE ARE YOU GOING?!
I'M LEAVING!
WE RENTED THIS HOUSE AND STUDIO TOGETHER TO RECORD OUR DEBUT ALBUM! YOU CAN'T JUST GO AWAY!
YES I CAN!
BEENNNY!!!
URREEEEEEKKK

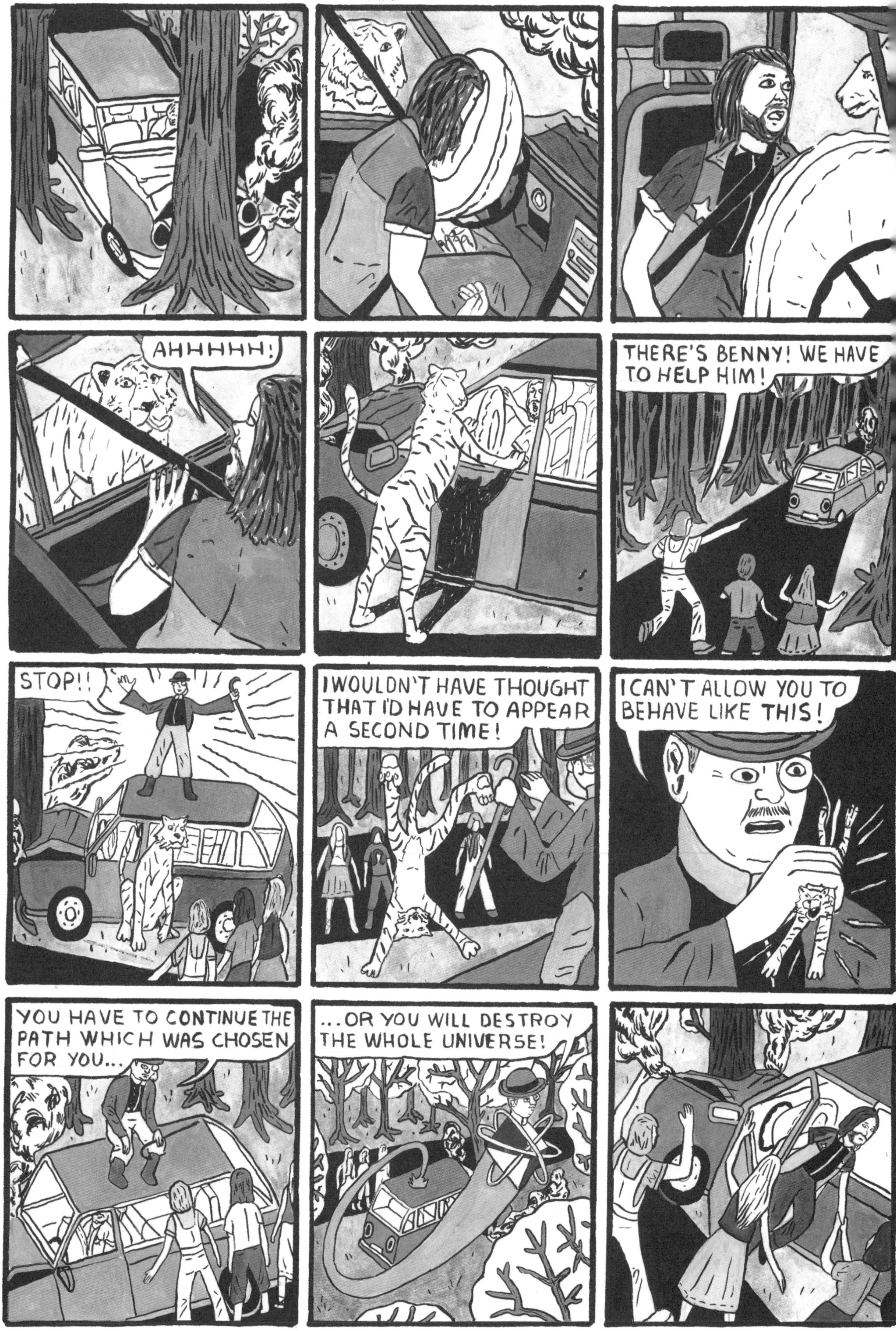
AHHHHH!
THERE'S BENNY! WE HAVE TO HELP HIM!
STOP!!
I WOULDN'T HAVE THOUGHT THAT I'D HAVE TO APPEAR A SECOND TIME!
I CAN'T ALLOW YOU TO BEHAVE LIKE THIS!
YOU HAVE TO CONTINUE THE PATH WHICH WAS CHOSEN FOR YOU...
...OR YOU WILL DESTROY THE WHOLE UNIVERSE!

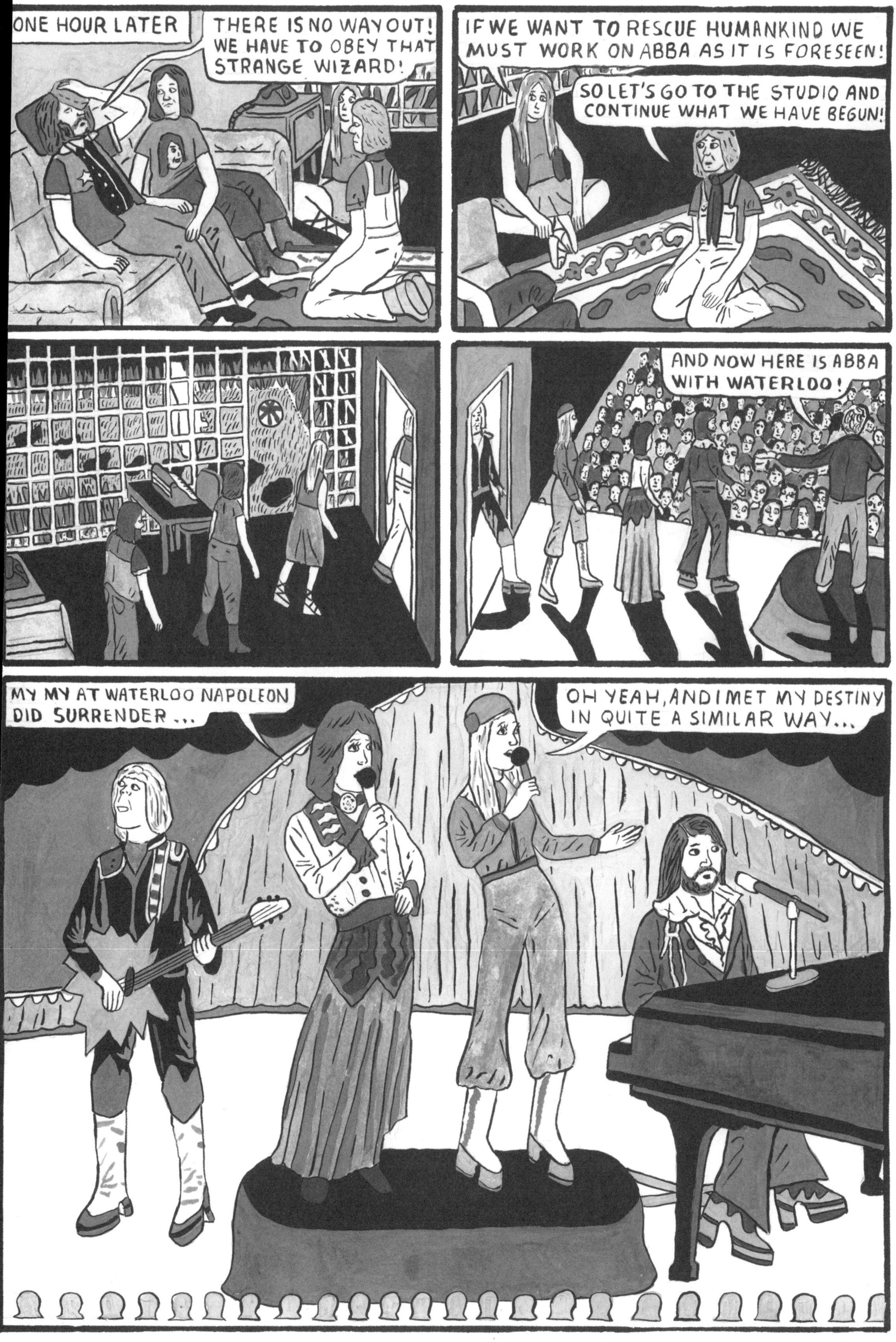
ONE HOUR LATER
THERE IS NO WAY OUT! WE HAVE TO OBEY THAT STRANGE WIZARD!
IF WE WANT TO RESCUE HUMANKIND WE MUST WORK ON ABBA AS IT IS FORESEEN!
SO LET'S GO TO THE STUDIO AND CONTINUE WHAT WE HAVE BEGUN!
AND NOW HERE IS ABBA WITH WATERLOO!
MY MY AT WATERLOO NAPOLEON DID SURRENDER ...
OH YEAH, AND I MET MY DESTINY IN QUITE A SIMILAR WAY...

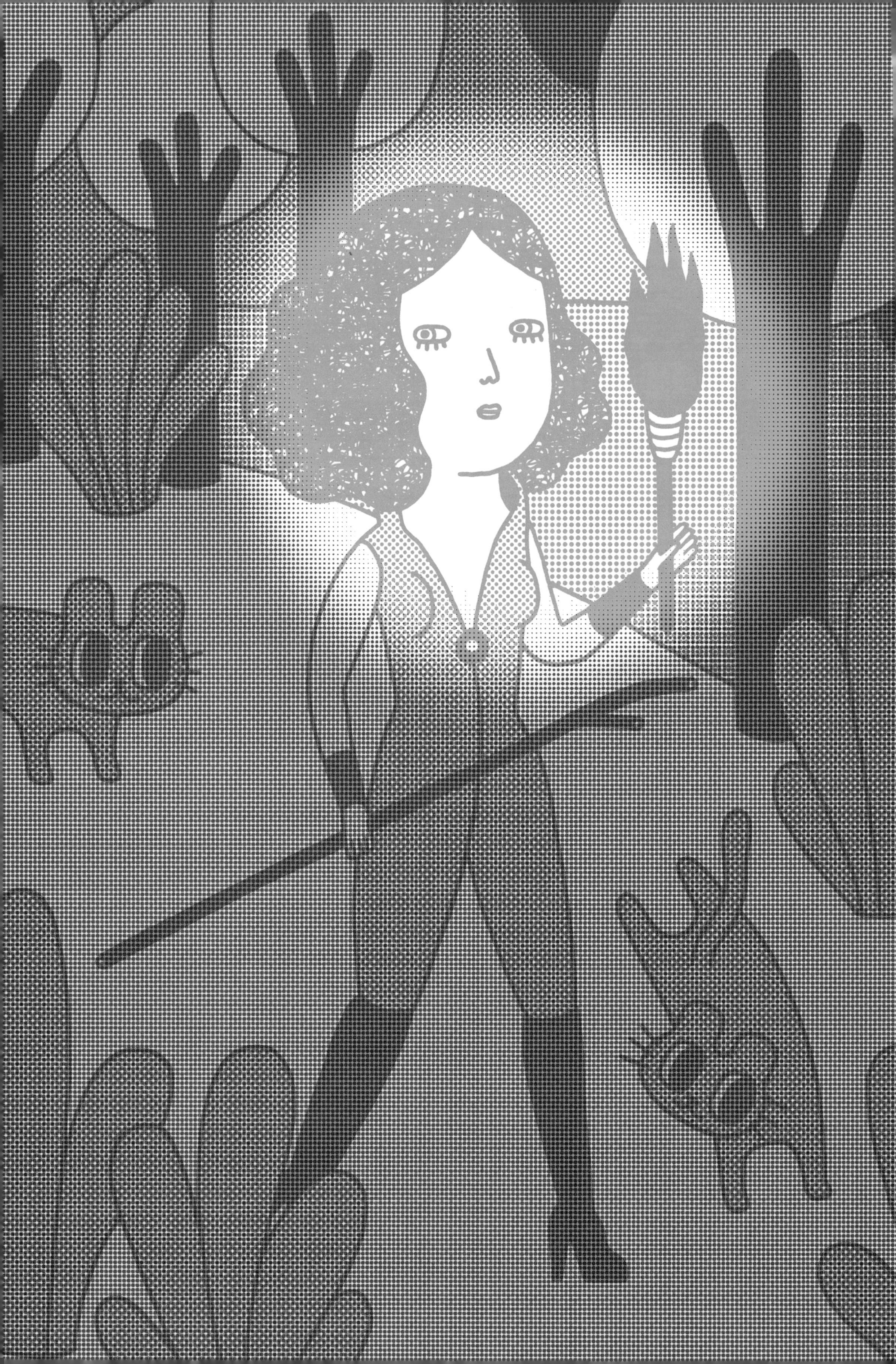

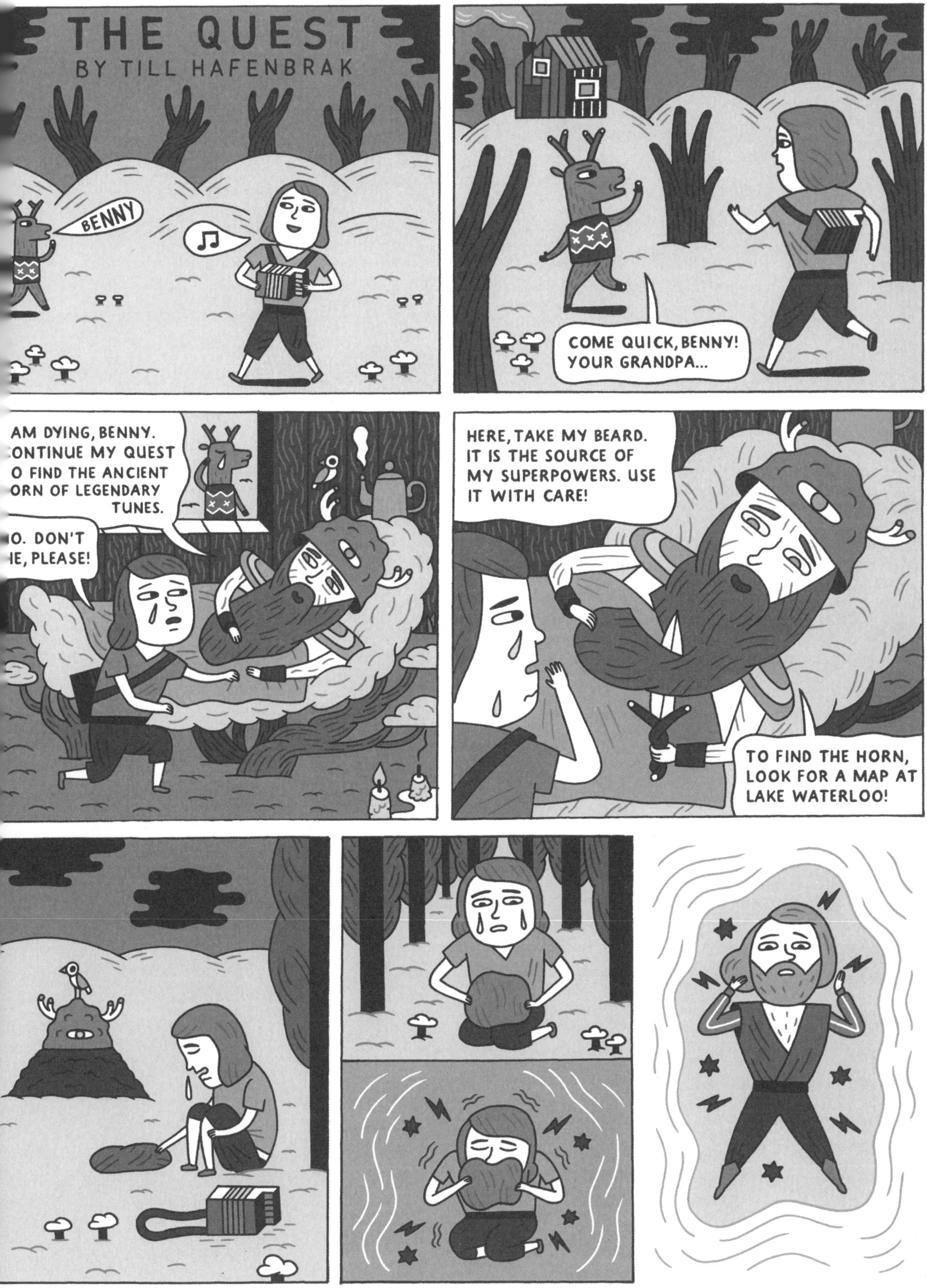
THE QUEST
BY TILL HAFENBRAK
BENNY
COME QUICK, BENNY! YOUR GRANDPA...
AM DYING, BENNY. ONTINUE MY QUEST O FIND THE ANCIENT ORN OF LEGENDARY TUNES.
O. DON'T IE, PLEASE!
HERE, TAKE MY BEARD. IT IS THE SOURCE OF MY SUPERPOWERS. USE IT WITH CARE!
TO FIND THE HORN, LOOK FOR A MAP AT LAKE WATERLOO!

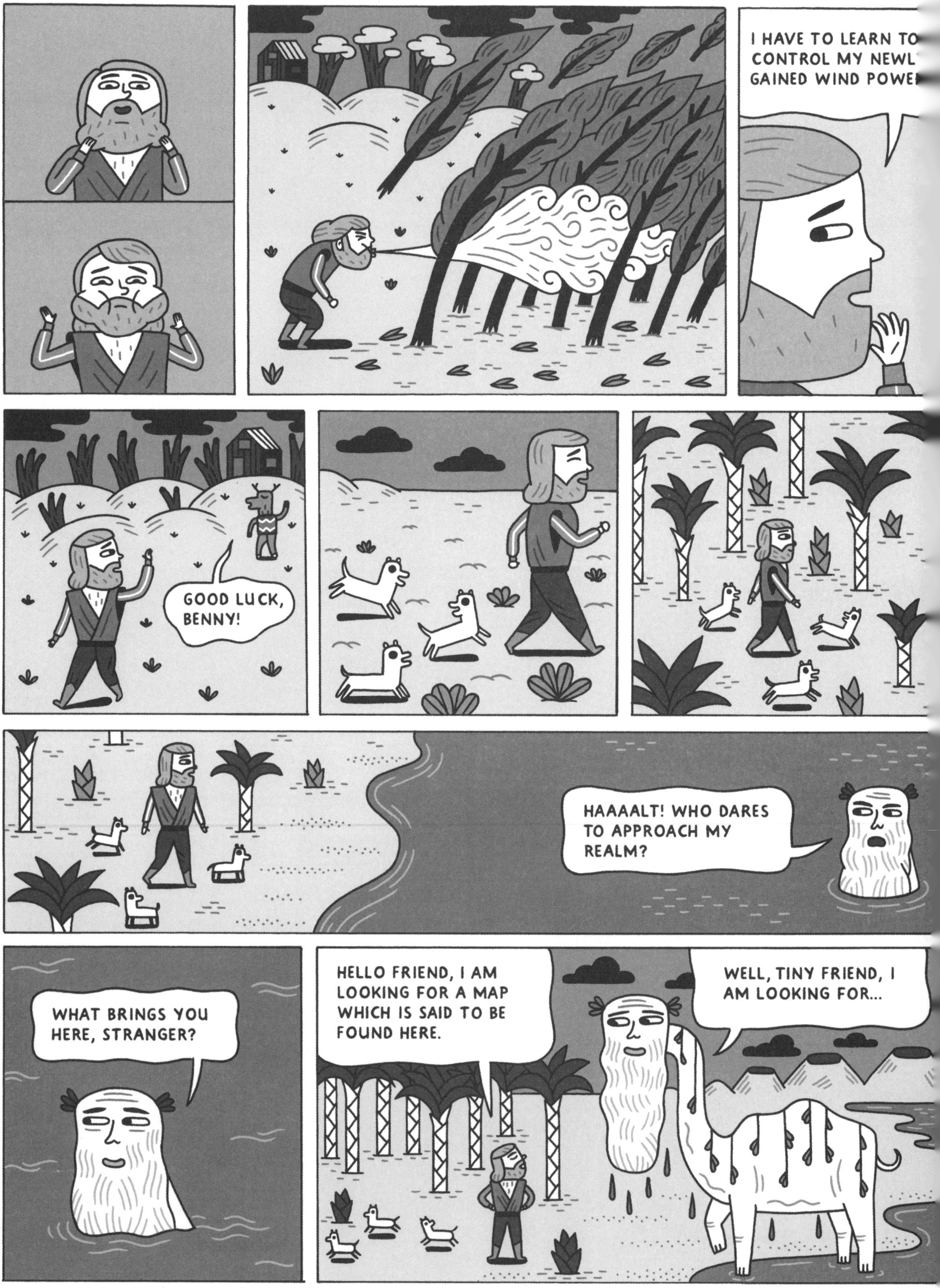
I HAVE TO LEARN TO CONTROL MY NEWL GAINED WIND POWE
GOOD LUCK, BENNY!
HAAAALT! WHO DARES TO APPROACH MY REALM?
WHAT BRINGS YOU HERE, STRANGER?
HELLO FRIEND, I AM LOOKING FOR A MAP WHICH IS SAID TO BE FOUND HERE.
WELL, TINY FRIEND, I AM LOOKING FOR...

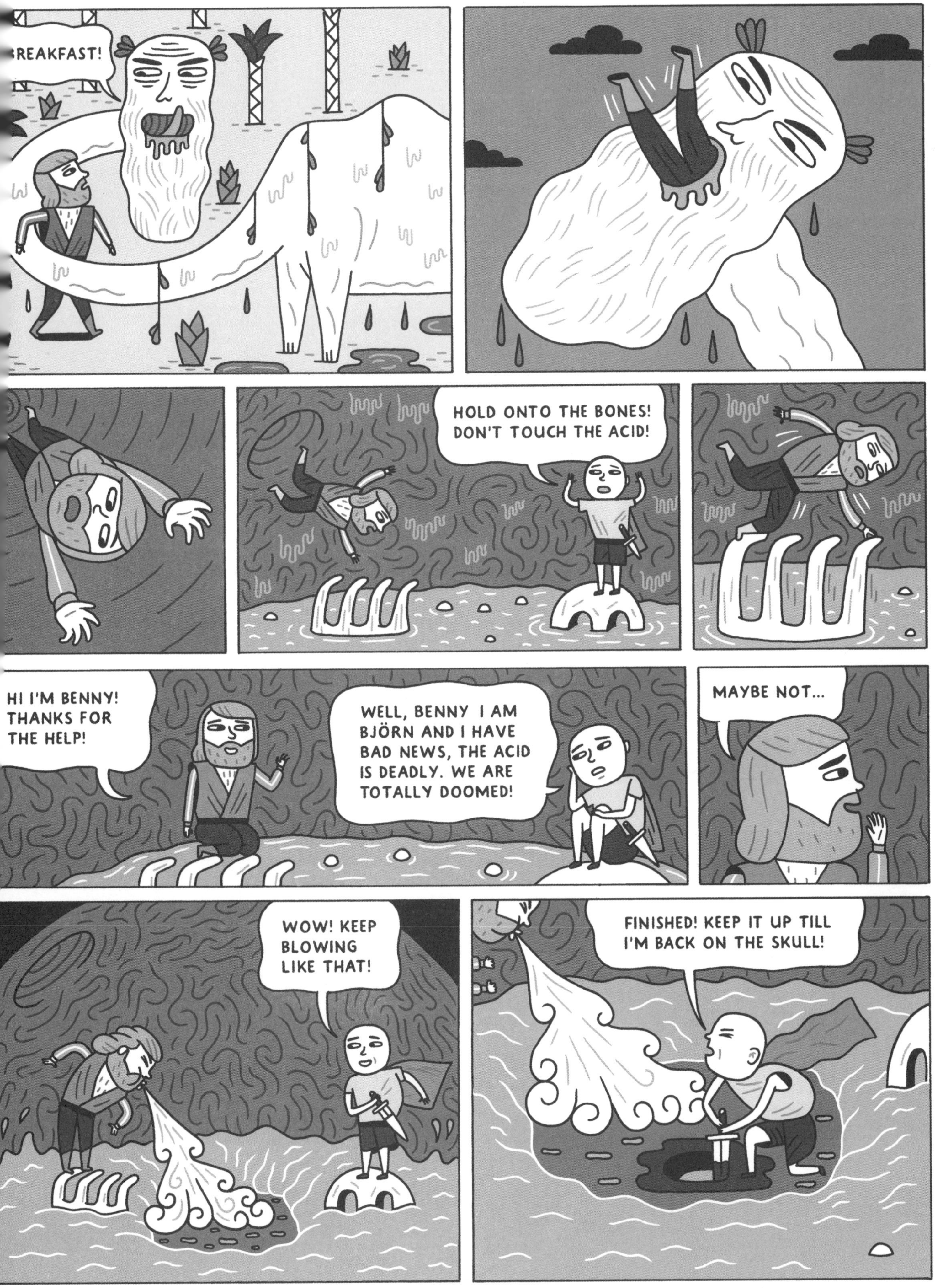
BREAKFAST!
HOLD ONTO THE BONES! DON'T TOUCH THE ACID!
HI I'M BENNY! THANKS FOR THE HELP!
WELL, BENNY I AM BJÖRN AND I HAVE BAD NEWS, THE ACID IS DEADLY. WE ARE TOTALLY DOOMED!
MAYBE NOT...
WOW! KEEP BLOWING LIKE THAT!
FINISHED! KEEP IT UP TILL I'M BACK ON THE SKULL!

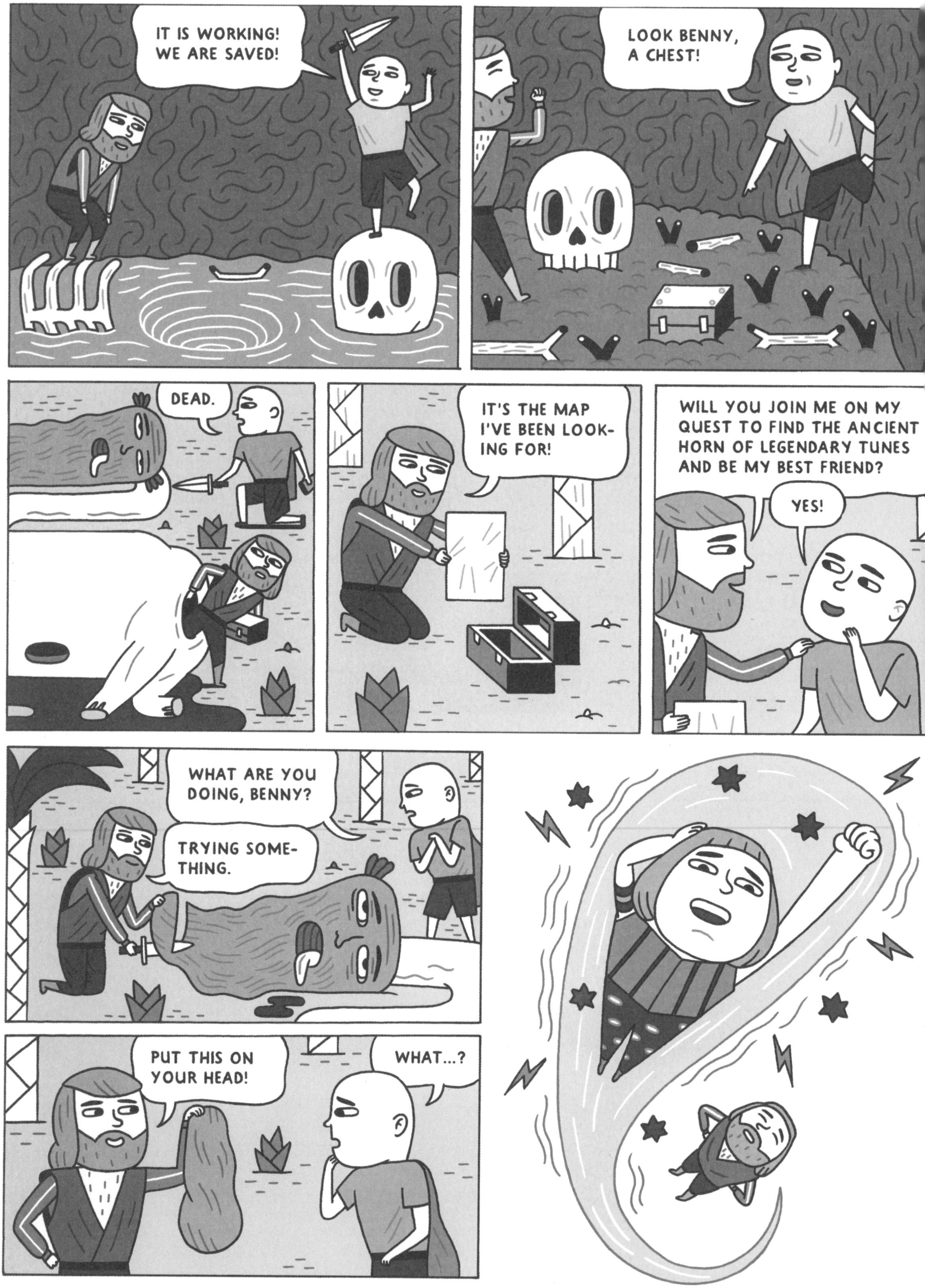
IT IS WORKING! WE ARE SAVED!
LOOK BENNY, A CHEST!
DEAD.
IT'S THE MAP I'VE BEEN LOOK-ING FOR!
WILL YOU JOIN ME ON MY QUEST TO FIND THE ANCIENT HORN OF LEGENDARY TUNES AND BE MY BEST FRIEND?
YES!
WHAT ARE YOU DOING, BENNY?
TRYING SOME-THING.
PUT THIS ON YOUR HEAD!
WHAT...?

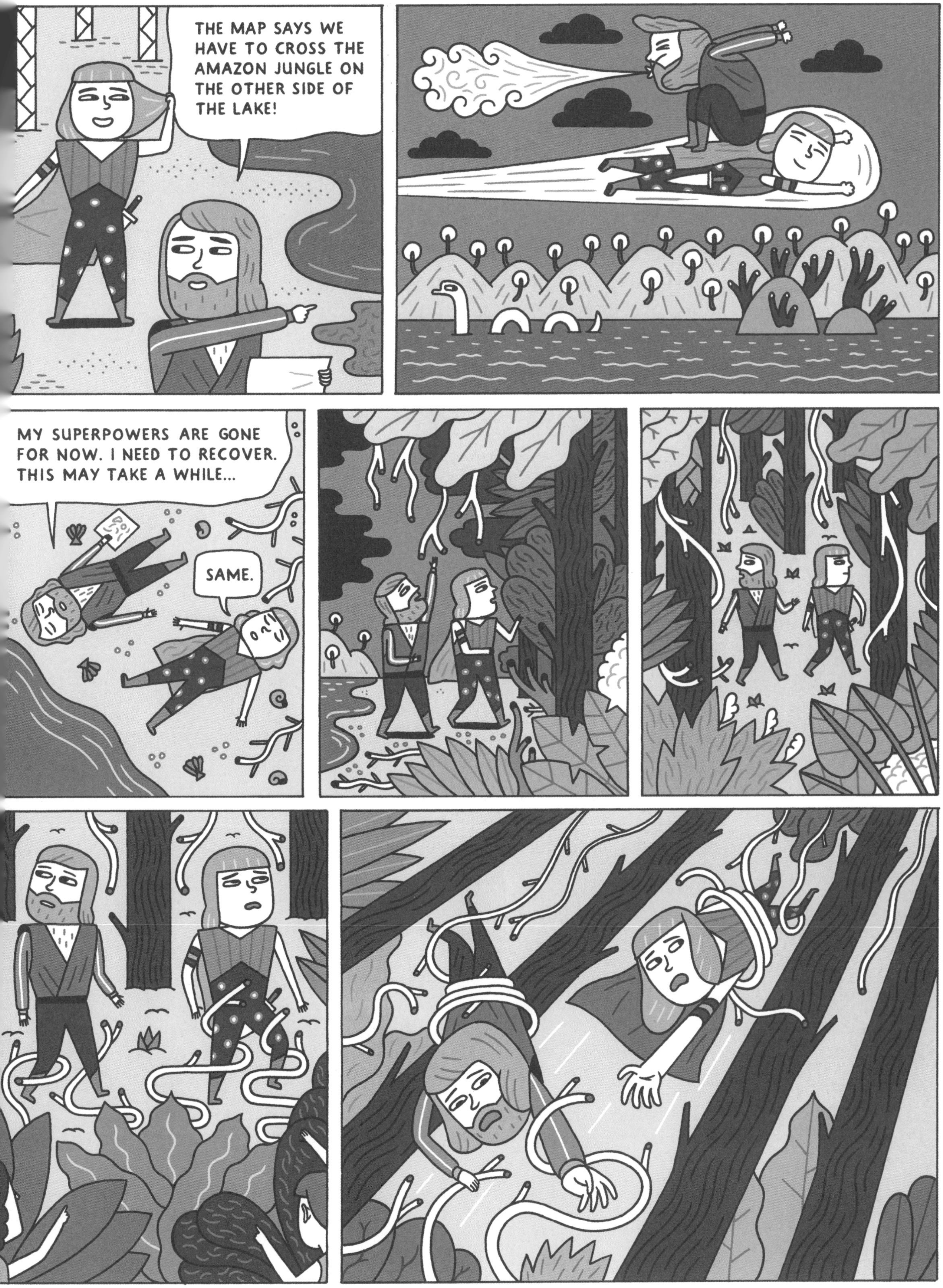
THE MAP SAYS WE HAVE TO CROSS THE AMAZON JUNGLE ON THE OTHER SIDE OF THE LAKE!
MY SUPERPOWERS ARE GONE FOR NOW. I NEED TO RECOVER. THIS MAY TAKE A WHILE...
SAME.

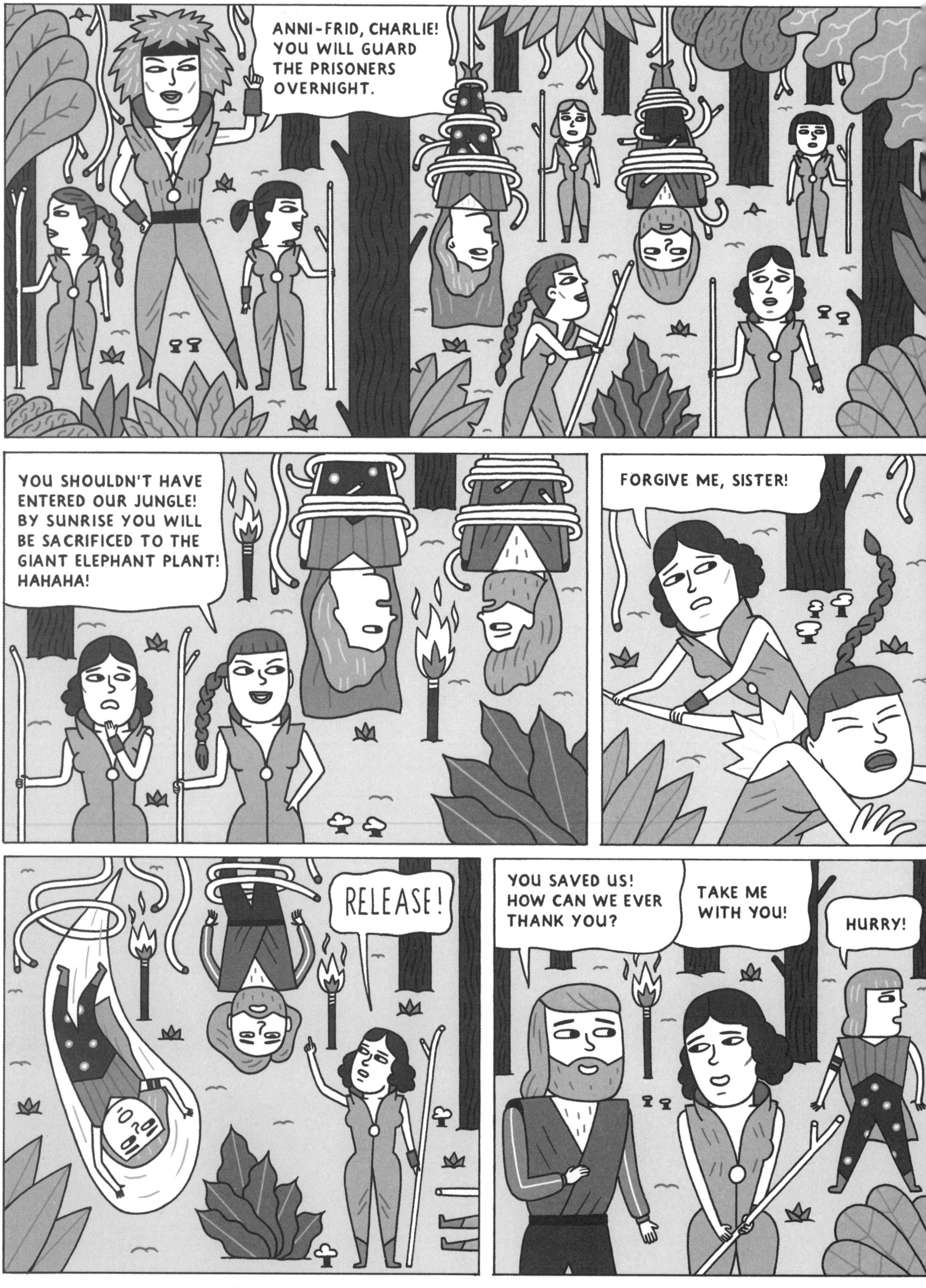
ANNI-FRID, CHARLIE! YOU WILL GUARD THE PRISONERS OVERNIGHT.
YOU SHOULDN'T HAVE ENTERED OUR JUNGLE! BY SUNRISE YOU WILL BE SACRIFICED TO THE GIANT ELEPHANT PLANT! HAHAHA!
FORGIVE ME, SISTER!
RELEASE!
YOU SAVED US! HOW CAN WE EVER THANK YOU?
TAKE ME WITH YOU!
HURRY!

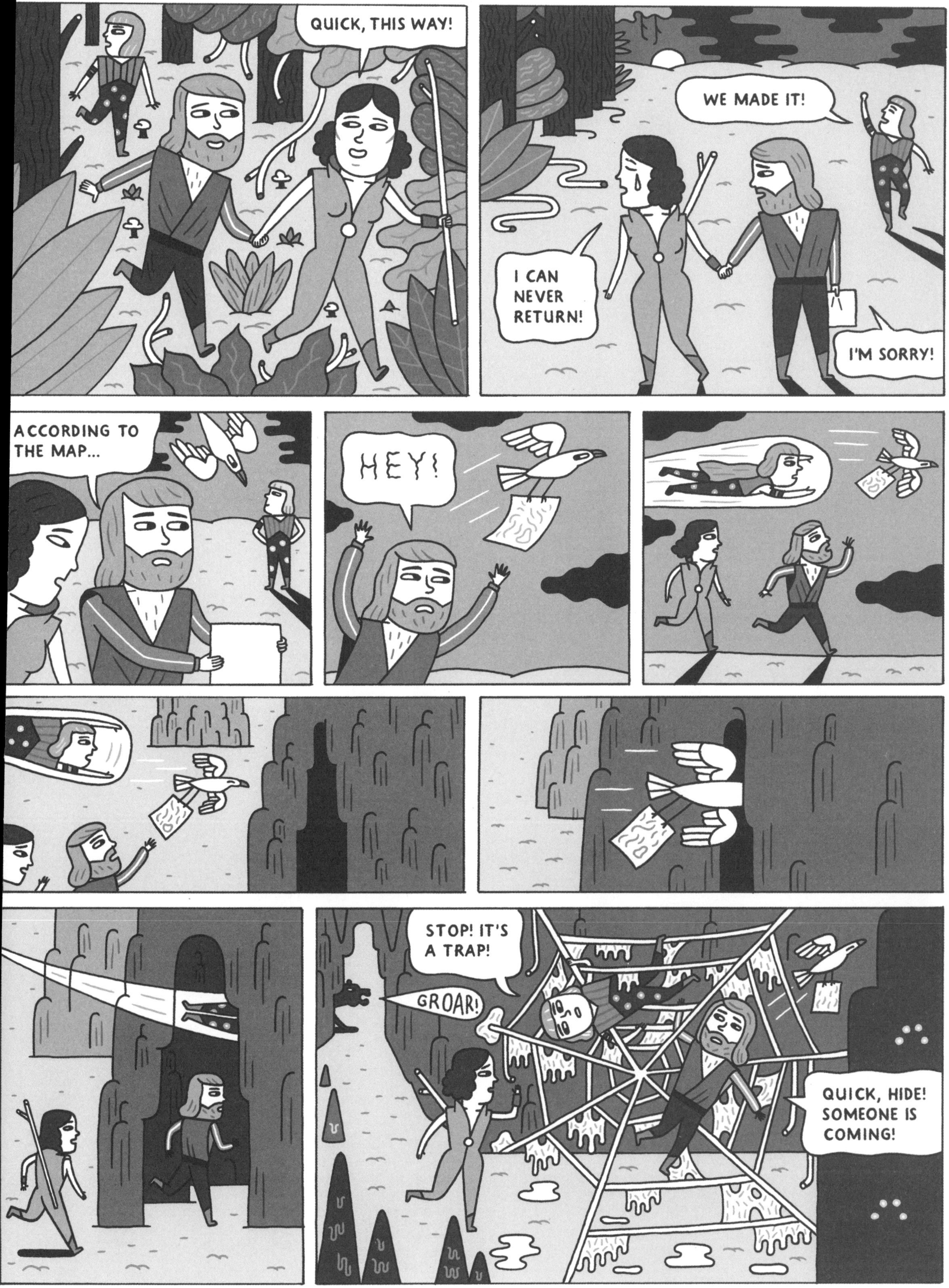

QUICK, THIS WAY!
WE MADE IT!
I CAN NEVER RETURN!
I'M SORRY!
ACCORDING TO THE MAP...
HEY!
STOP! IT'S A TRAP!
GROAR!
QUICK, HIDE! SOMEONE IS COMING!

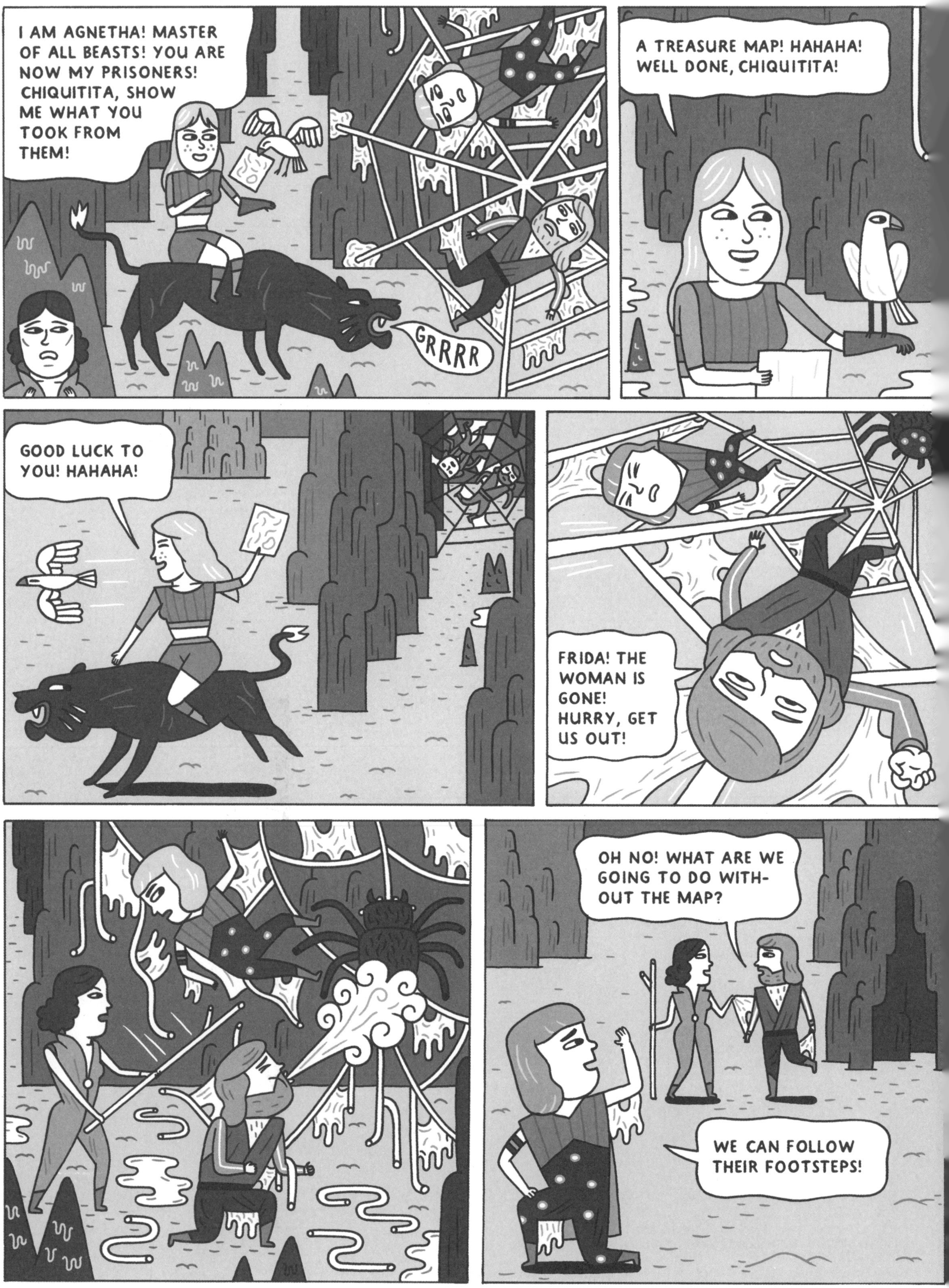
I AM AGNETHA! MASTER OF ALL BEASTS! YOU ARE NOW MY PRISONERS! CHIQUITITA, SHOW ME WHAT YOU TOOK FROM THEM!
GRRRR
A TREASURE MAP! HAHAHA! WELL DONE, CHIQUITITA!
GOOD LUCK TO YOU! HAHAHA!
FRIDA! THE WOMAN IS GONE! HURRY, GET US OUT!
OH NO! WHAT ARE WE GOING TO DO WITH-OUT THE MAP?
WE CAN FOLLOW THEIR FOOTSTEPS!

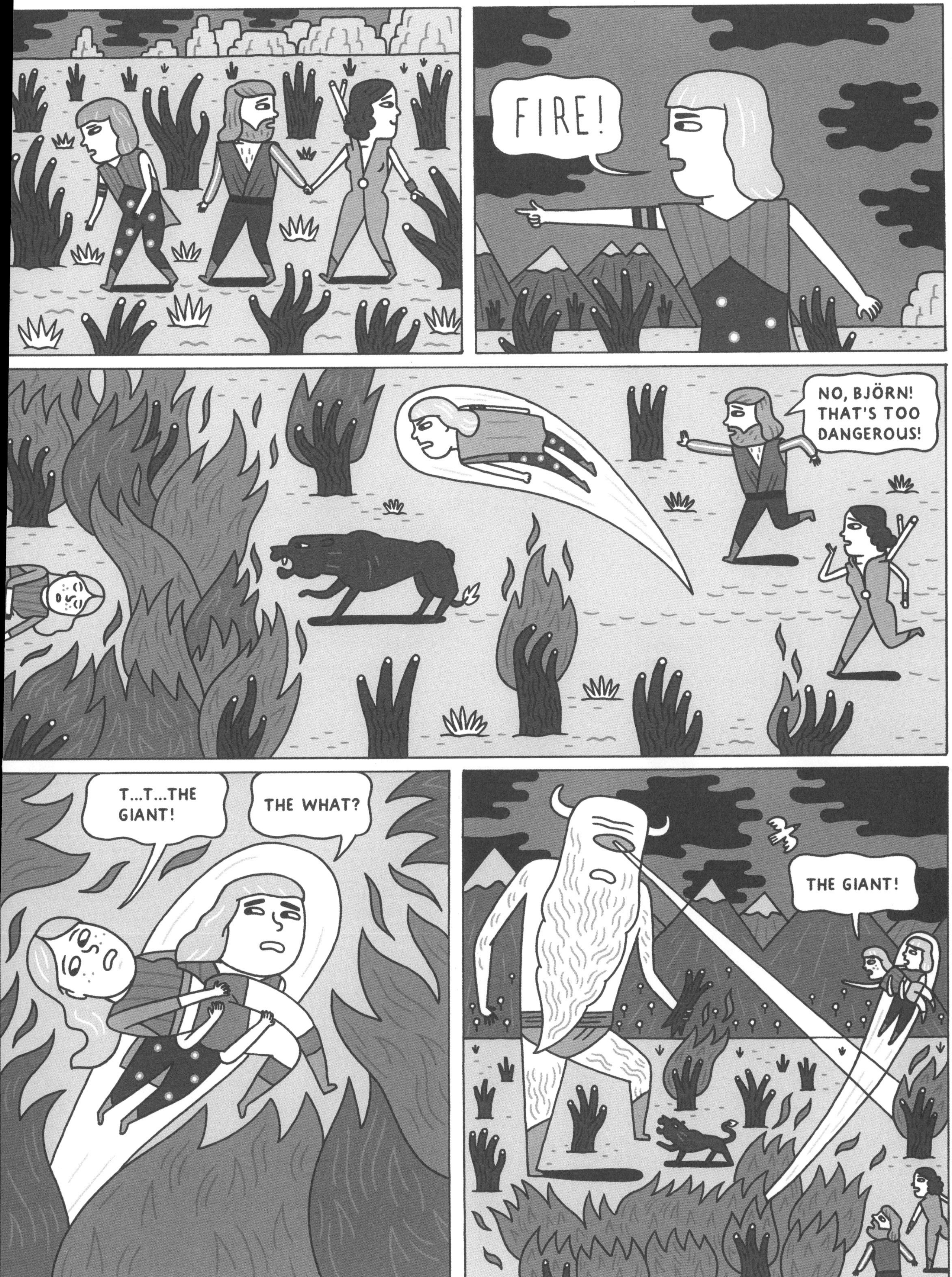
FIRE!
NO, BJÖRN! THAT'S TOO DANGEROUS!
T...T...THE GIANT!
THE WHAT?
THE GIANT!

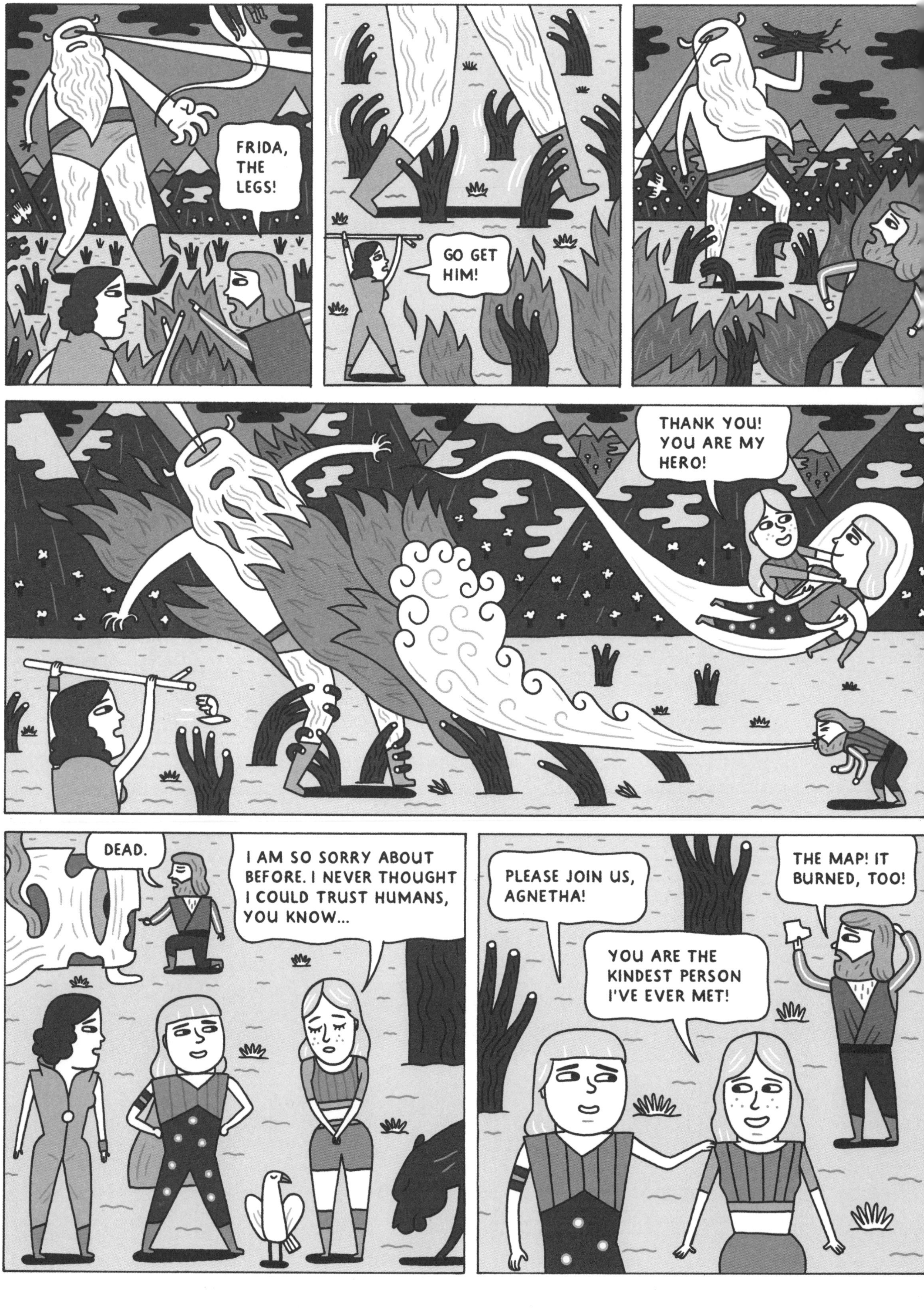
FRIDA, THE LEGS!
GO GET HIM!
THANK YOU! YOU ARE MY HERO!
DEAD.
I AM SO SORRY ABOUT BEFORE. I NEVER THOUGHT I COULD TRUST HUMANS, YOU KNOW...
PLEASE JOIN US, AGNETHA!
YOU ARE THE KINDEST PERSON I'VE EVER MET!
THE MAP! IT BURNED, TOO!

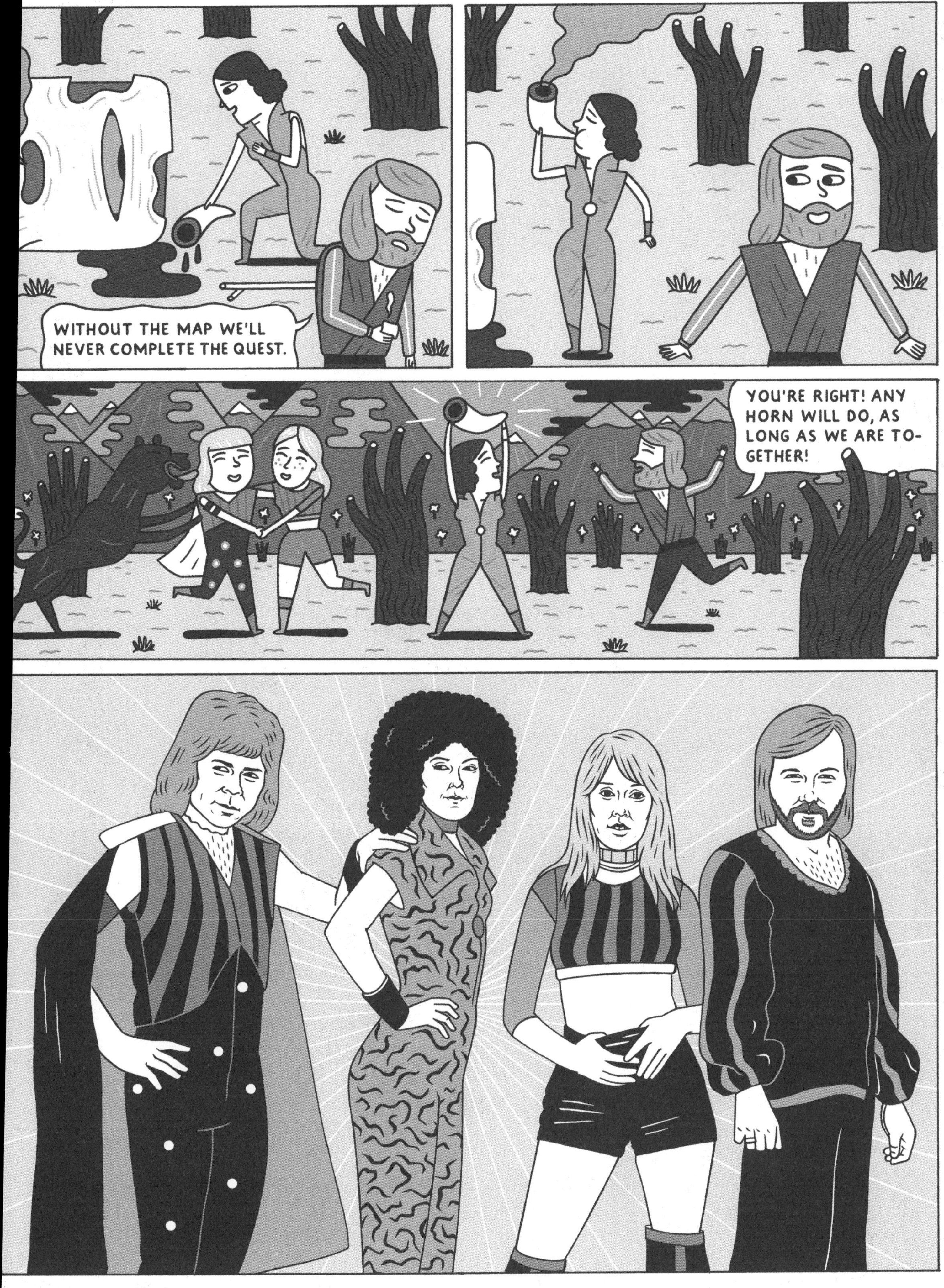
WITHOUT THE MAP WE'LL NEVER COMPLETE THE QUEST.
YOU'RE RIGHT! ANY HORN WILL DO, AS LONG AS WE ARE TO-GETHER!

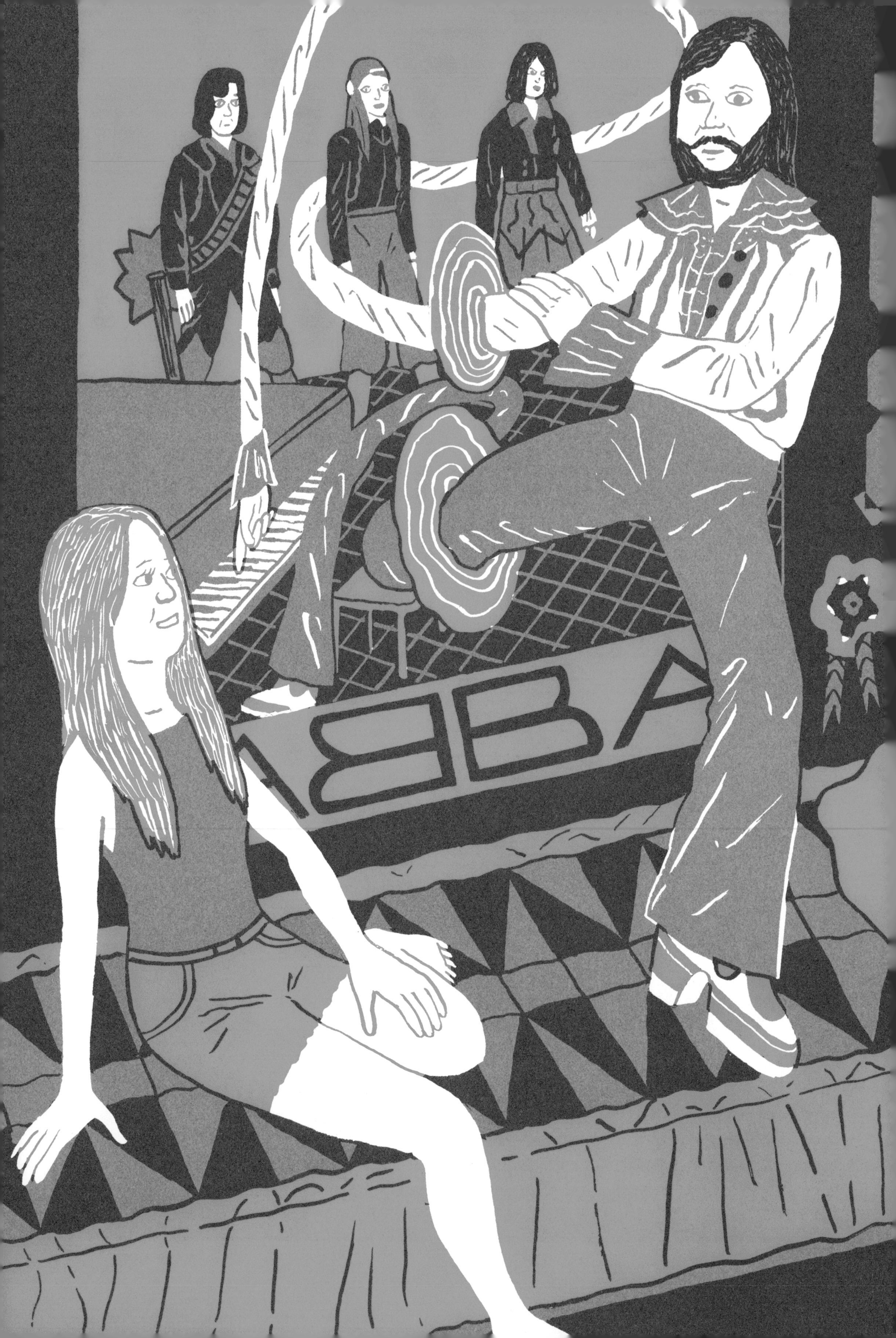
BBA

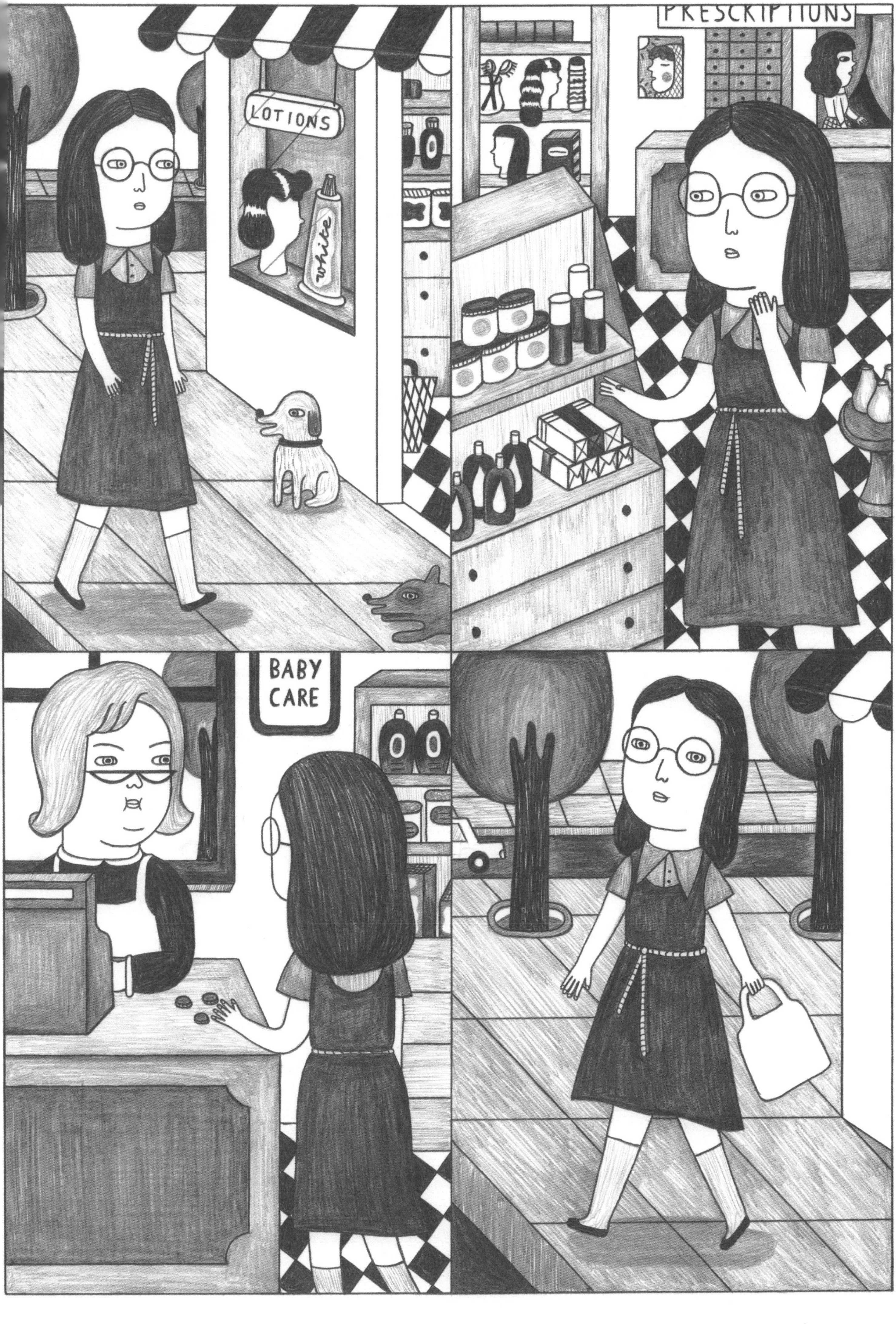
LOTIONS
white
PRESCRIPTIONS
BABY CARE

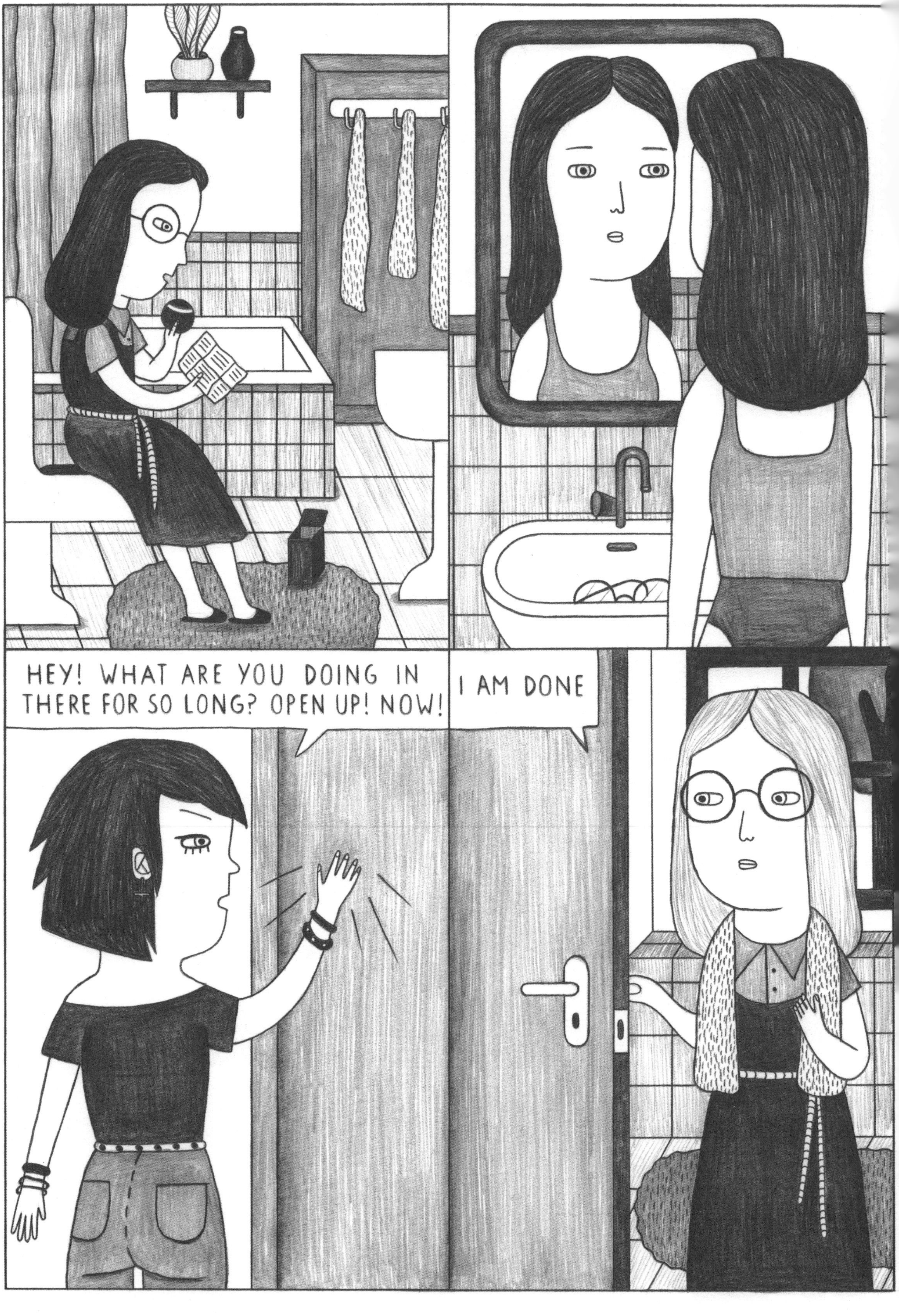
HEY! WHAT ARE YOU DOING IN THERE FOR SO LONG? OPEN UP! NOW!
I AM DONE

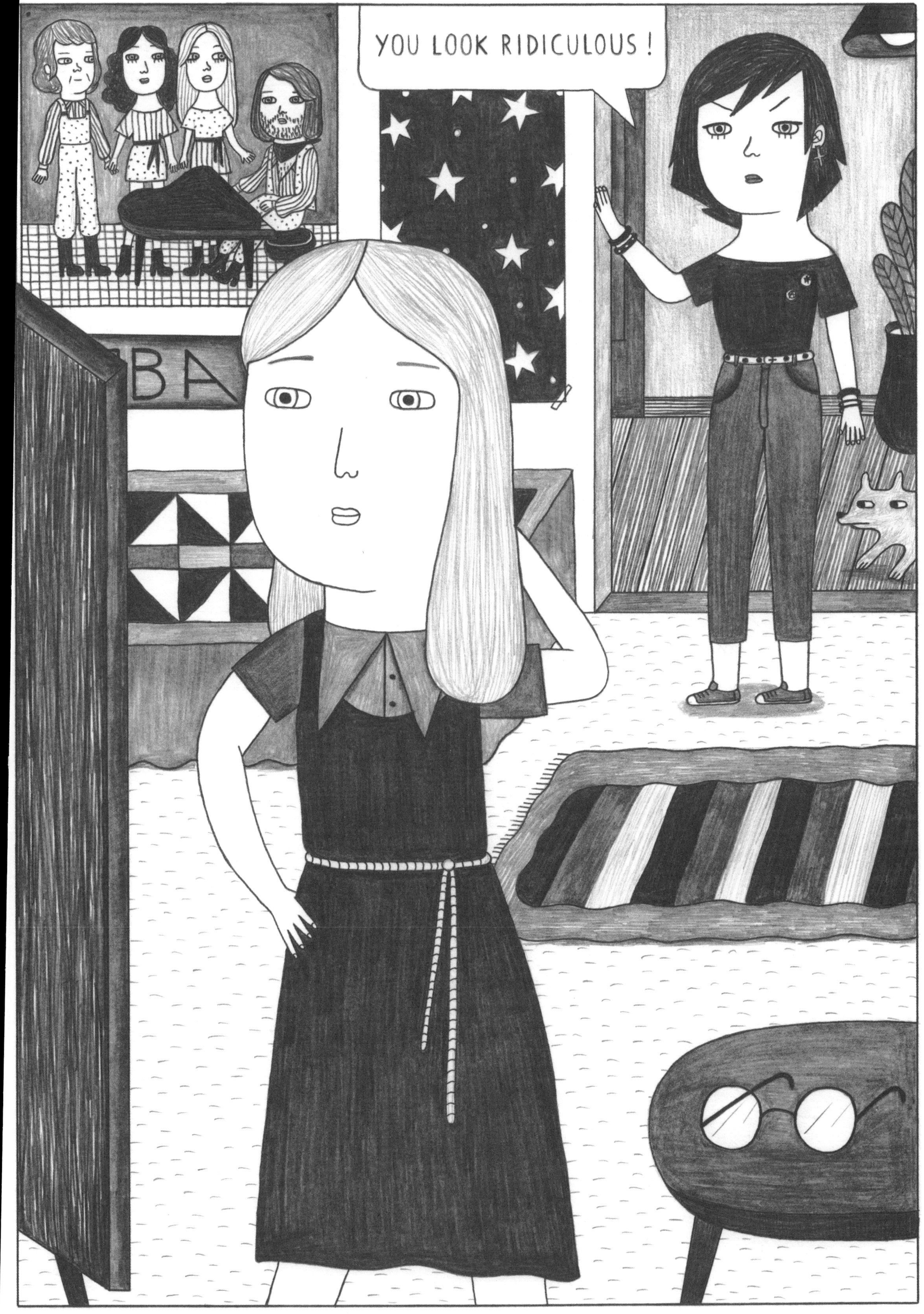
YOU LOOK RIDICULOUS !

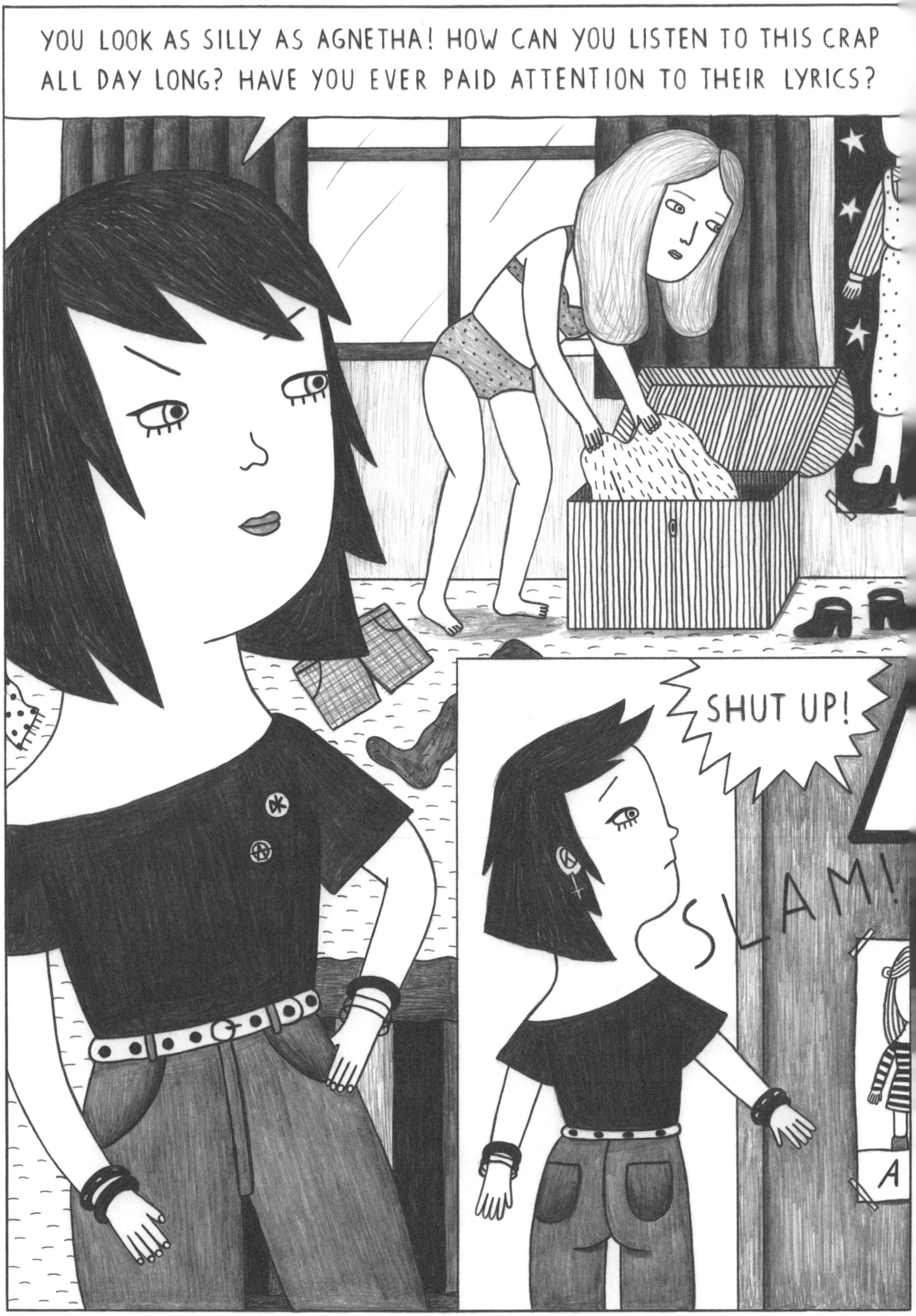
YOU LOOK AS SILLY AS AGNETHA! HOW CAN YOU LISTEN TO THIS CRAP ALL DAY LONG? HAVE YOU EVER PAID ATTENTION TO THEIR LYRICS?
SHUT UP!
SLAM!

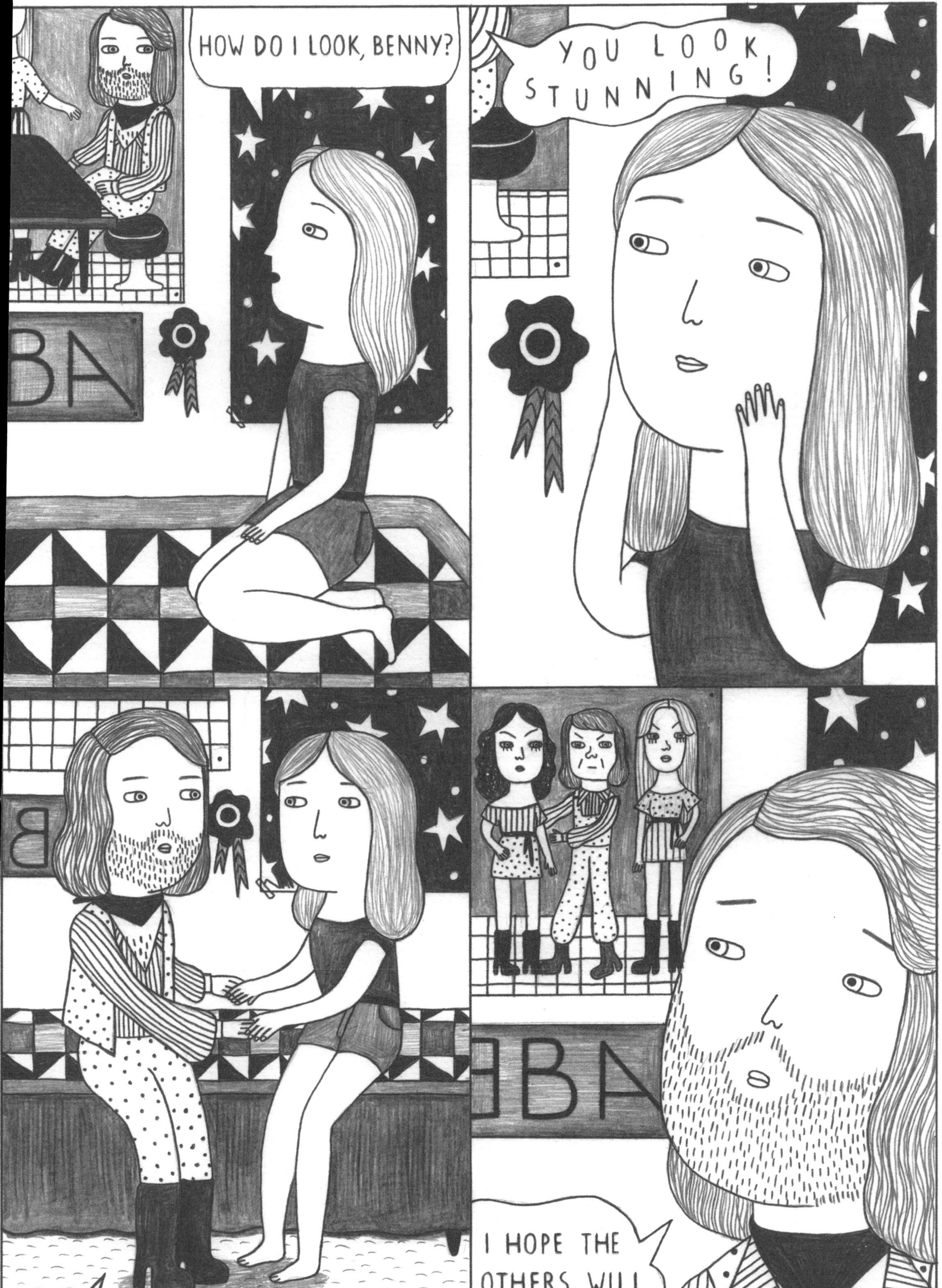
HOW DO I LOOK, BENNY?
YOU LOOK STUNNING!
OUR LOVE IS BIGGER THAN ABBA
I HOPE THE OTHERS WILL UNDERSTAND

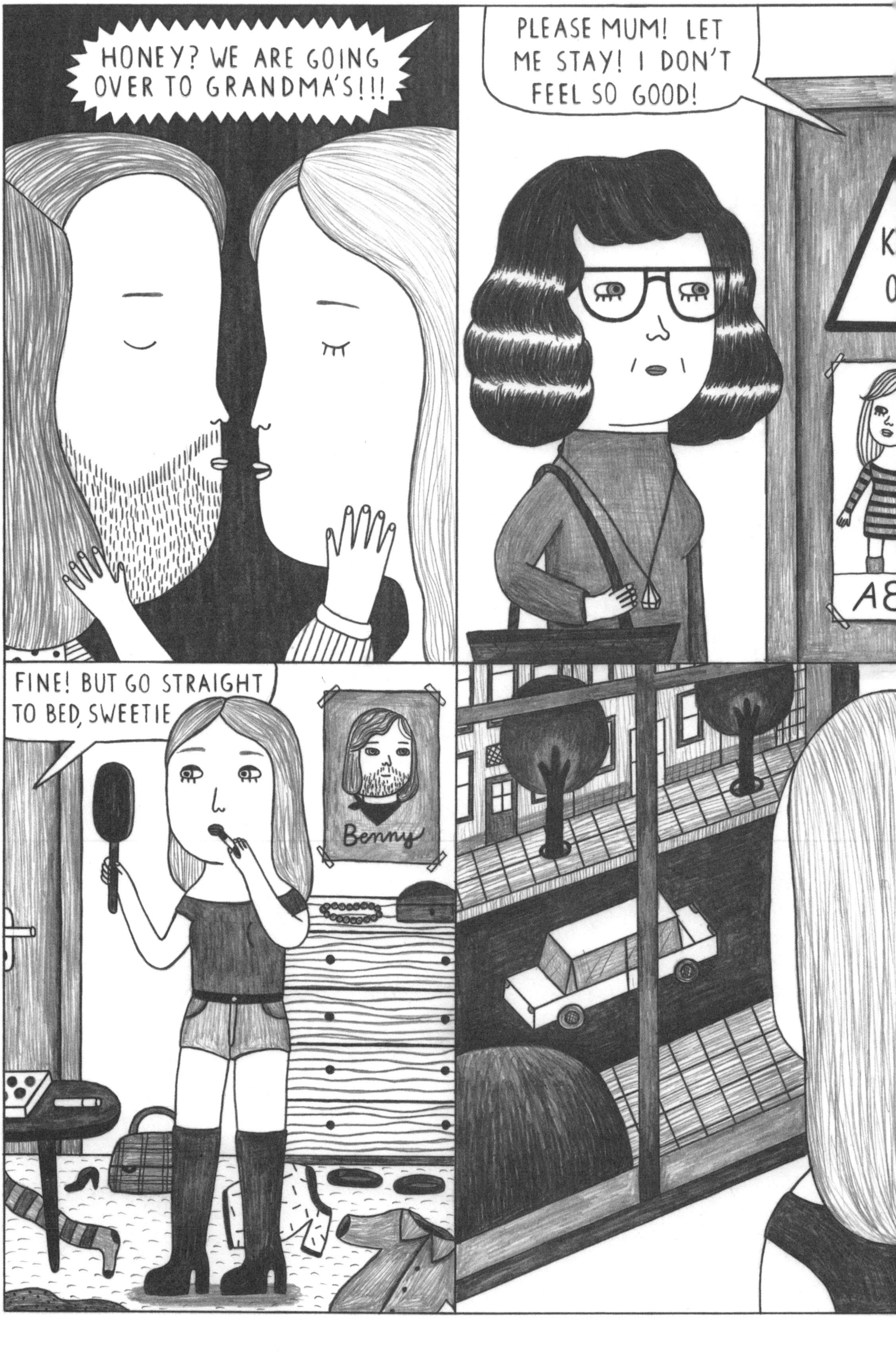
HONEY? WE ARE GOING OVER TO GRANDMA'S!!!
PLEASE MUM! LET ME STAY! I DON'T FEEL SO GOOD!
FINE! BUT GO STRAIGHT TO BED, SWEETIE
Benny

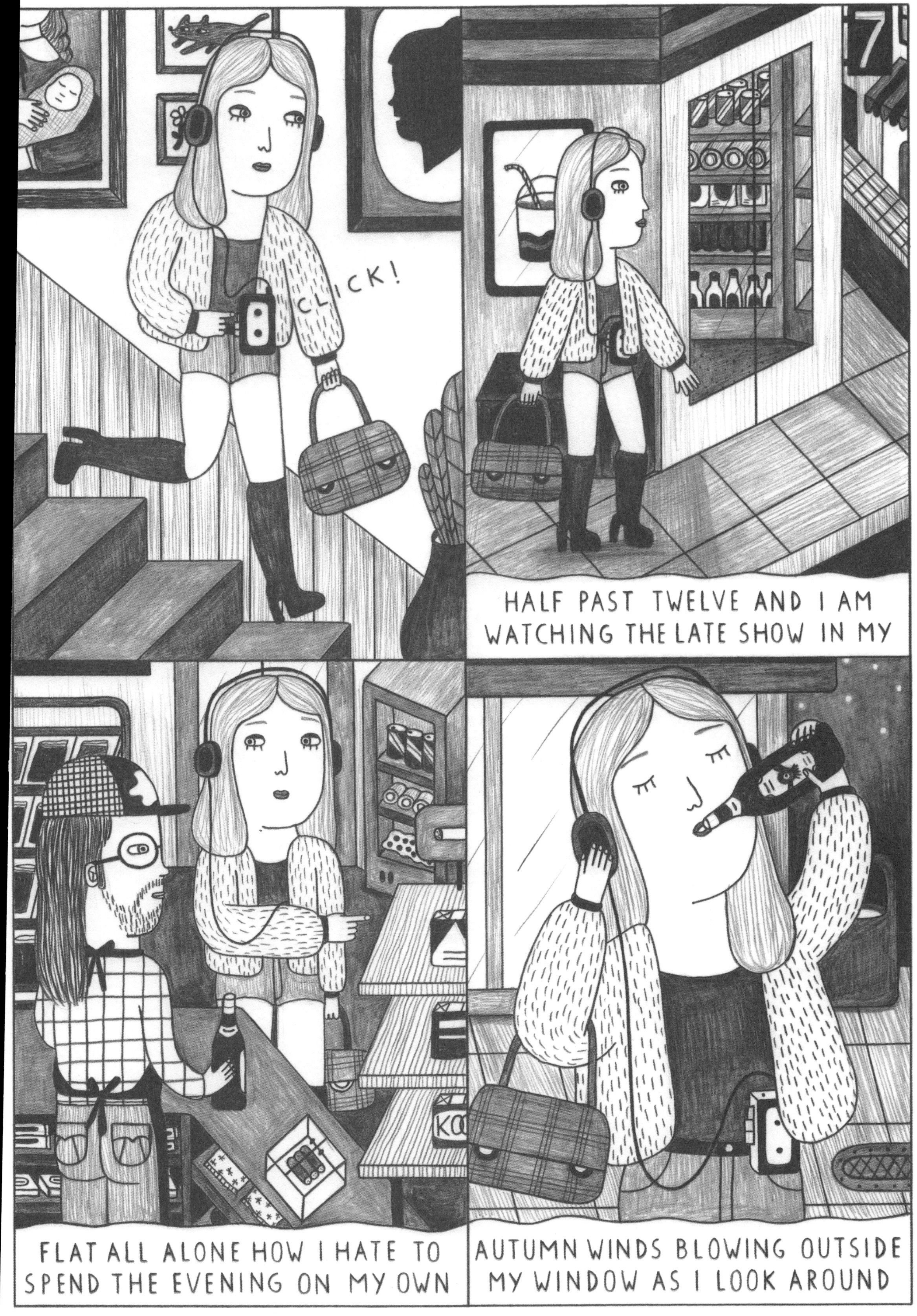
CLICK!
HALF PAST TWELVE AND I AM WATCHING THE LATE SHOW IN MY
FLAT ALL ALONE HOW I HATE TO SPEND THE EVENING ON MY OWN
AUTUMN WINDS BLOWING OUTSIDE MY WINDOW AS I LOOK AROUND

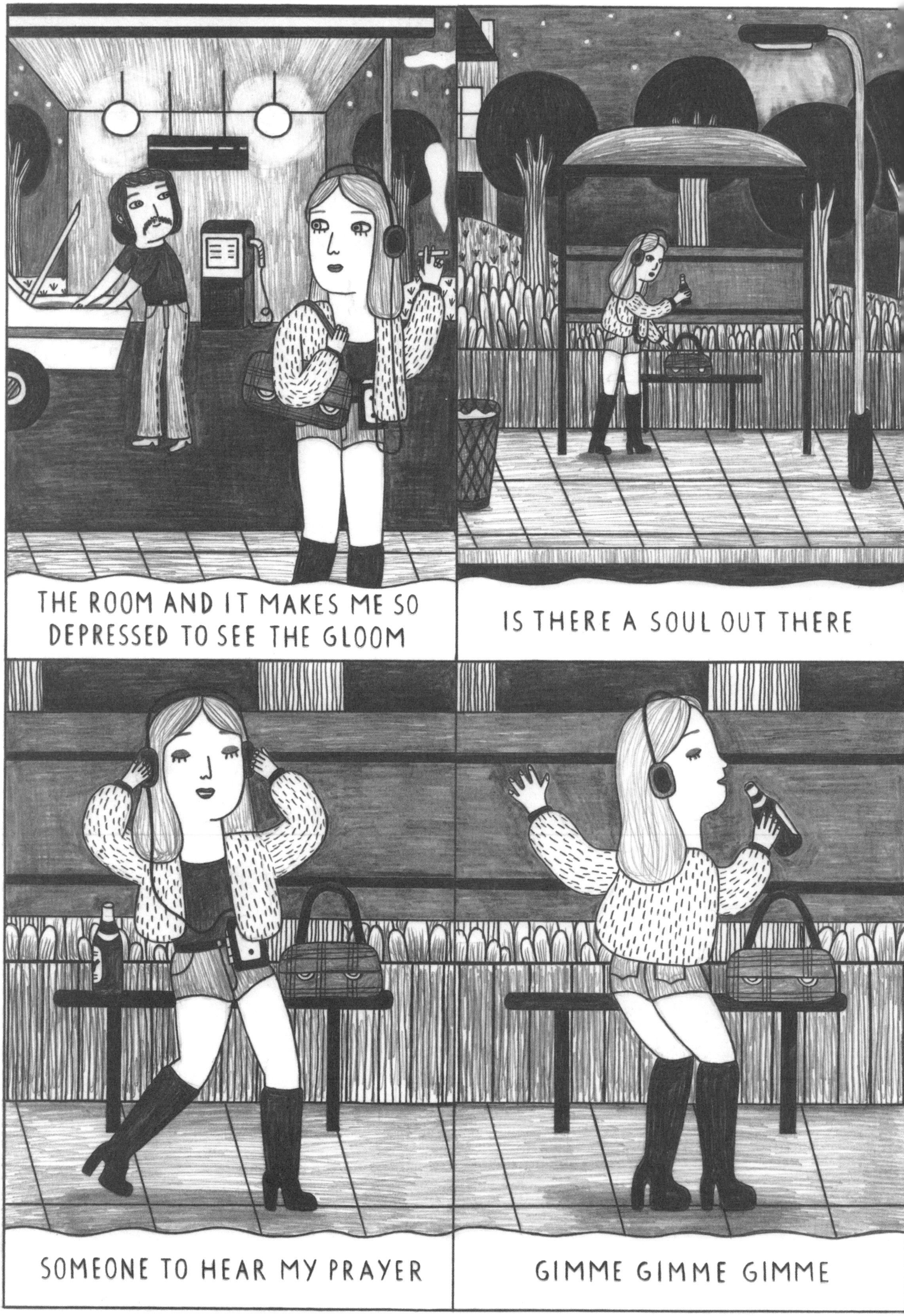
THE ROOM AND IT MAKES ME SO DEPRESSED TO SEE THE GLOOM
IS THERE A SOUL OUT THERE
SOMEONE TO HEAR MY PRAYER
GIMME GIMME GIMME

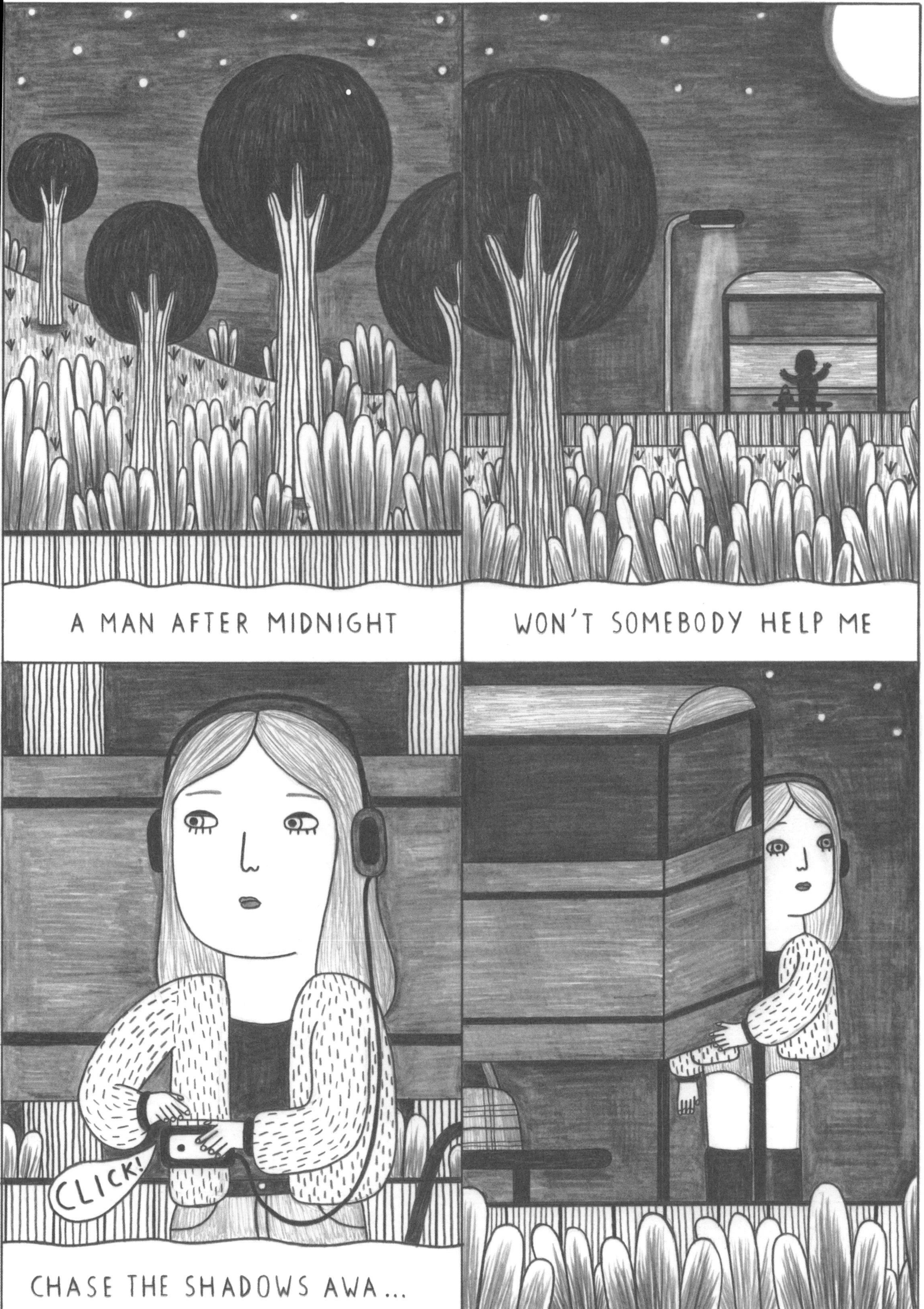
A MAN AFTER MIDNIGHT
WON'T SOMEBODY HELP ME
CLICK!
CHASE THE SHADOWS AWA...

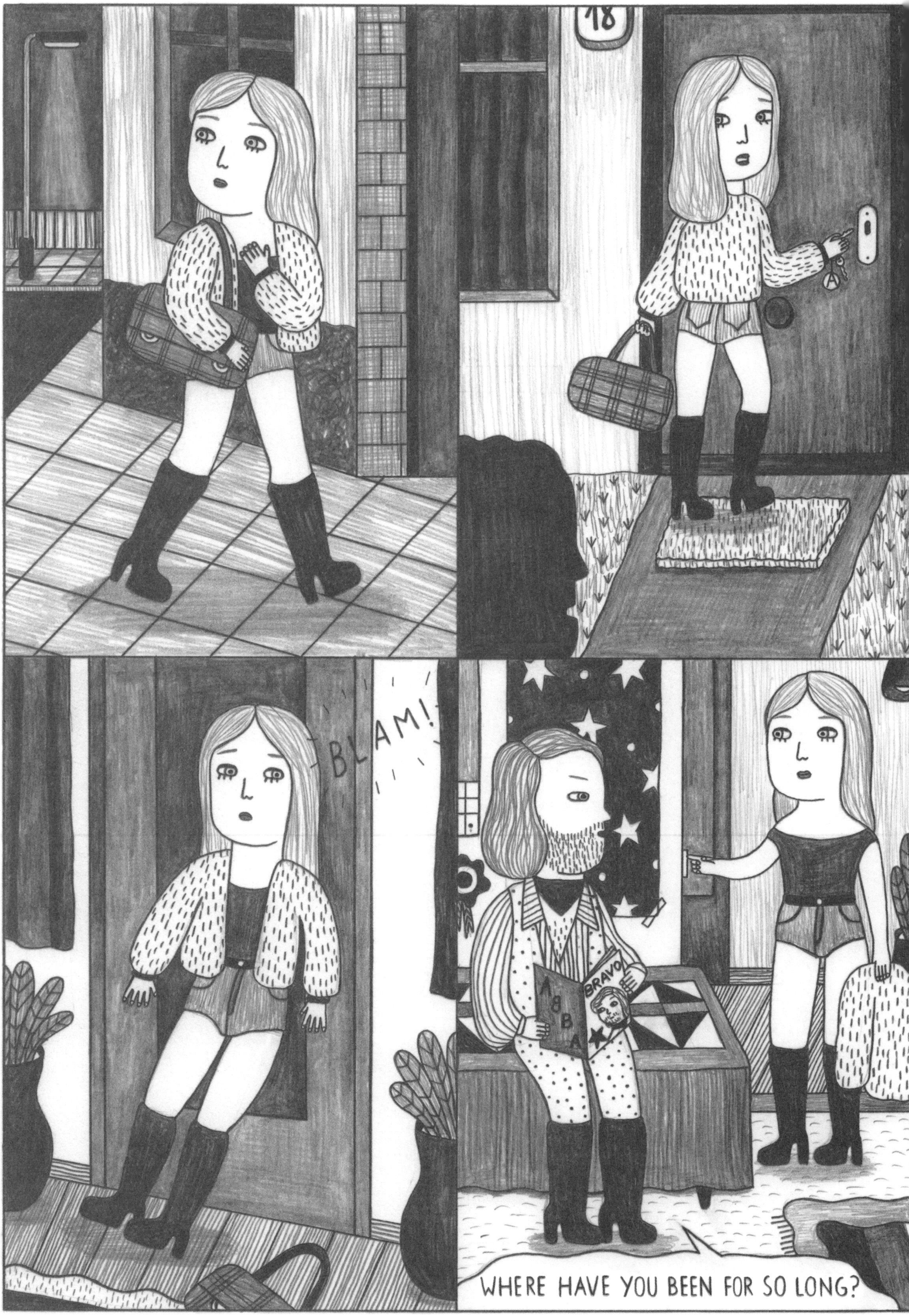
18
BLAM!
ABBA
BRAVO
WHERE HAVE YOU BEEN FOR SO LONG?

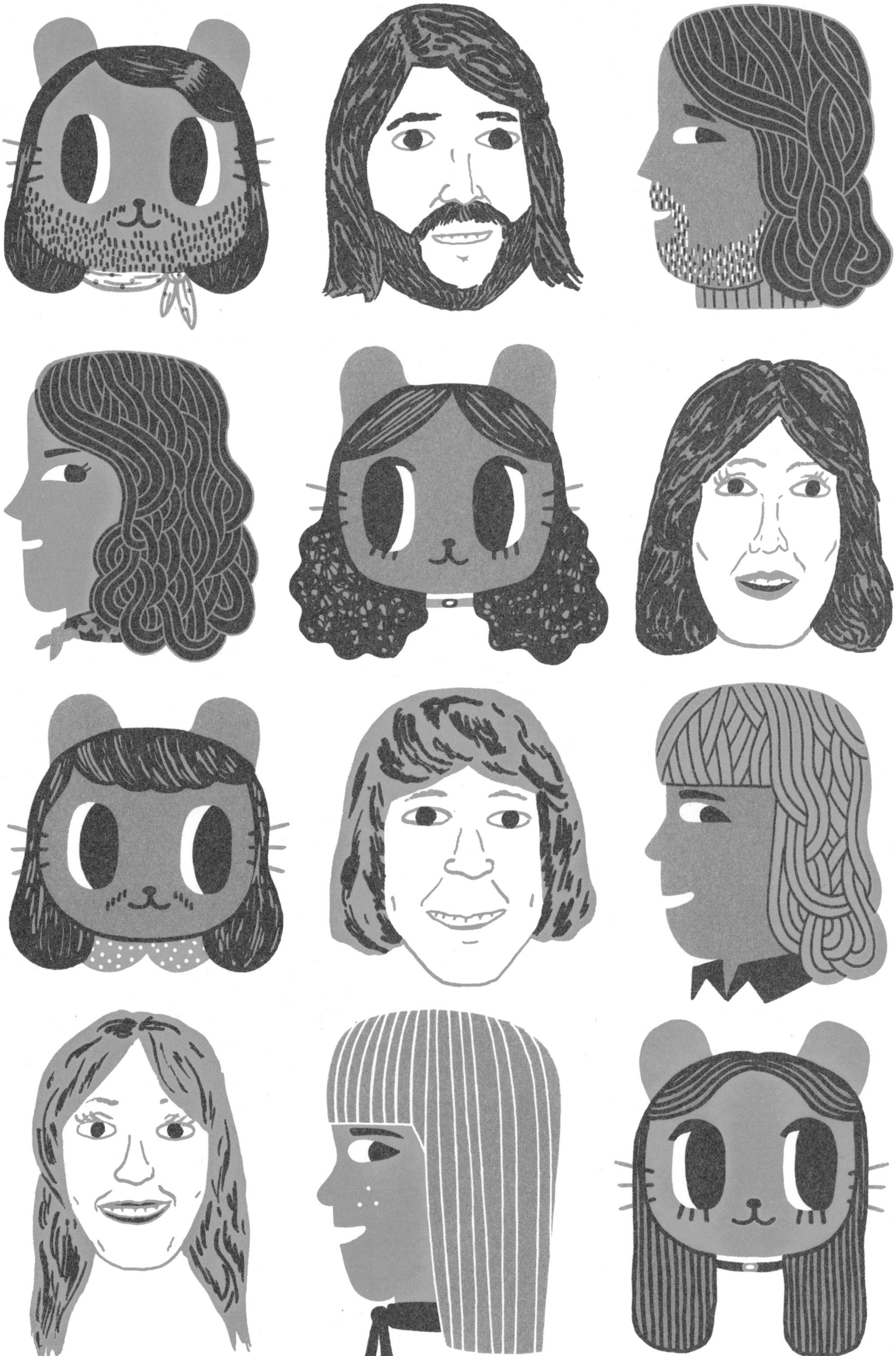

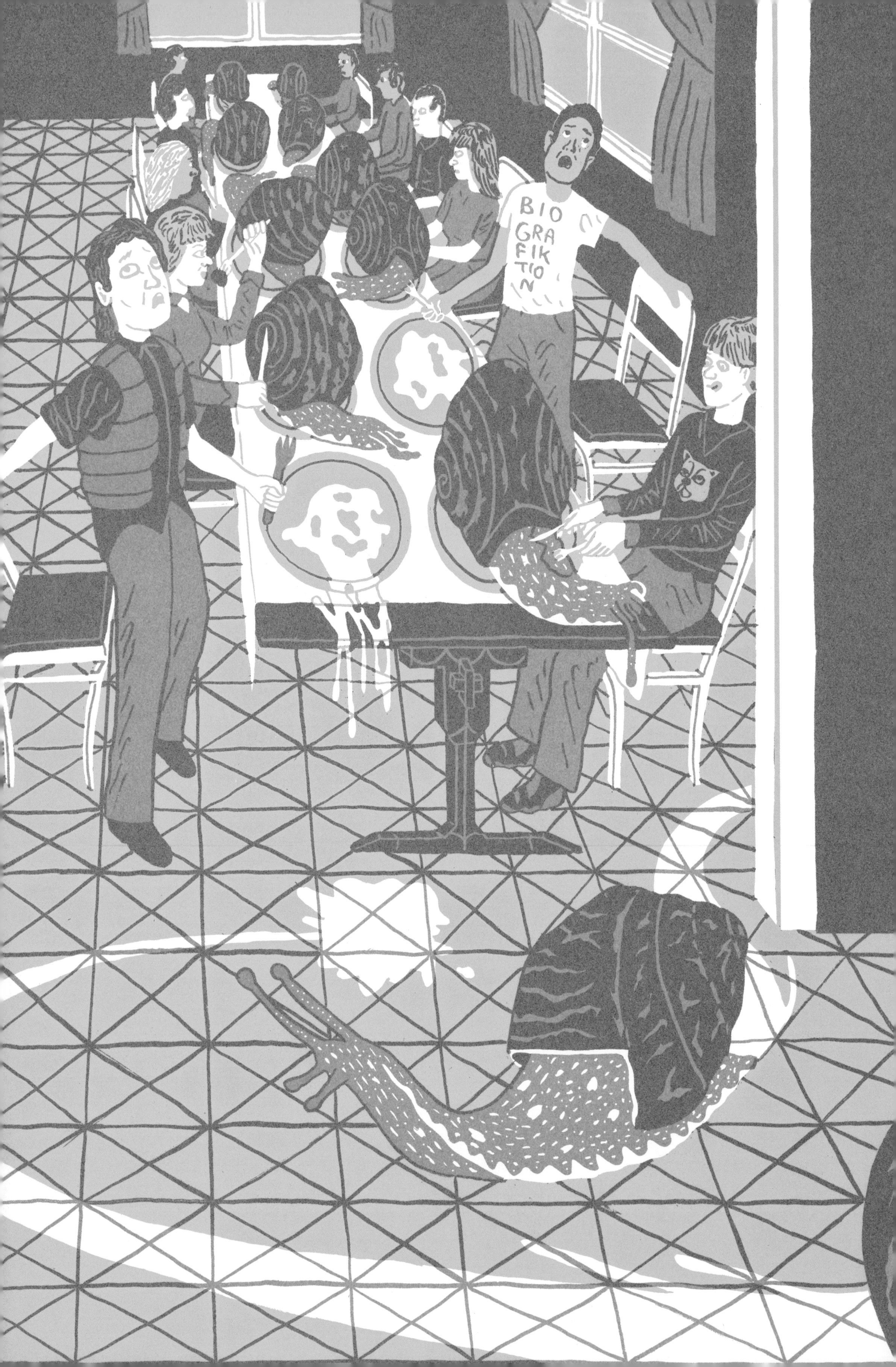
BIO
GRA
FIK
TIO
N

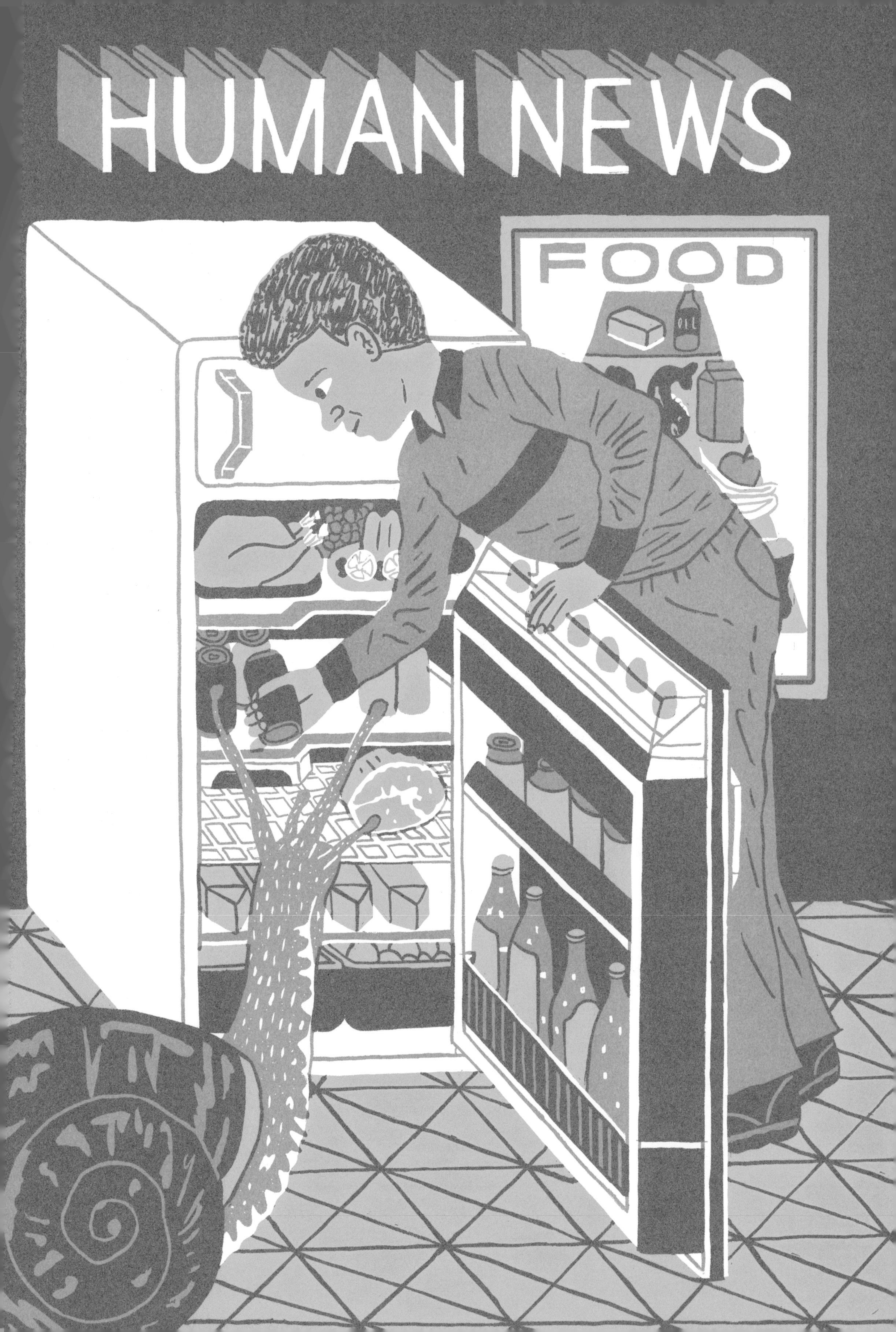
HUMAN NEWS
FOOD
OIL

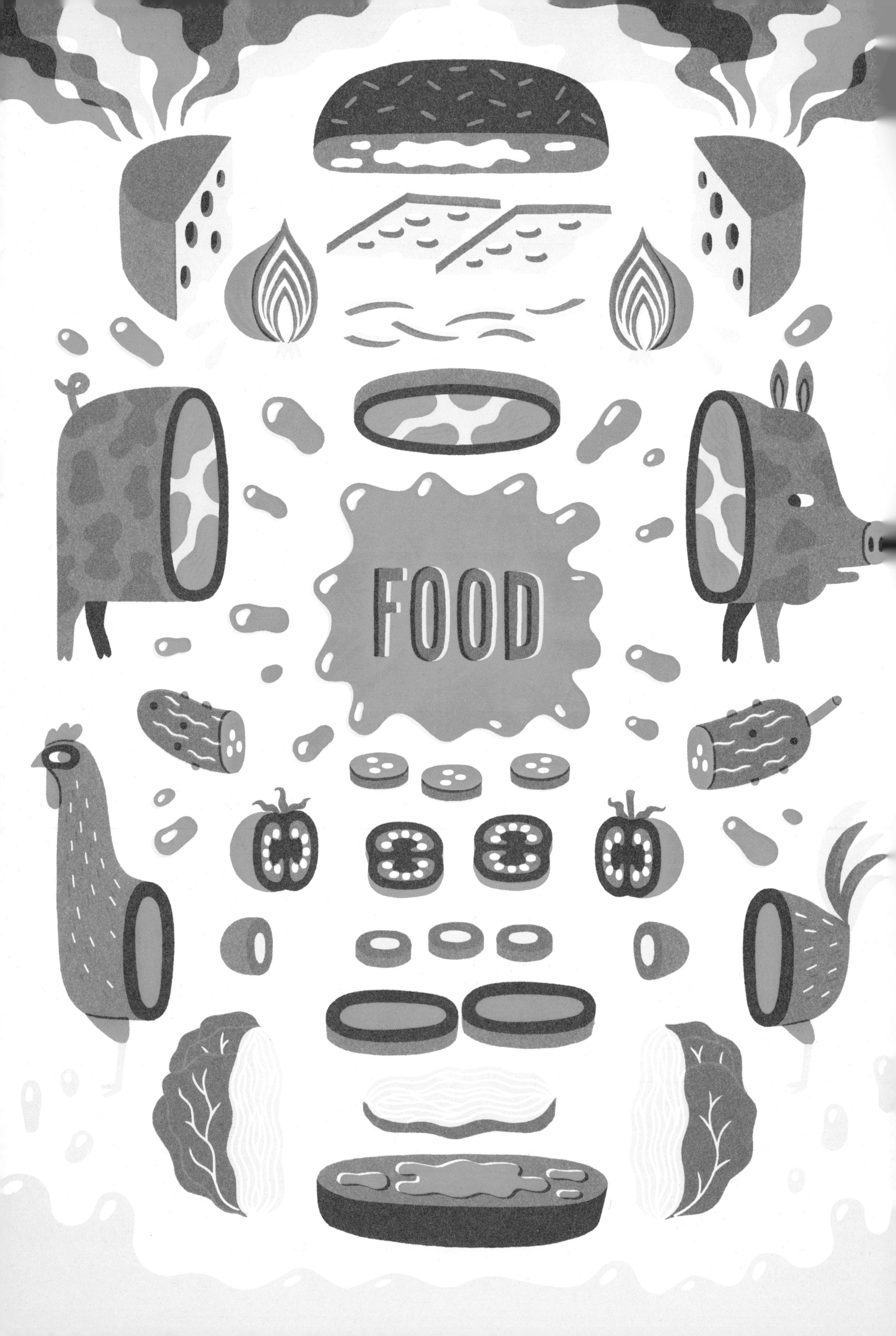
FOOD

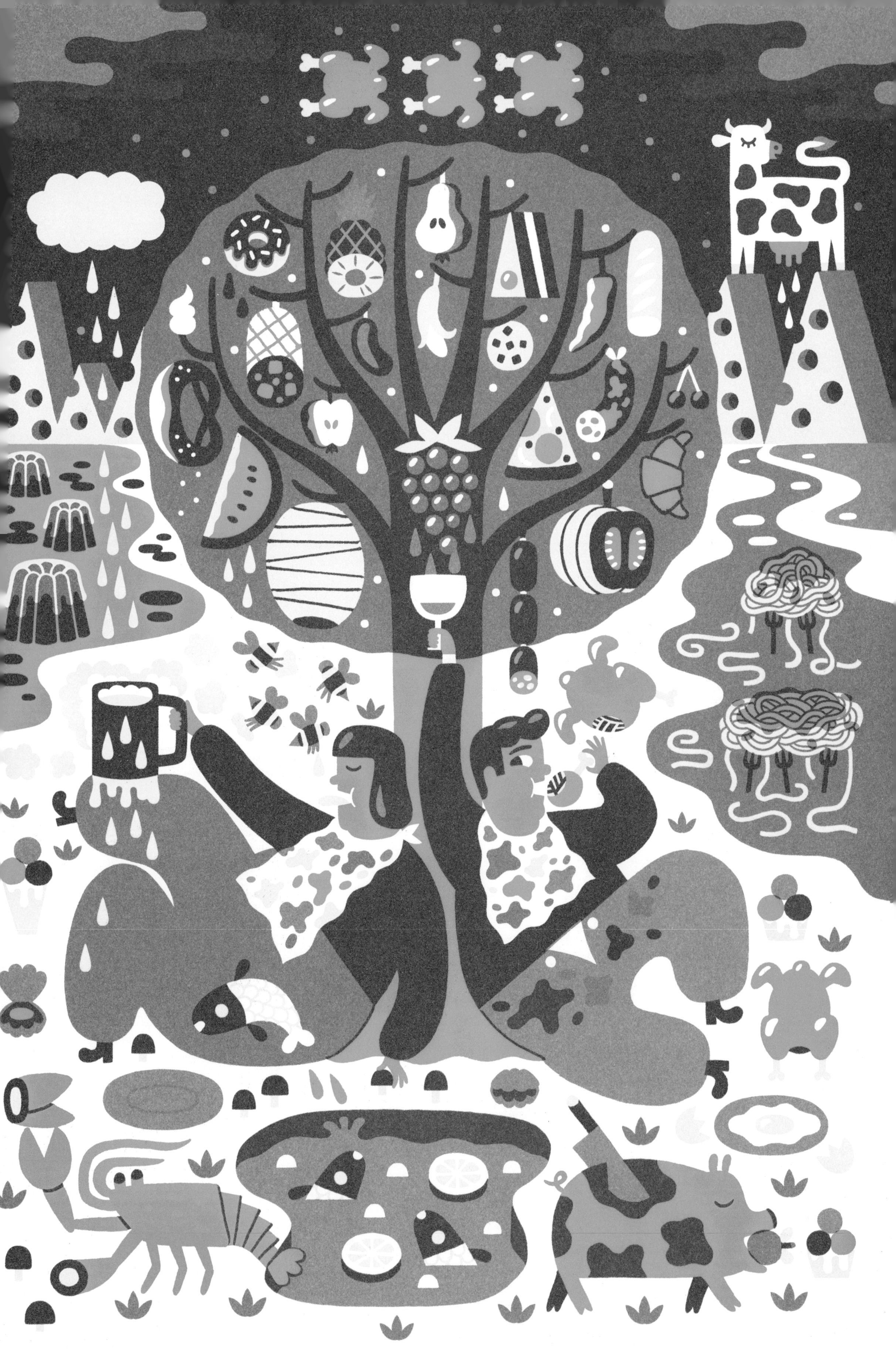

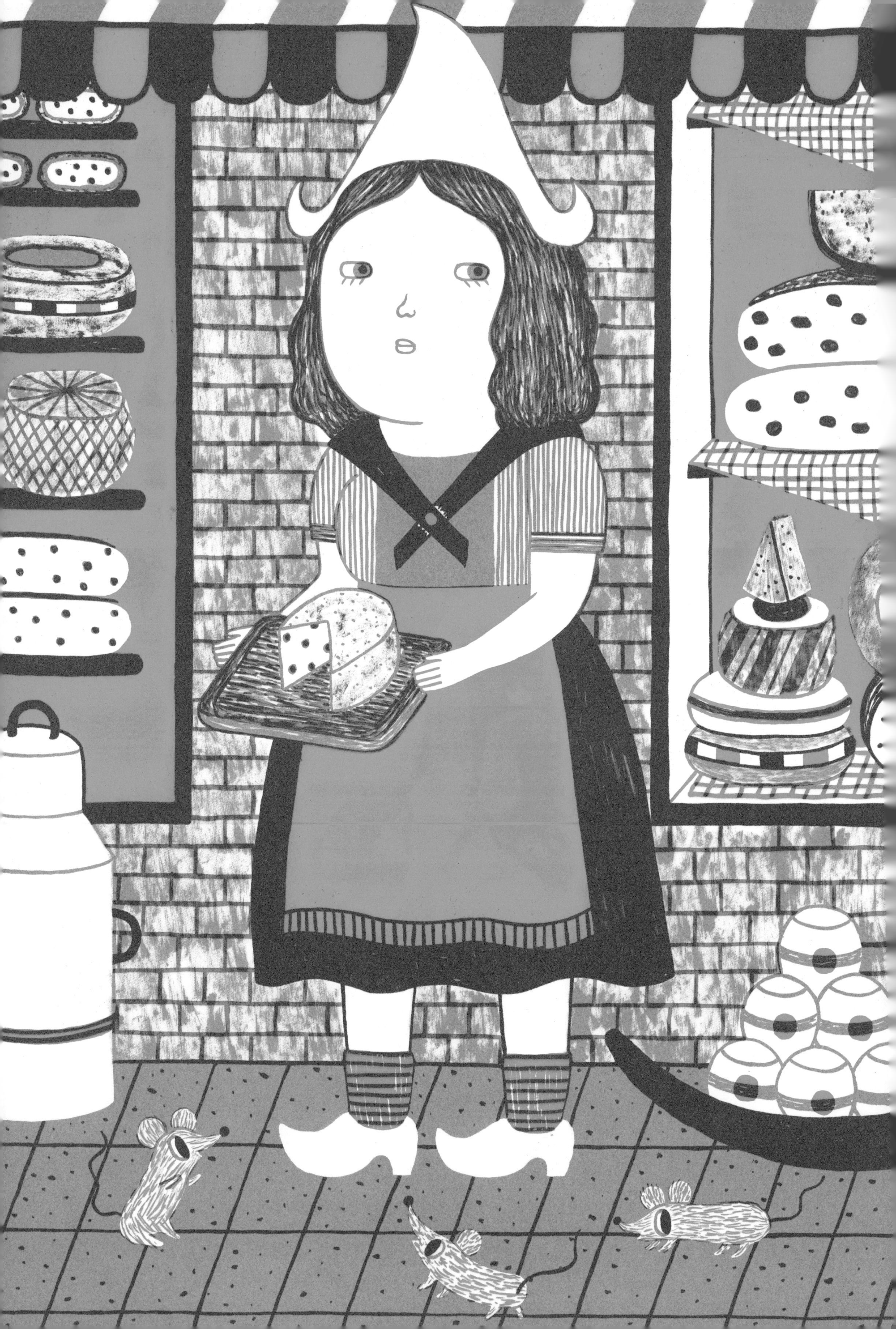

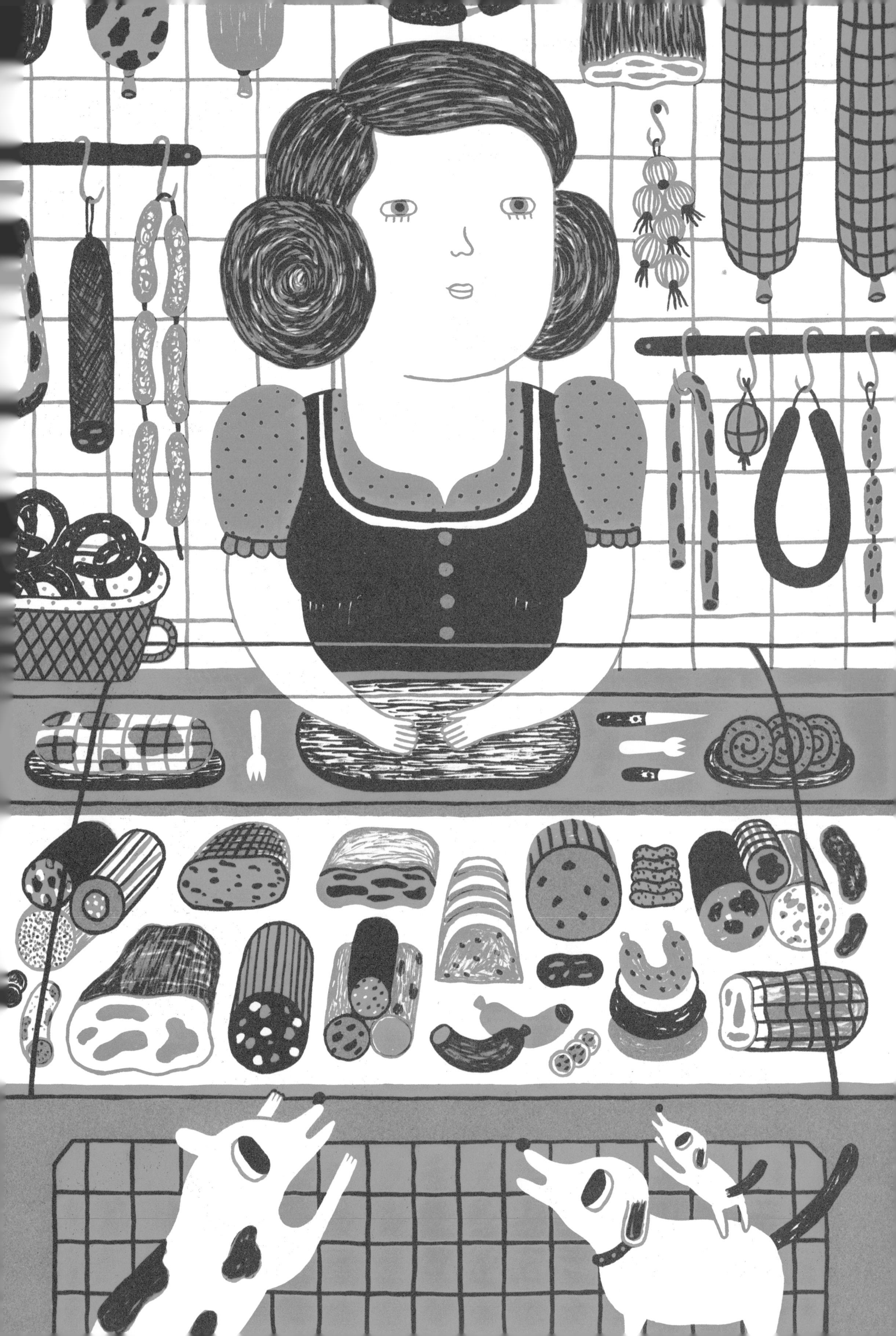

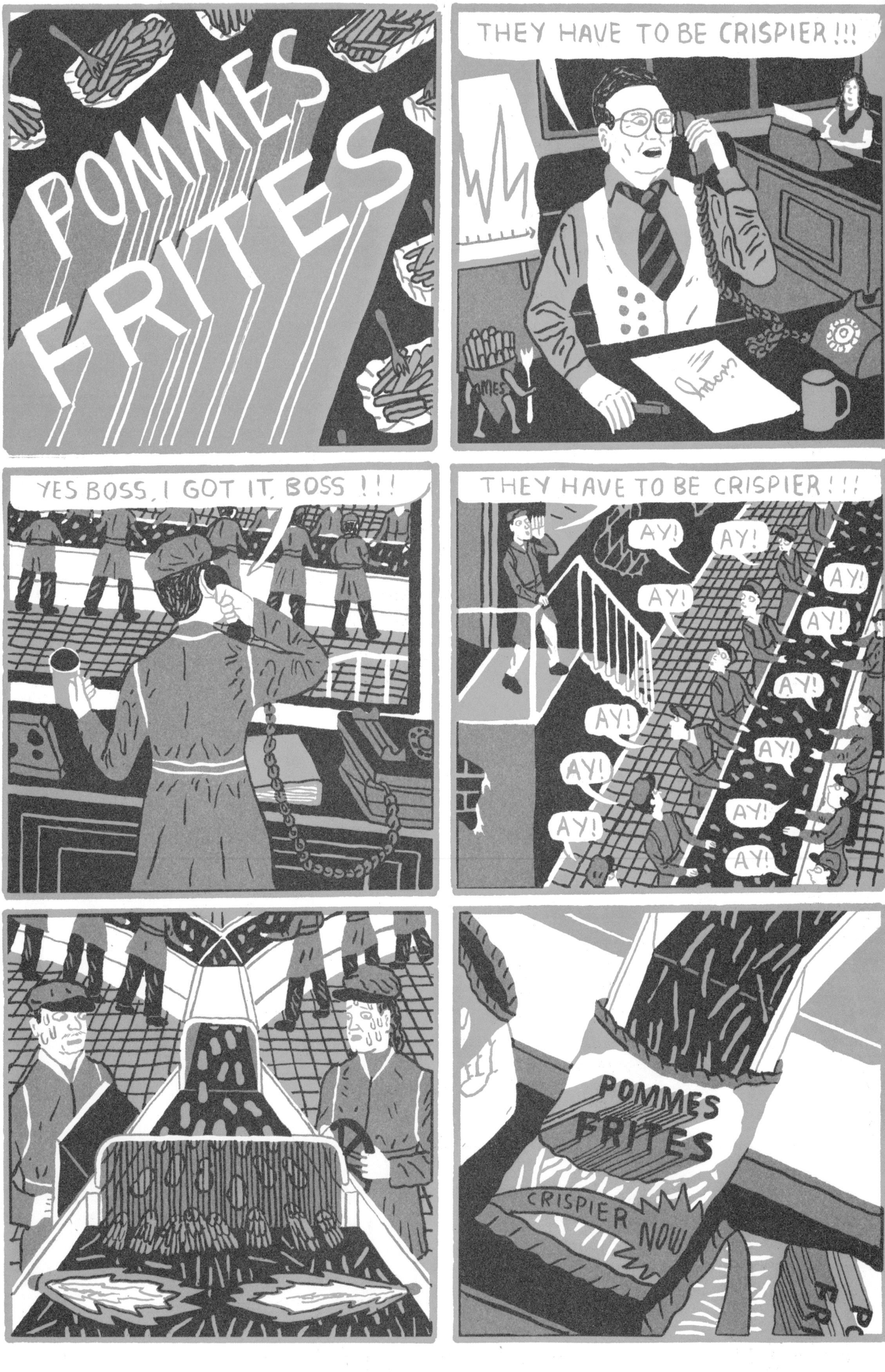
POMMES FRITES
THEY HAVE TO BE CRISPIER!!!
YES BOSS, I GOT IT, BOSS!!!
THEY HAVE TO BE CRISPIER!!!
AY!
AY!
AY!
AY!
AY!
AY!
AY!
AY!
AY!
AY!
AY!
AY!
POMMES FRITES
CRISPIER NOW

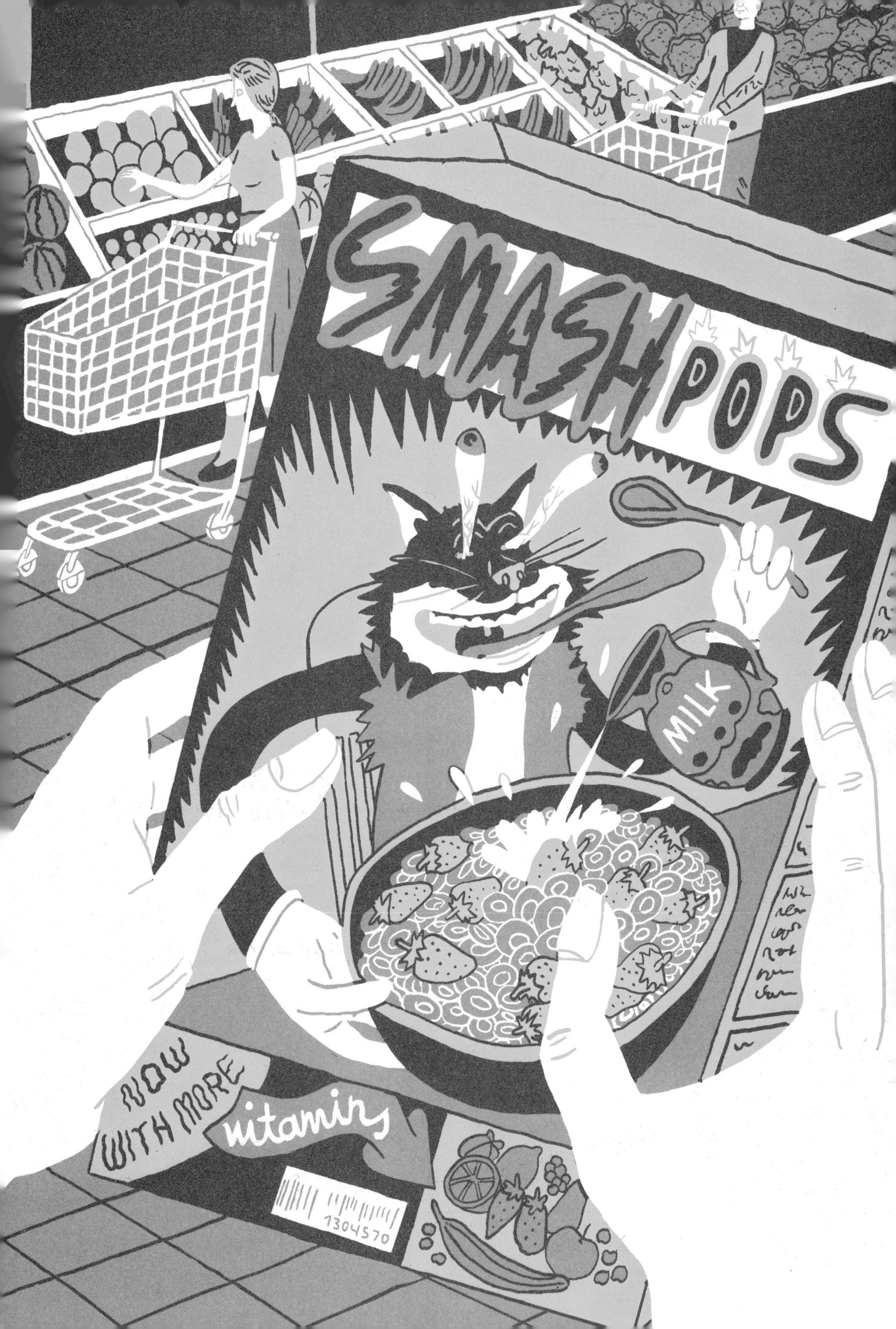
SMASH POPS
MILK
NOW WITH MORE
vitamins
1304570

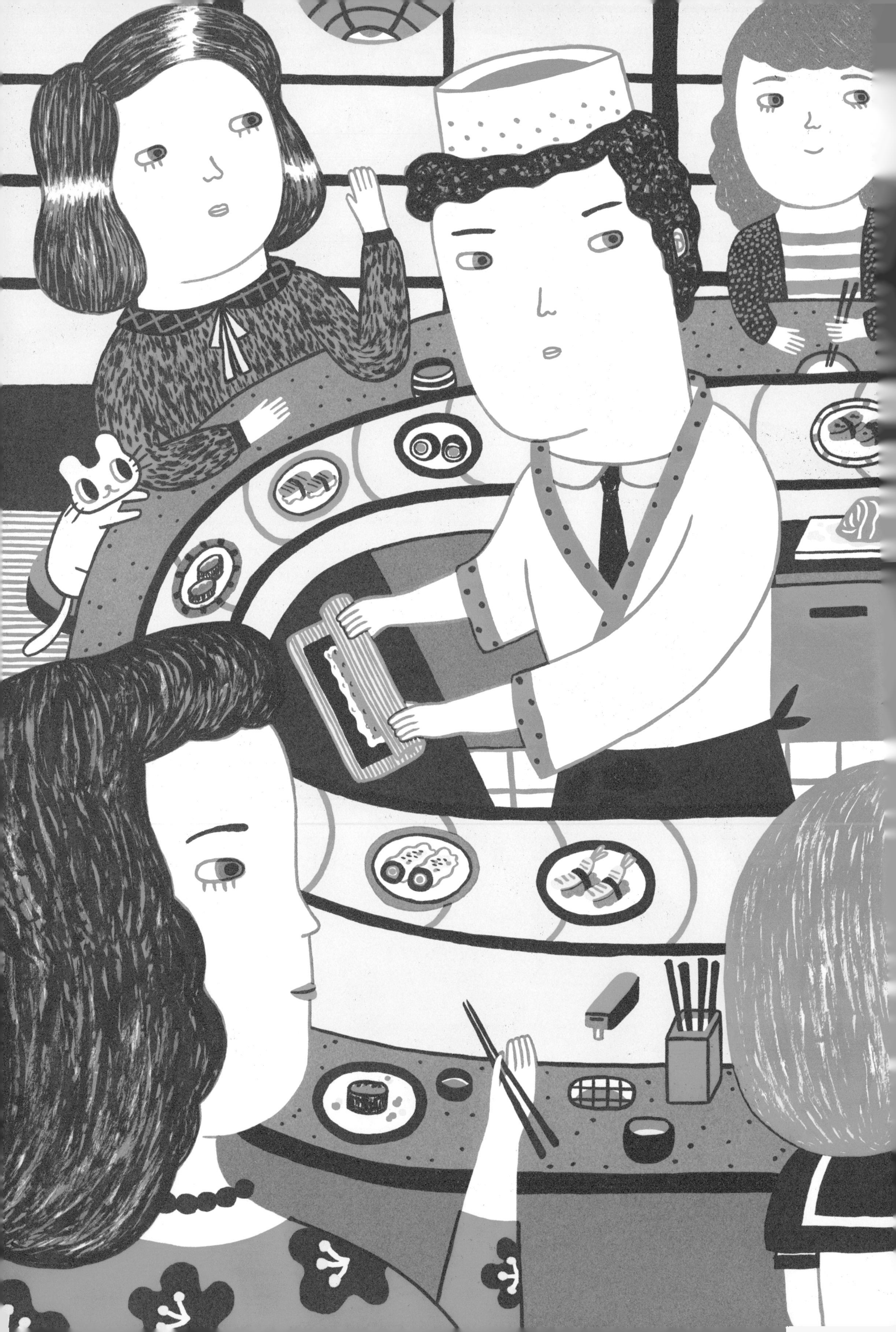

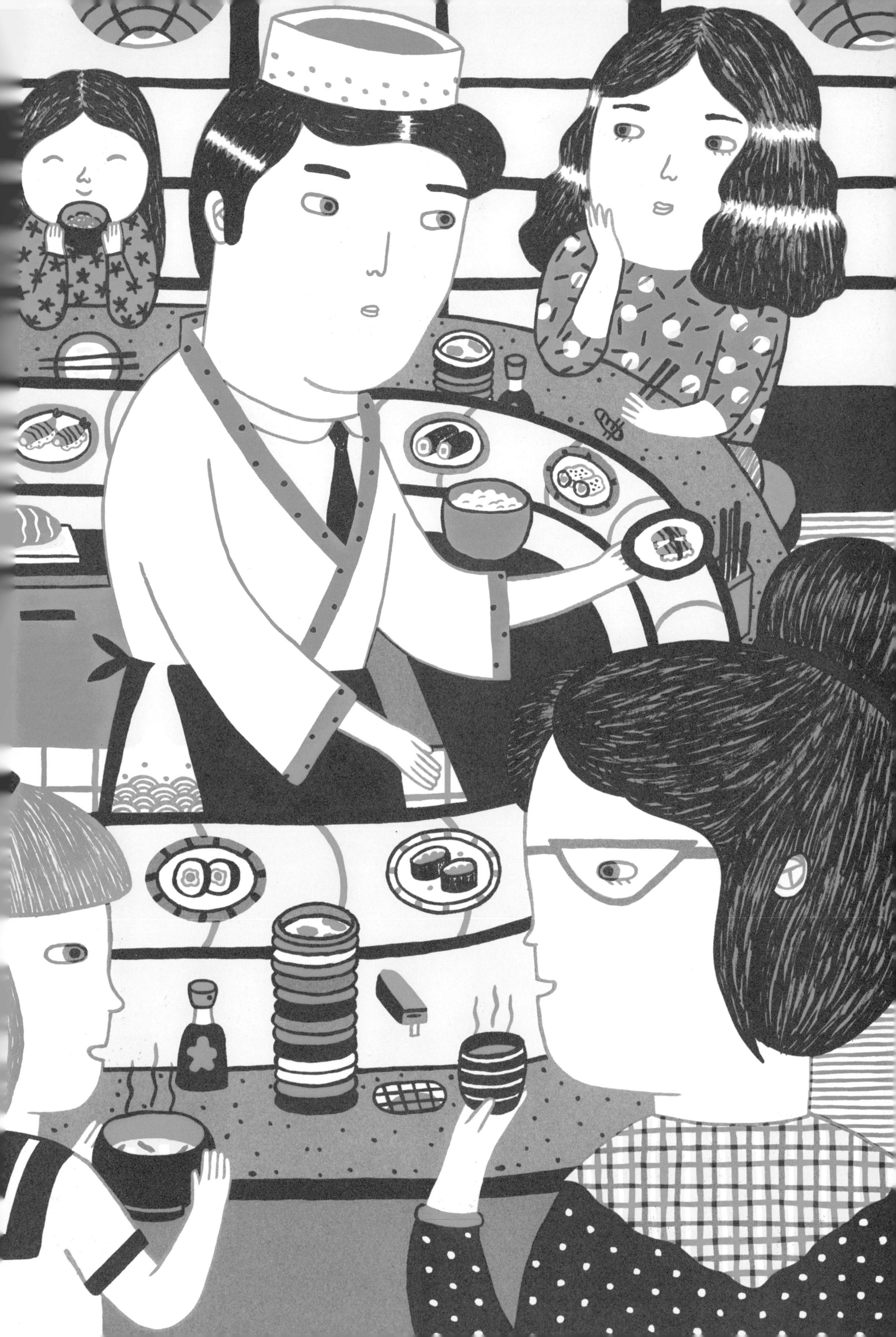

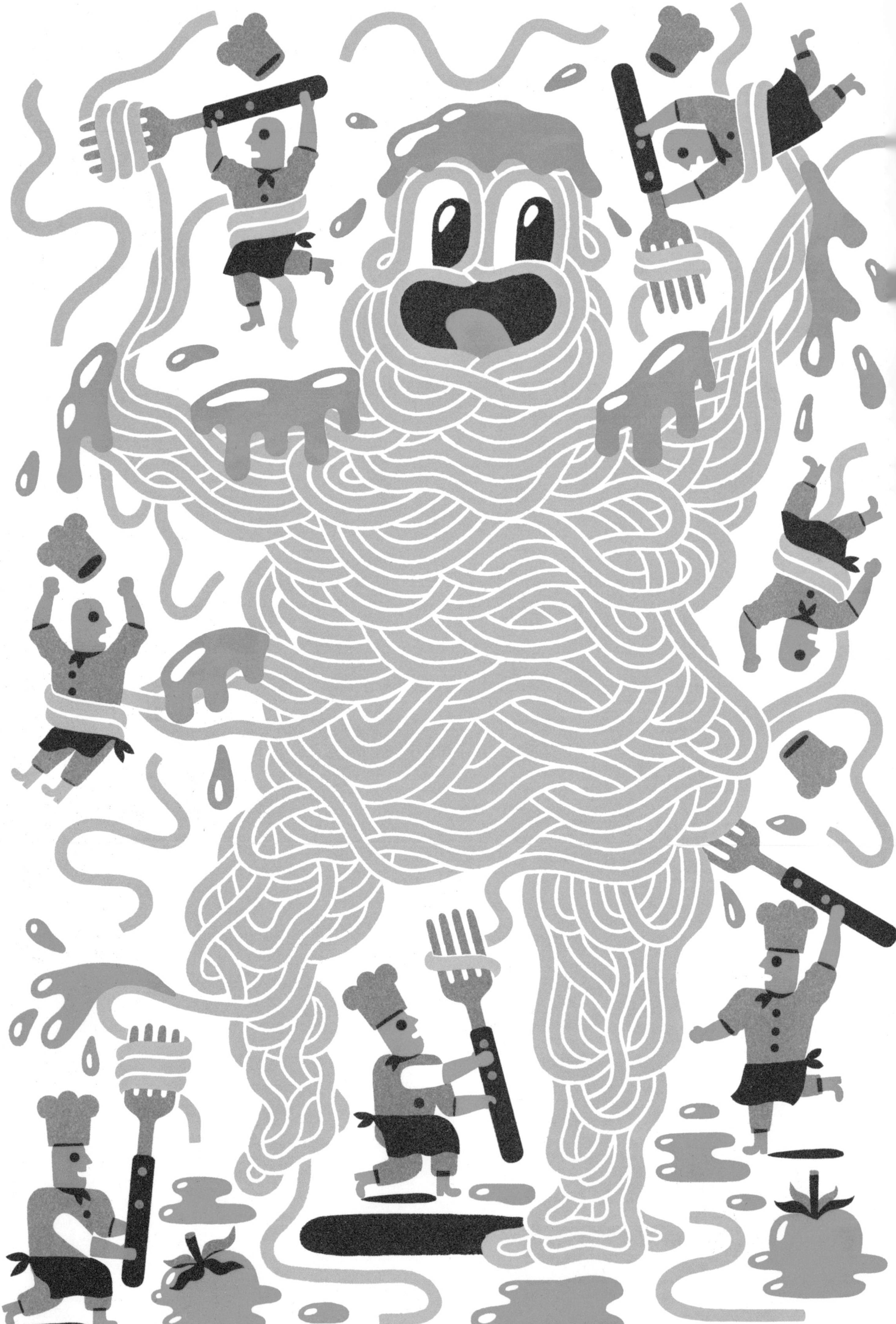

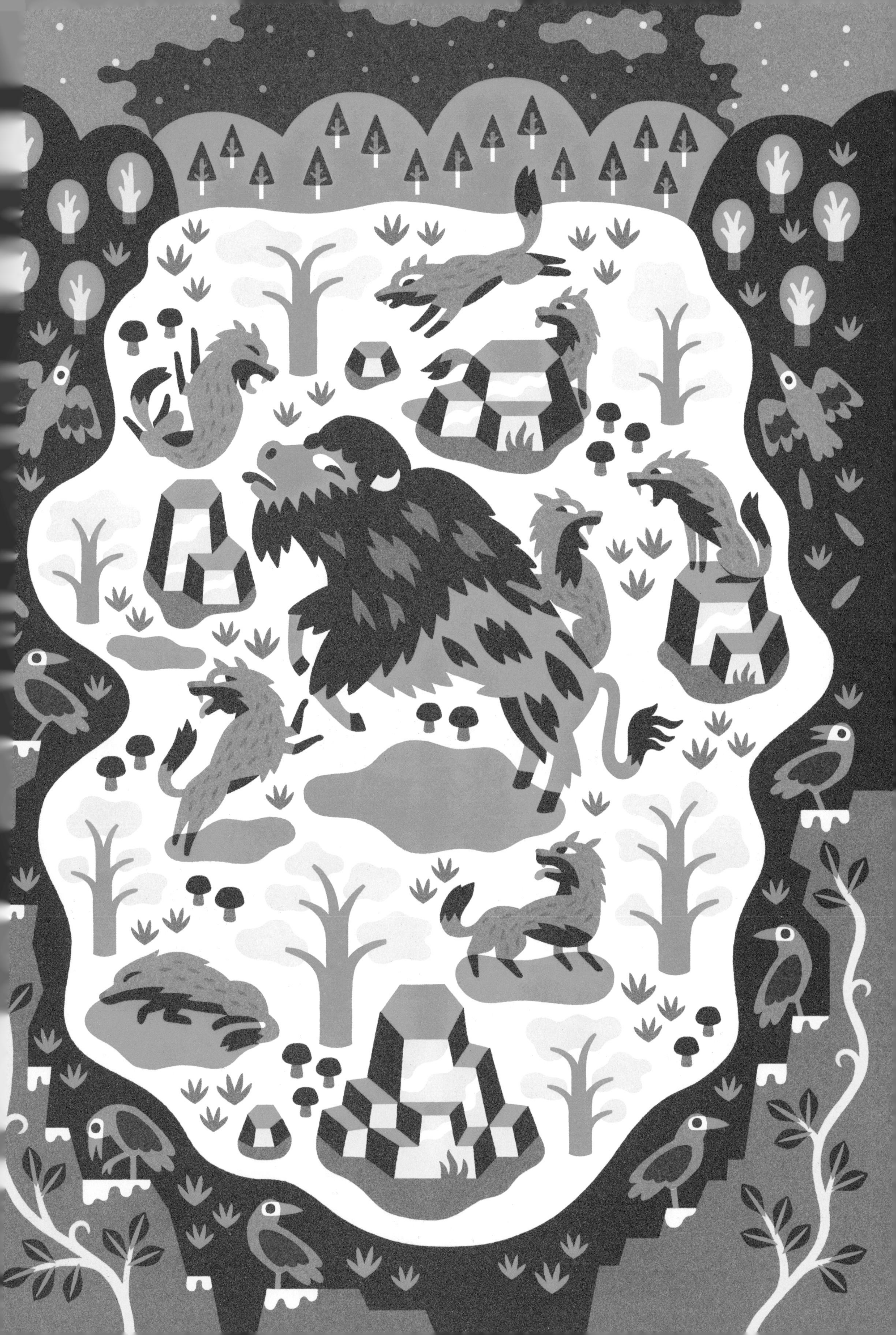

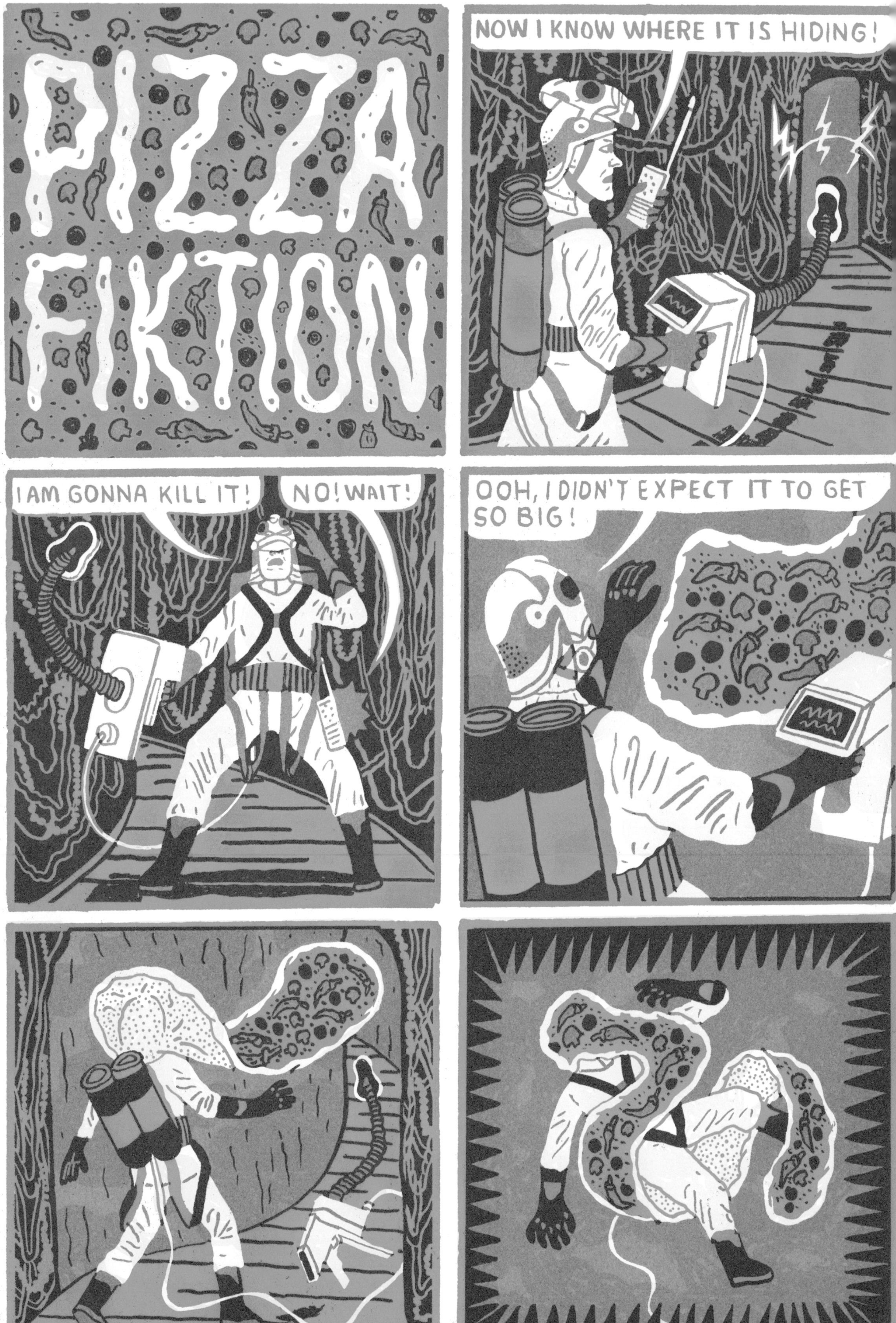
PIZZA FIKTION
NOW I KNOW WHERE IT IS HIDING!
I AM GONNA KILL IT!
NO! WAIT!
OOH, I DIDN'T EXPECT IT TO GET SO BIG!

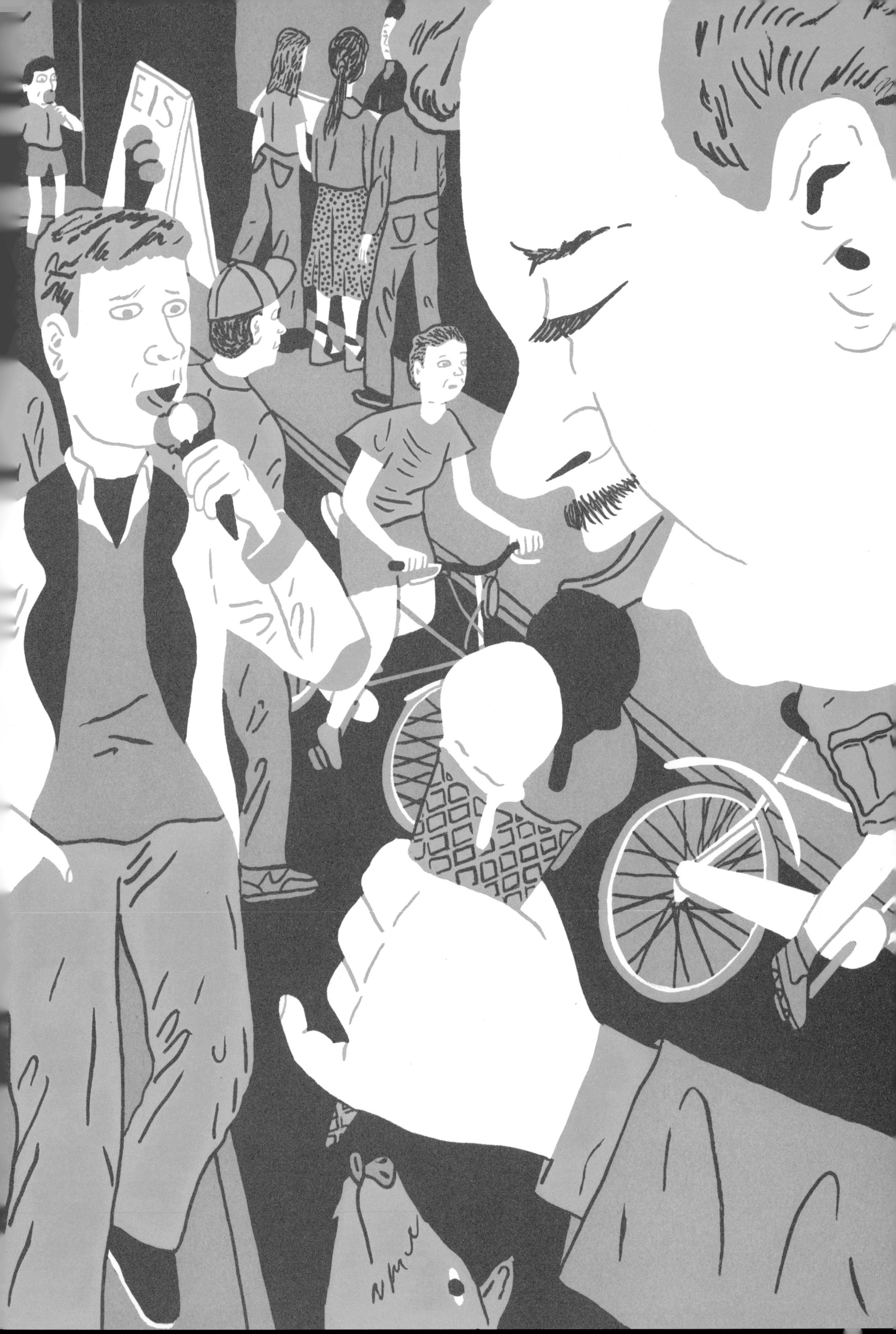
EIS

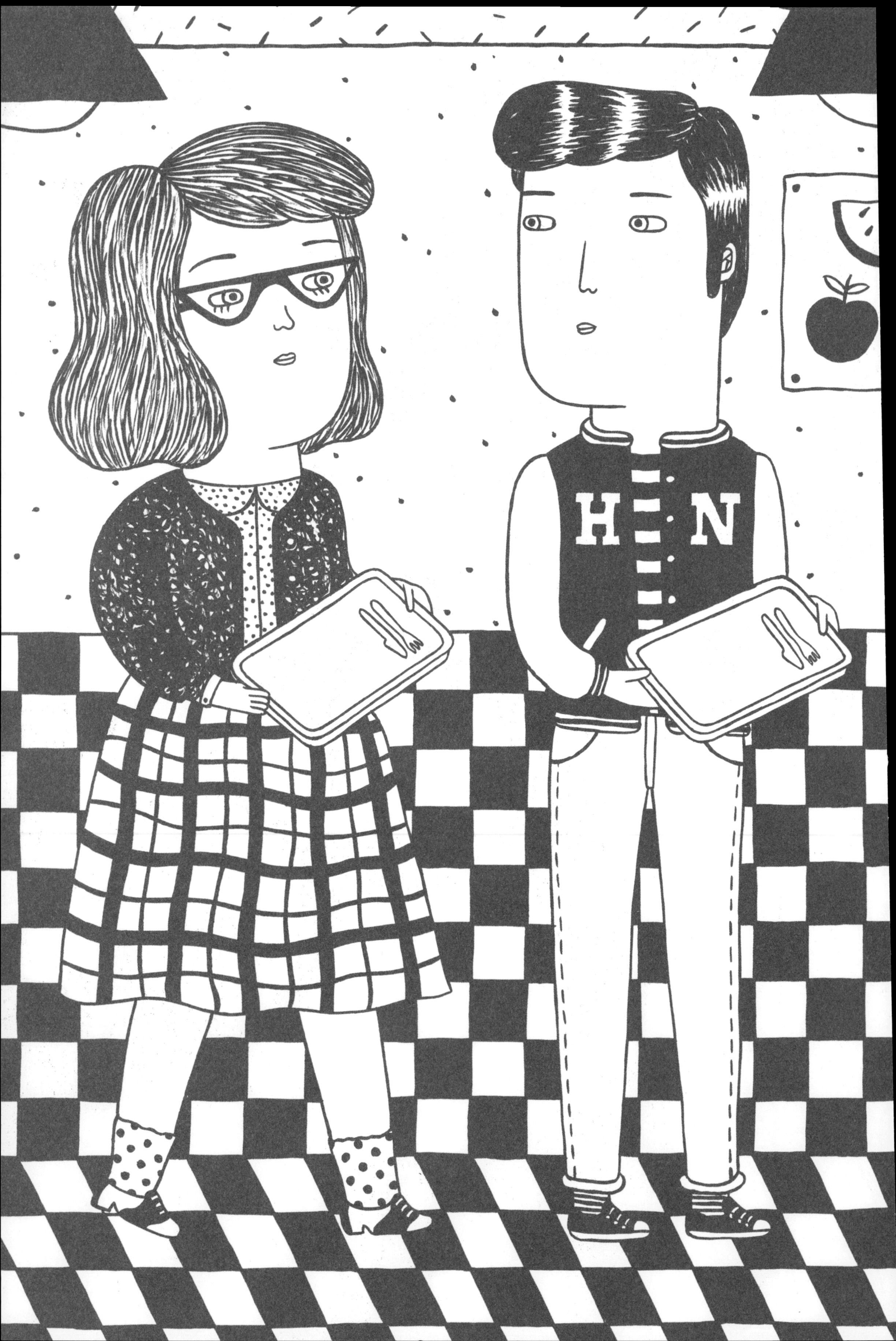
H N

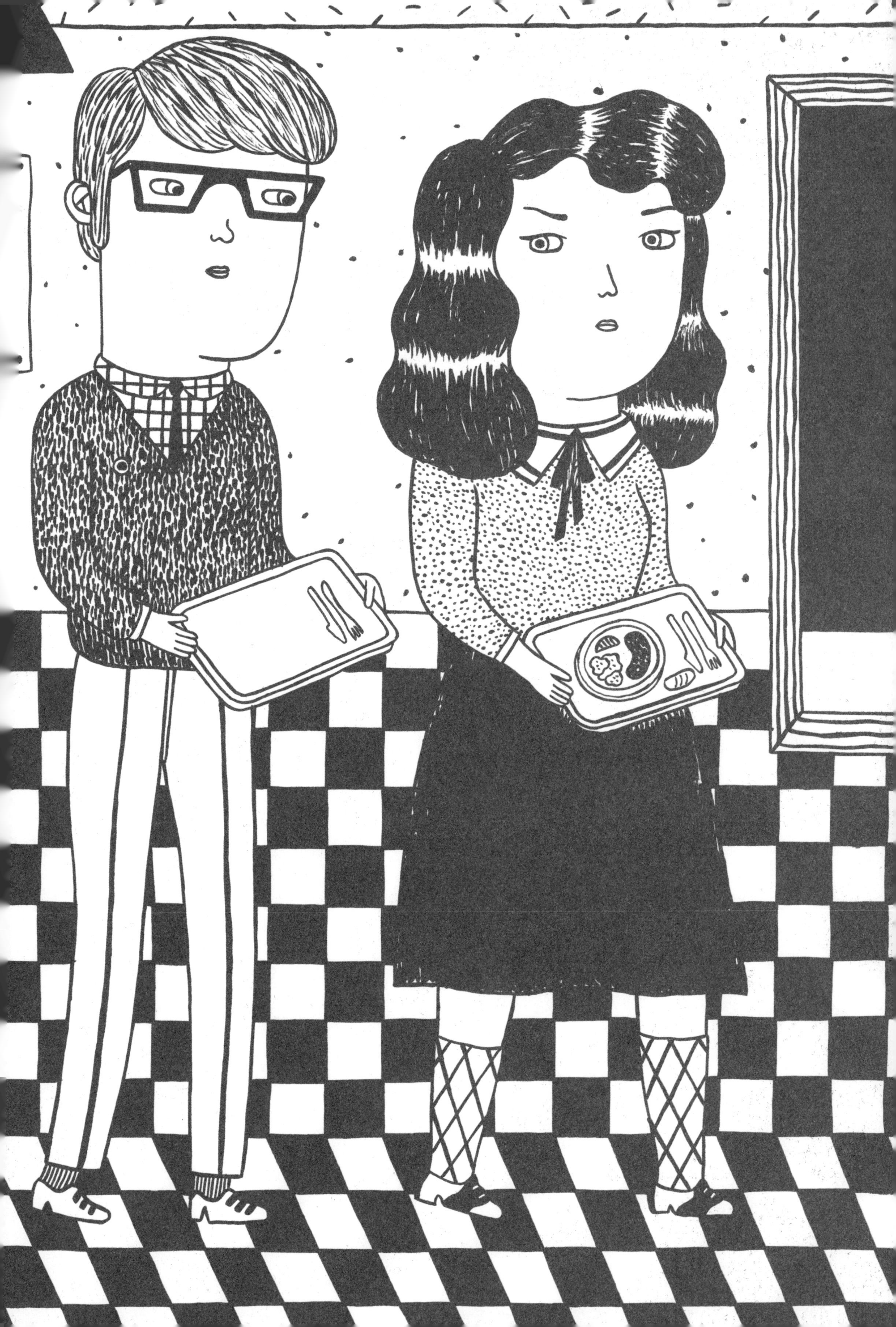

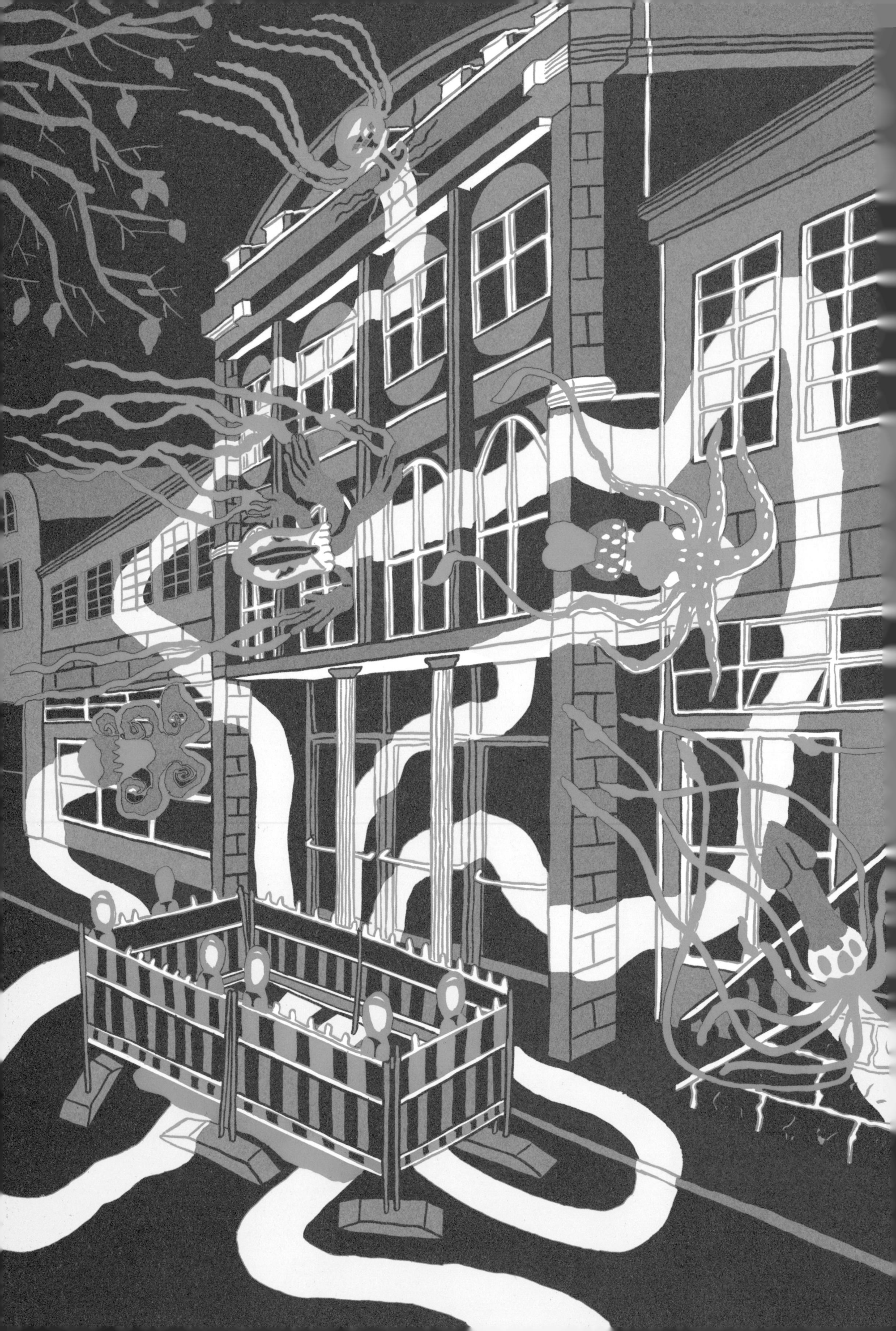

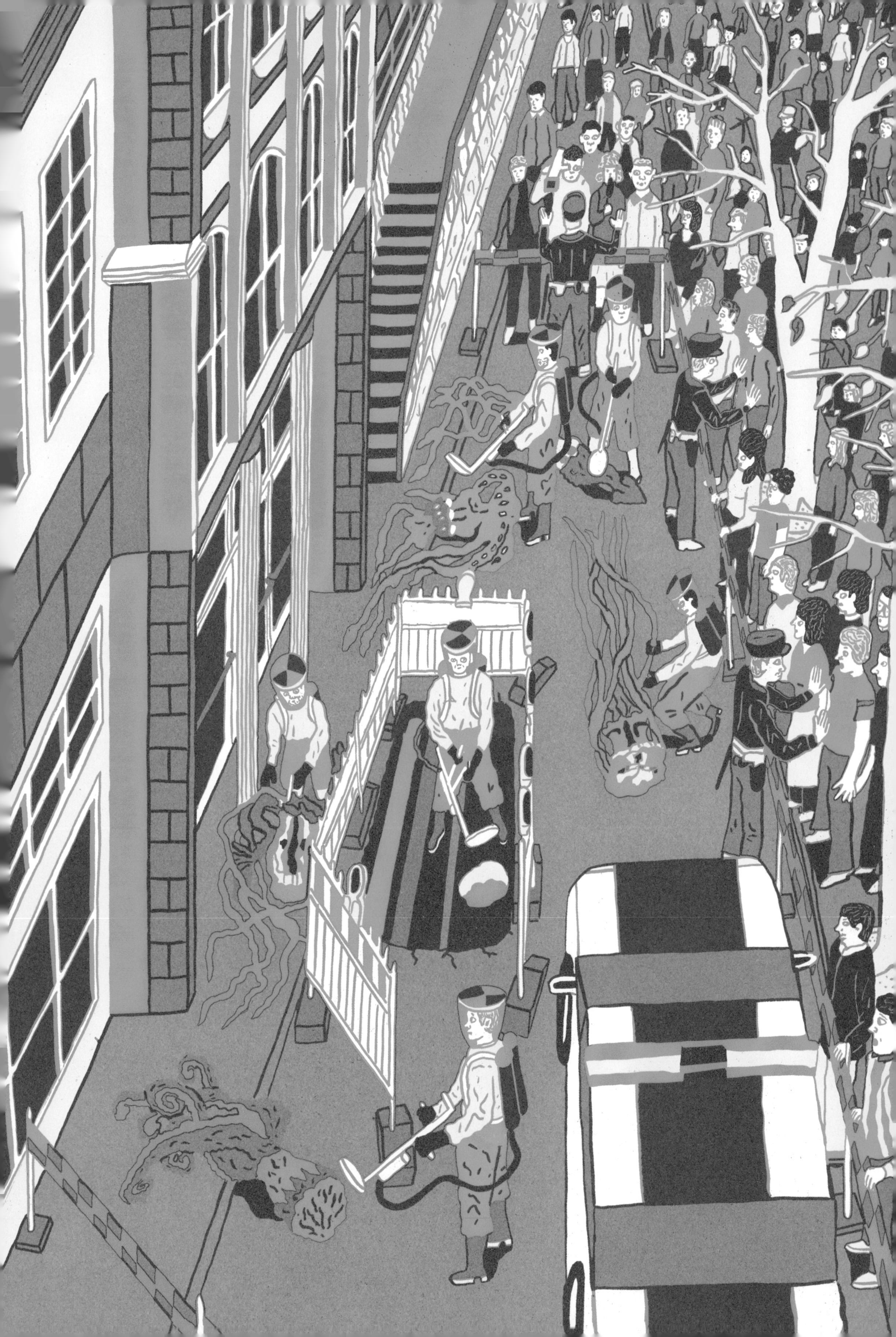

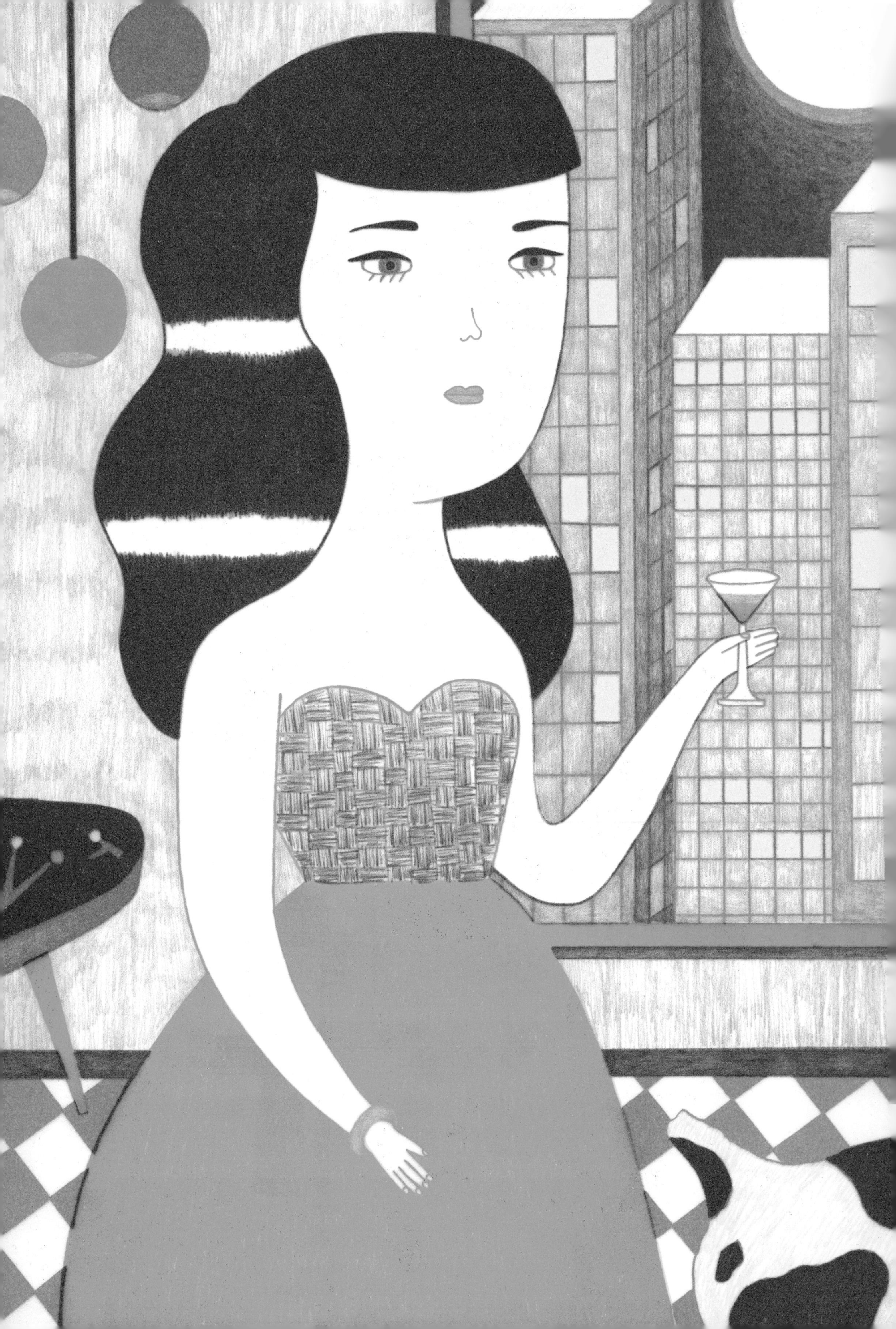

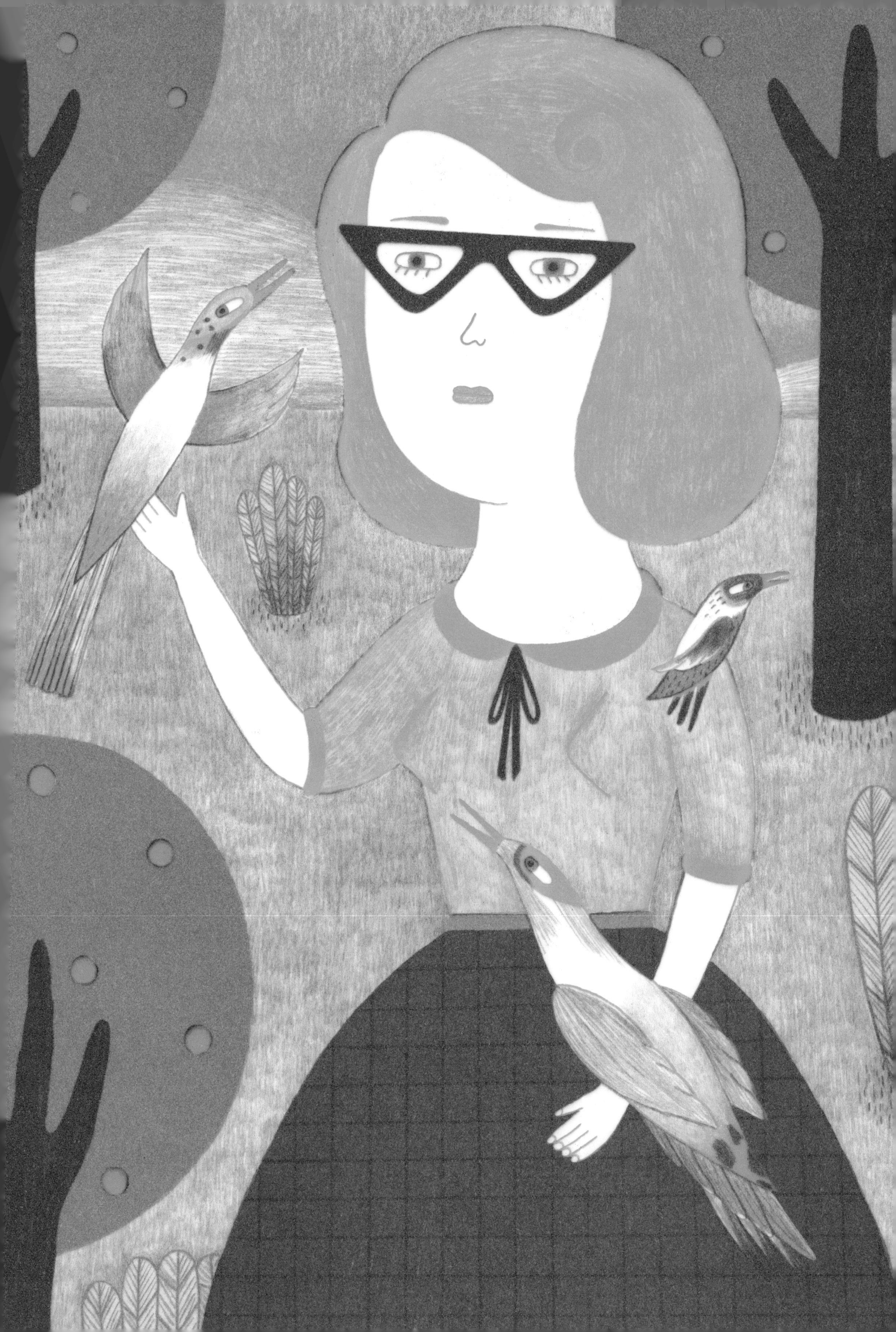

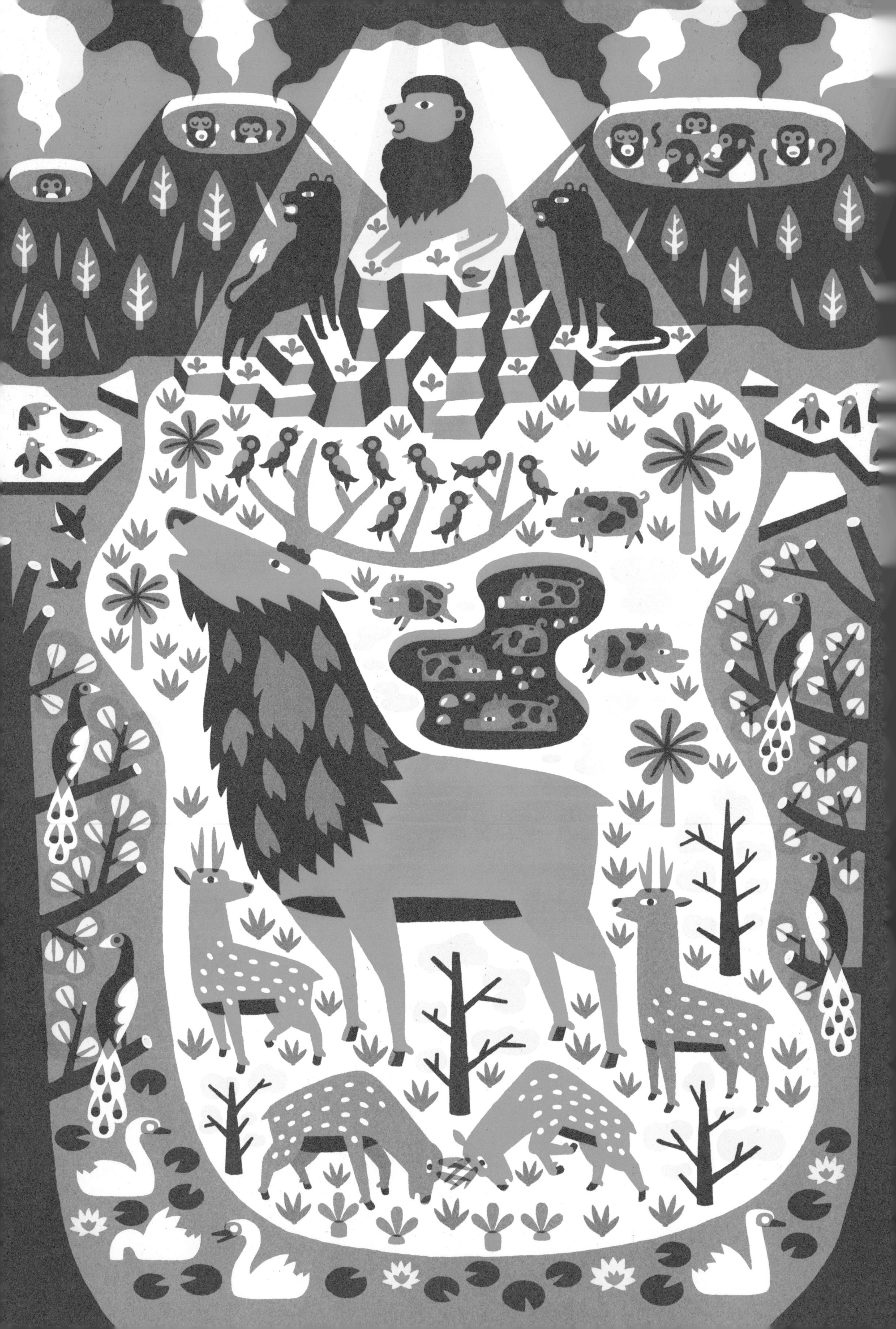

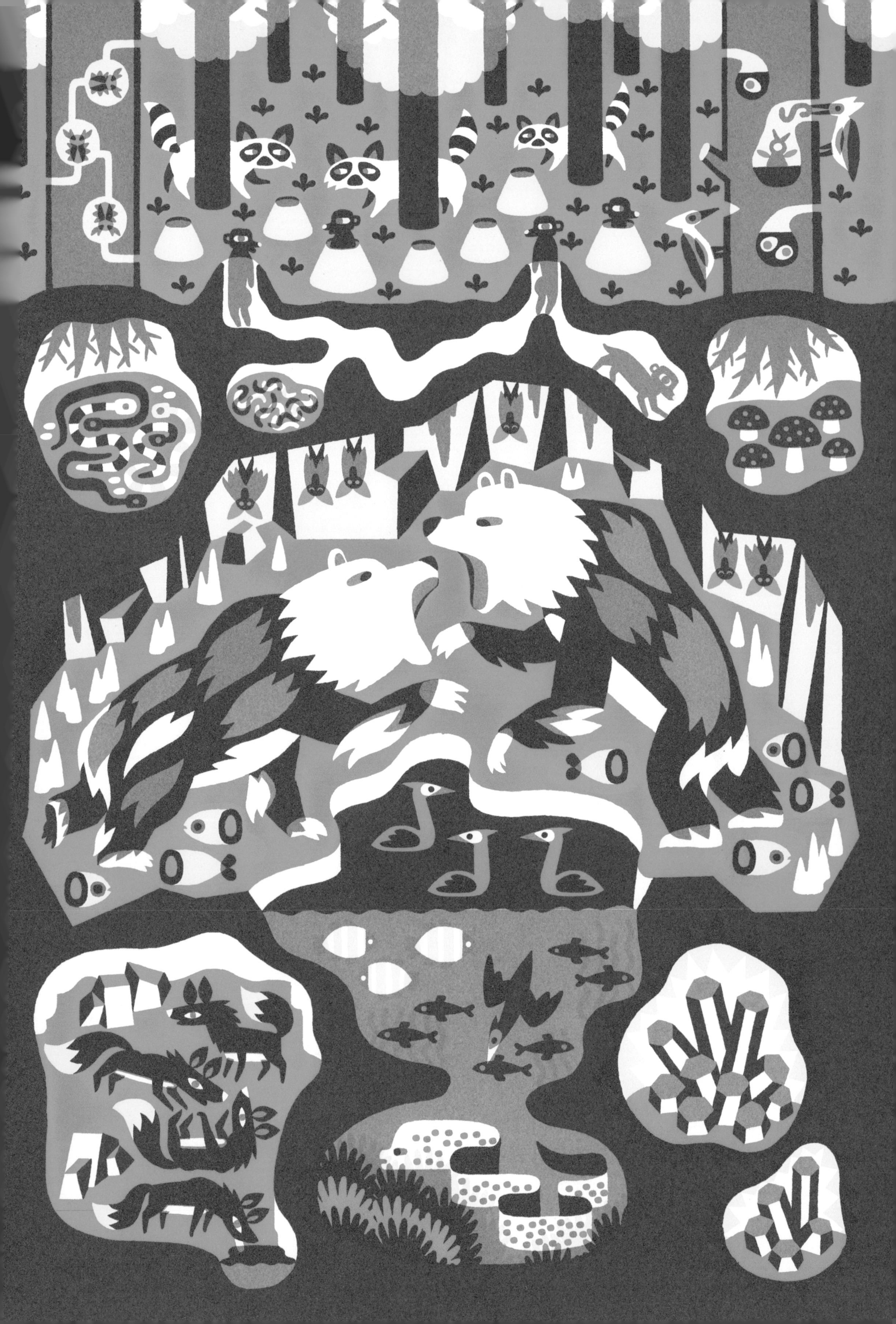

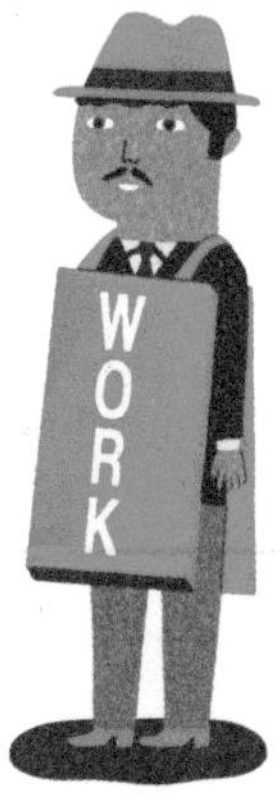
WORK

Disclaimer: This is a work of fiction. Names, characters, places and incidents are either products of the author's imagination or are used fictitiously. Any resemblance to actual events, places, or persons, living or dead, is entirely coincidental.

Published by: Nobrow Ltd. 62 Great Eastern Street, London, EC2A 3QR

Printed in Spain by Imago on FSC paper

ISBN: 978-1-907704-52-9

Order from www.nobrow.net